How Not to Hate
Your Husband After
Kids

ALSO BY JANCEE DUNN

Cyndi Lauper: A Memoir

*Why Is My Mother Getting a Tattoo? And Other Questions
I Wish I Never Had to Ask*

But Enough About Me

Don't You Forget About Me

How Not to Hate Your Husband After Kids

Jancee Dunn

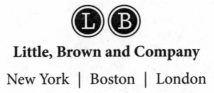

Little, Brown and Company

New York | Boston | London

Little, Brown and Company
Hachette Book Group
1290 Avenue of the Americas, New York, NY 10104
littlebrown.com

First Edition: March 2017

Little, Brown and Company is a division of Hachette Book Group, Inc. The Little, Brown name and logo are trademarks of Hachette Book Group, Inc.

The publisher is not responsible for websites (or their content) that are not owned by the publisher.

The Hachette Speakers Bureau provides a wide range of authors for speaking events. To find out more, go to hachettespeakersbureau.com or call (866) 376-6591.

ISBN 978-0-316-26710-6
LCCN 2016946111

10 9 8 7 6 5 4 3 2 1

LSC-C

Printed in the United States of America

You carry all the ingredients

To turn your existence into joy

Mix them, mix

Them!

—HAFIZ

CONTENTS

Contents

AUTHOR'S NOTE

••••••••••••••••••••••••••

THIS BOOK is written for parents and partners who define their marriages as "good" or "satisfactory" but feel they could be better. However, if you are experiencing problems in your marriage that arise from serious issues such as mental illness, physical altercations, or substance abuse, seek professional help.

I have changed all the names of the friends I have interviewed for this book to protect their privacy.

How Not to Hate Your Husband After Kids

Introduction:
Maters Gonna Hate

When you have a baby, you set off an
explosion in your marriage, and when the
dust settles, your marriage is different from
what it was.

—NORA EPHRON

When I was six months pregnant with my daughter, I had lunch with a group of friends, all of whom were eager to pass along their hard-won scraps of parental wisdom. In the quiet café they noisily threw them down, with much gesturing, like street-corner dice players on a hot streak. There were so many tips flying at me that I was forced to write them on a napkin. *Bring flip-flops for nasty shower at hospital,* I scribbled. *Huggies wipes are nice, thick. Freeze maxi pads in water for postpartum 'roid-sicles.*

"Oh, and get ready to hate your husband," said my friend Lauren. I looked up from writing *If gas, pump baby's legs like bicycle.* Wrong, I told her calmly. I listed various reasons why our relationship was solid: We had been together for nearly a decade. We were heading toward middle age, and squabbling requires siphoning precious energy from waning reserves. Most important, we were peaceable, semi-hermetic writers who startled at loud noises, running madly away like panicked antelope.

I looked around at my friends' carefully composed faces as they tried not to smirk. Over the course of a few months, I had already been privy to hundreds of parental decrees: *Say good-bye to a good night's sleep. You'll never have sex again, and trust me, it will be a relief. Natural childbirth? You'll beg for that epidural, especially if your pelvis separates like mine did.*

My favorite edict was supplied by my friend Justin, father of three. "Better see all the movies you can now," he said, shaking his head mournfully. "When the baby comes? Not gonna happen."

I squinted at him. Parenthood was so overwhelming that I wouldn't be able to sit on my couch and watch a movie? Ever?

•••••••••••••••••••••••••••

As it turns out, my friend Justin was wrong—I was watching movies the week after I gave birth.

But my friend Lauren was right.

Soon after the baby was born, my husband and I had our first screaming fight as new parents. To be more precise, it was I who screamed.

What set me off was embarrassingly trivial, yet the source of a baffling amount of conflict in the first few weeks of parenthood: whose turn it was to empty the Diaper Genie. On that day, it was Tom's. The coiled bag had grown to the size of a Burmese python, and was about to spring like the snake-in-a-nut-can gag. The stench enveloped our small Brooklyn apartment.

"Please empty that thing," I called to him as I sat on the couch, breastfeeding the baby. "The fumes are making me dizzy."

"In a minute, hon," he said from the bedroom, his robotic voice a tip-off that he was playing chess on his computer. He has a handful of programmed responses on call, like tugging the string on an action doll: *That's interesting; Huh, really?* and *Oh wow, sounds great* (his response when I told him I had a suspicious growth on my leg).

In seconds, I was flooded with molten rage. I carefully put the baby down, barged into the bedroom, and seared him with contemptible, juvenile invective, terms that had not crossed my lips since I was a New Jersey teen in the '80s. Dickwad. Asshole. Piece-a-shit. The force of my anger surprised both of us. Almost immediately, I was filled with shame. True, I was reeling from hormones, sleep deprivation, and a sudden quadrupling of cleanup and laundry. But I love my husband — enough to have had him impregnate me in the first place. I knew within two weeks of meeting him that I wanted to marry him; he was the most interesting person I had ever met. I was charmed by the way he would blush and stammer when we talked, prompting me to lean in more closely just for the fun of making everything worse. During our tranquil nights at home in the early days of our marriage, I was often reminded of Christopher Isherwood's description of a couple reading: "the two of them absorbed in their books yet so completely aware of each other's presence."

I'm not sure what a dickwad is, exactly — but I know Tom isn't one. He's a sweet, caring spouse and father who spends hours with our daughter, Sylvie, patiently playing an eighth round of Go Fish.

He refuses her nothing: when she begs him to ride bikes at dawn on a freezing Saturday, his standard response is what I've termed *nokay.* "No." (Five seconds elapse.) "Okay." He is almost comically protective of his only child. One day at our local playground, an older girl was taunting Sylvie as Tom watched grimly from the sidelines.

Older girl: *You can't do the monkey bars! You're too small. You're not strong enough, like me!*

Sylvie does not answer, so the girl continues in a singsong voice: *You can't do it, you can't do it!*

Tom materializes next to the older child, who squints up at his six three frame. *Right. Let's see you do it, then.*

The child swings through three bars, falls, then hastily jumps back on.

Tom, with Vulcan calm: *You fell off. Which is cheating. You're the one who can't do the monkey bars.* Older child backs away.

Playground disputes aside, Tom finds fighting physically unbearable: the moment my voice begins to rise, he turns light gray and retracts into himself like a stunned gastropod. While I have threatened divorce and called him every name in the book, he has never — I mean never — done the same to me. It gives me no satisfaction to holler at a kind, gentle chess player who enjoys reading and bird-watching in his spare time.

And did the Diaper Genie actually need to be emptied right away? Were we really ready to haul out the HazMat suits? It could have waited until Tom had finished his game. But from that day on, my resentment has been on a constant lochia-like drip. Our daughter is now six, and Tom and I still have endless, draining fights. Why do I have the world's tiniest fuse when it comes to the division of childcare and household labor?

I am baffled that things have turned out this way. I fully assumed that my very evolved husband and I, both freelance writers who work from home, would naturally be in tune. When we were a duo, he handled all the cooking while I did most of the housework; we grocery shopped and did laundry *à deux*. When I became pregnant, he confidently informed me he was ready for diaper duty.

Surely, we would figure everything out organically, as we always had.

I had read the encouraging news that modern men, unlike the distant breadwinners of previous generations, are more invested in their children than ever before. A Pew Research Center study shows that today's working dads are as likely as working moms to say they would prefer to be home with their kids. We live in an era in which fathers-to-be throw all-male "man showers" for their babies (according to one party-gear designer, a popular theme is "barbecue, babies, and beer"). Websites aimed solely at dads are on the rise, such as Fatherly.com, which features, alongside more standard content (an illustrated guide to high fives, tips from a Navy SEAL on how to dominate hide-and-seek), numerous articles on how to raise strong daughters — a response, said the site's founders, to reader demand.

Fathers' attitudes about housework are changing, too. The same Pew study found that since 1965, the time that fathers spend doing household chores has more than doubled — from about four hours a week to roughly ten. Men, though, are selective about the ones they will do, according to sociologist Scott Coltrane. He has said that of the "big five" household tasks — cooking, meal cleanup, grocery shopping, housework, and laundry — men are more apt to balk at housework and laundry and more likely to go for cooking, meal cleanup, and grocery shopping.

Since Tom and I had already established fairly clear roles in our household — our generation is, arguably, the first to have expectations of splitting up the work — I assumed we would simply fashion new ones. But after our baby was born, we soon slid backward into the traditional roles we'd grown up seeing, which were clearly more ingrained than I'd thought (we're just a grandma and grandpa away from the old model, after all). It wasn't by any grand design; it just sort of happened. I was making food for the baby, so I started doing all the family cooking and food shopping. I did the baby's laundry, so I began to throw in our clothes, too. When she was small, I stayed at home with her during the day and, out of habit, my caregiver duties gradually extended into the evening.

Our scenario is not uncommon: an Ohio State study of working couples who became first-time parents found that men did a fairly equal share of housework — until, that is, they became dads. By the time their baby had reached nine months, the women had picked up an average of thirty-seven hours of childcare and housework per week, while the men did twenty-four hours — even as both parents clocked in the same number of hours at work. When it came to childcare, moreover, dads did more of the fun stuff like reading stories, rather than decidedly less festive tasks such as diaper duty (not to mention that they did five *fewer* hours of housework per week after the baby arrived).

To their credit, the new fathers seemed to be clueless that they weren't keeping up with the burgeoning workload, says study coauthor Sarah Schoppe-Sullivan. "We were surprised at the inaccuracies," she tells me. "Both parents feel like they are doing a ton more work after the baby is born, but for men, that perception is especially inaccurate."

These days, Tom does around 10 percent of our household chores. He maintains that he is consistent: as a bachelor, he did 10 percent of *his* household chores. (I can vouch for that: in our early days of dating, upon my first visit to his apartment, the only thing I found in his refrigerator was a furred 64-ounce jar of salsa from Chi-Chi's, a brand I was not even aware still existed).

I wish his 10 percent effort was enough, but it isn't. I feel like he's a guest at the hotel I'm running. I'm constantly taking a silent feminist stand to see if he'll step up and lend a hand. The score-keeping never ends. Adding to my resentment is that on weekends, Tom somehow manages to float around in a happy single-guy bubble. A typical Saturday for him starts with a game of soccer with his friends or a five-hour bike ride (he seemed to take up endurance sports right around the time our baby's umbilical cord was cut, like the sound of the snip was a starter's pistol to get the hell out of Dodge).

This is followed by a leisurely twenty-minute shower, a late breakfast, a long nap, and then a meandering perusal through a variety of periodicals. Meanwhile, I am ferrying our daughter to birthday parties and playdates. On weekend evenings, Tom doesn't check with me before he meets friends for drinks; he just breezes out the door with the assumption that I'll handle bath time and bed. Yet whose fault is that? In my deranged quest to Do It All, I have allowed this pattern to unfold — so is it fair of me to get angry when he ducks (or, as I view it, "skulks") into the bedroom for a nap?

And so I fume, and then unleash the beast at the slightest provocation. A typical scenario: I am in the kitchen, simultaneously cooking dinner, checking our daughter's homework, and emptying both her school lunch bag and the dishwasher. Tom heads into the kitchen and I brighten — *Oh, good, some help!* — but no, he is only wending through the typhoon in order to reach the refrigerator to pour himself a glass of wine.

> TOM (OPENING FRIDGE, FROWNING): There's no wine left?
>
> ME (DISTRACTED): I guess not.
>
> TOM (WITH SLIGHTLY MORE URGENCY): You didn't get wine today?
>
> ME: Oh, so now I manage the storerooms? My apologies, Lord Grantham! I'll alert the staff!
>
> TOM: No, I just meant that you were at the store earlier, and...
>
> ME (NOW ENRAGED): I know what you meant, Dickwad!

As this little contretemps is unfolding, our daughter runs over, stands protectively in front of Tom, and tells me not to yell at Daddy. "We're just working something out, honey," I say quickly. In one of the many parenting books I keep piled on my bedside table, I read that if you squabble in front of children, you should make an elaborate point of making up, so that they can witness your "healthy conflict resolution." "Here," I tell her. "I'll hug Daddy. We fight sometimes, but we always make up, because we love each other! You see?"

I move in for a hug. My back is toward her, so she doesn't see that as I embrace my husband, I scowlingly give him the finger and mouth, *Fuck you!*

Of course, I overreacted. And Tom could have gone down to the store without an Edwardian harrumph and purchased a new bottle of wine. Instead, I've become this lurking harridan who waits for her husband to screw up (I suppose the legal phrase for this is "entrapment"). But when I explode — making a conscious choice to vent, rather than consider my daughter's anxiety — is my "victory" worth it? My concern for her wellbeing turns out to be unsettlingly selective. While I carefully apply sunscreen to the back of her neck and shield her from the harms of too much sugar by scrutinizing the label of her Nature's Path EnviroKidz Organic Lightly Frosted Amazon Flakes, I apparently feel free to trash her sense of peace by yelling horrible names at her father.

We save our best selves for our children.

•••••••••••••••••••••••••••

What makes me especially sad about our endless bickering is that it drags down what is by all accounts a pretty wonderful life. Our daughter is goofy and easygoing (bursting with excitement over the Mother's Day present she bought me, she says, "I'll give you a hint — it's soap!"). We live in a serene converted church in Brooklyn. Tom's enviable magazine assignments barely classify as work: a mountain biking expedition to Mayan ruins where he drinks whiskey with shamans atop a pyramid, traipsing in remote Utah deserts in search of rare bird sounds, horseback riding in the pampas of Uruguay.

Meanwhile, I have, through careful maneuvering, carved out a part-time job as a freelance writer. During the six hours my daughter is at school, I park myself in front of the computer and industriously write about beauty and health for magazines such as *Vogue* (even if, in my limp ponytail and frayed yoga pants, I am easily the fashion bible's least glamorous employee). During those hours, I barely rise from my chair — but the payoff is that when school is out at 3, I close my computer for the day and transform into a stay-at-home mom. Because I'm so demonically focused, my work output roughly equals that of my former job as a music writer at *Rolling Stone* magazine — I may have spent nine hours daily in the office, but a full third of it was dedicated to web-surfing, gossiping with coworkers, and debating what to have for lunch (if we weren't on deadline, twenty minutes could be devoted to the topic of *will Mexican food make us too drowsy?*).

These days, a delightfully surreal workday might involve dropping my daughter at school — a three-minute walk through a leafy park — hopping on the F train to Manhattan to meet up with Jennifer Lopez, and then heading back to Brooklyn in time for school pickup. Whenever I interview celebrities, I often warm them up with a softball question in which I have them describe for me the happiest time of their lives. If they are parents, their inevitable answer is this: *Oh, the period of time when my children were small, no question.* I am fully aware that this should be a golden era for me and Tom — we have our health, fulfilling jobs, the child we have longed for. And we are squandering it.

Our situation is certainly not unique: this simmering resentment dominates mom blogs. Get a group of mothers together, uncork a bottle or three of sauvignon blanc, and the scattered sniping will soon rise to a thunderous crescendo of complaint as everyone clamors to share their stories:

My husband works all week, so on weekends, he tells me he doesn't want to "deal with" our sons. I'm amazed that he doesn't notice that I'm basically radiating hatred all the time.

I'm emptying the dishwasher and Brian starts grabbing my boobs. I've had kids pawing me all day long, so that's not hot. If you want some action, help me unload the dishes, idiot.

My husband tries to get out of changing diapers by saying I'm the "expert."

I'm so tired of asking Andrew to do things around the house. No one has to ask me. You know why? Because I just get on with it.

I'd divorce Jason, but he drops off the kids at school in the mornings.

A friend just wrote me this: "I'm running on 5 hrs sleep and irrational anger at Adam while cortisol pumps itself into my breast milk. He just asked me what I wanted for our anniversary, and I tell him a weekend at a hotel, alone. I wasn't kidding. The words 'weekend alone' feel like porn to me."

Perhaps the single most widely cited piece of research on marriage and children comes from eminent couples therapists Julie and John Gottman. They found that 67 percent of couples see their marital satisfaction plummet after having a baby. No surprise there: your bundle of joy brings a boatload of additional stresses such as hormonal zigzagging, work schedule upheavals, money worries (the cost of diapers alone is panic-inducing), a sex drought, and, as one paper I read pointed out, "increased interactions with medical professionals."

And the significance of chronic sleep deprivation on a new parent's temper cannot be overestimated. Lack of sleep makes us focus on negative experiences, pick fights, and become irrational. Research shows that after sleep deprivation, the emotional part of the brain, the amygdala, is much more reactive. Normally, the more rational prefrontal cortex works to put everything into context, but when your brain is sleep deprived, this relationship breaks down — and often, so do you. Suddenly, your responses are way less controlled — and you rip your husband a new one when he unthinkingly slams a door after you've just gotten the baby to nap.

When people miss sleep for one night, they feel the effects the next day — but one study shows that if sleep loss continues, people report that they actually feel just fine: I got this! You know what? I don't even need sleep! When I chat with Matthew Walker, director of UC Berkeley's Sleep and Neuroimaging Laboratory, he compares this mind-set to that of stubbornly confident drunk drivers. "After five drinks, they may think they're fine to drive home, but they're markedly impaired in their brain function," he says. "The same is true of sleep: when people regularly get less than seven hours, we can measure significant cognitive impairment."

Before I had a baby, I would roll my eyes when I'd hear a new mom lamenting that she didn't have time to shower for days on end. *Please,* I'd think. *Doesn't a newborn sleep all the time? Drama!* Now that I'm a mother, I roll my eyes when I hear the oft-repeated advice urging moms to "nap when the baby naps." The effort required to keep a tiny new being alive is bizarrely immense — and, at least when it comes to childcare and housework, women are bearing the brunt of it. Over a quarter century ago, Berkeley sociologist Arlie Hochschild called this disparity the "stalled revolution," and it still holds true: while the lives of women, who now make up almost half of the US labor force, have radically changed, the behavior of their mates has not changed quite as much.

Working mothers are now the top earners in a record 40 percent of families with kids — yet a University of Maryland study found that married mothers are still doing nearly three and a half times as much housework as married fathers. And when you've been picking up nonstop after a two-year-old, your husband's formerly innocuous habit of shedding his socks into a bounceable ball shape — within view of the hamper — is suddenly deeply irritating.

Comedian Dena Blizzard, a New Jersey mom, says she would bristle when her husband would return home from work, look around at the chaos wrought by their three children, and ask her, "What happened here? Who pulled all this stuff out?" "Every day, he would say it," she tells me. "I'm like, 'Oh, this? Yeah, I pulled all this shit out. I was really bored today, so I thought I'd throw everything on the floor.'"

Then he would follow with the question dreaded by stay-at-home mothers worldwide: *What did you do all day?* "I did a hundred things, but none of them added up to anything," Blizzard says. "I vacuumed, I called Poison Control because my son ate a plant, and I think I took a shower. I'd tell him, 'We have three kids. This is as far as we got.' He would always be surprised. It was hard not to want to punch him in the face."

Sociologist Michael Kimmel, director of the Center for the Study of Men and Masculinities (yes, this exists) at Stony Brook

University, says that men tend to pitch in more with childcare than with housework—but as with housework, they're selective about the kind of childcare that they will do. "What happens in a lot of middle-class families is that Dad becomes the Fun Parent," Kimmel tells me. "So Dad takes the kids to the park on Saturday mornings to play soccer, and Mom cleans the breakfast dishes, makes the beds, does the laundry, makes lunch. Then the kids come home at noon and say, 'Oh my gosh, we had such a great time with Dad in the park—he's awesome!'"

This unfair dynamic is neatly summed up in an article from the satirical online newspaper the *Onion:* "Mom Spends Beach Vacation Assuming All Household Duties in Closer Proximity to Ocean." As the "mom" puts it, "I just love that I can be scrubbing the bathroom, look out the window, and see the tide coming in. We should do this every year!"

And even though fathers have stepped up considerably in sharing childcare duties—since the 1960s, nearly tripling the time they spend with their children—mothers still devote about twice as much time to their kids as fathers do. Perhaps it's not surprising that in the US government's American Time Use Survey, women reported feeling significantly more fatigued than fathers in all four major life categories—work, housework, leisure, and childcare. (I read these statistics and think of Tina Fey's tip in *Bossypants* for carving out "me time" after a baby: "Say you're going to look for the diaper cream and then go into your child's room and just stand there, until your spouse comes in and curtly says, 'What are you doing?'")

When journalist Josh Katz crunched the numbers from the most current Time Use Survey, he found that even when men didn't *have* jobs, they still did half the amount of housework and childcare that women did. A large survey of US mothers by NBC's *Today* program revealed that for nearly half of them, their husbands were a bigger source of stress than their children. Some of them commented that the fathers acted more like kids than equal partners.

"If I let my husband and baby have their way, I'd never pee, brush my teeth, shower, or eat again," says Leyla, a friend of a friend. When she went out one night for an hour-long meeting, she soon received a text from her husband about their daughter that read, ominously: *Witching hour just began but don't worry.* Moments later, a more urgent message arrived: *This is the worst I've ever heard it.* "Seconds later my phone beeps," she says. "He has sent an iPhone recording of the baby screaming bloody murder." Leyla quickly said her good-byes and hurried out the door. The iPhone, alas, is every parent's electronic parole bracelet — and in life, there is no "airplane mode."

I certainly feel like Tom's mother when I have to nag him to do a task — especially when he treats it as an option by saying, "In a minute," or simply ignores me completely. (At least he doesn't do what my friend's husband does: salute and shout, "Aye-aye, sir," to make their kids laugh. At her.) Darby Saxbe, a psychology professor at the University of Southern California, explains to me that couples often fall into a pattern of demand and retreat — most often, the woman demands and the man retreats. This dynamic has arisen, she says, because men have less to gain by changing their behavior, while women are more likely to want to alter the status quo — which means they also initiate more fights.

My friend Jenny, mother of two, recalls one Saturday morning when it became clear that the baby had a dirty diaper. "My husband chirped, 'Your turn — I did the last one,'" she says. "As a stay-at-home mom, I was up a ballpark three thousand lifetime diaper changes on this guy. I think my head rotated 360 degrees."

When men do help around the house, says Pamela Smock, a sociology professor at the University of Michigan (with the very term *help*, she says, indicating that we have quite a way to go), they often choose chores with a "leisure component." This would include yard work, driving to the store to pick up something, or busily reordering the family Netflix queue — quasi-discretionary activities that have a more flexible timetable than more urgent jobs such as hustling the kids out the door for school or making dinner (and often, many of those "leisure component" chores involve getting out of the house).

Smock, a leading expert on the changing American family, who is equally at home discussing gender inequality as she is true crime novels and '70s rock bands, says that on top of basic duties such as cooking and cleaning, women do countless invisible tasks. This is the time-gobbling labor that will likely never show up on any sort of time use study. One is "kin work," which Smock defines to me as "giving emotional support to relatives, buying presents and sending cards, handling holiday celebrations, things like that." (Which is why a certain page in the gift book *Porn for New Moms* always gets a laugh: a smiling, hunky man sits at a desk and says, *I'll be right there, hon. I'm just finishing the last of the baby shower thank-you cards.*)

Then there's "emotion work," the constant checking on the wellbeing of everyone in the household: Is your tween still feeling excluded in the school cafeteria? The dog seems under the weather —

is it time to get his kidney medication refilled? Did your husband hash out that issue with his boss? Yet another kind of invisible work is called "consumption labor" — buying the kids' underwear and school supplies, researching the car seat and the high chair. "This often falls to the woman," says Smock, "unless you're talking about big-ticket items like a large-screen TV and the refrigerator."

Let us not forget the schlepping: a study in the journal *Transportation* found that women shoulder most of the load in the drearily named "average daily household support travel time" category (the school run, grocery shopping, hauling kids to piano lessons). Women do this an average of eleven minutes more per day than men — even when both spouses are breadwinners.

Perhaps the least visible but most pervasive job is that of household manager. "That one is constant," Smock says. "It's the person who remembers everything: that Joey needs to have a dentist appointment, what foods each child likes, that a babysitter needs to be hired for the weekend. If a mother is handing her husband a grocery list, he is given credit for going shopping, but she has done the work of constructing the list. Giving direction to the husband is labor. It's in every area in terms of childcare, and it's always going on in your brain, even if you're not aware of it."

And mothers resent it, says New York psychotherapist Jean Fitzpatrick. "What I hear most often from women," she says, "is 'I do not want to be the boss here, I do not want him coming to me and asking me. I want *him* to take ownership.'"

My friend Marea says that this is a constant struggle in her house. "Oh, if I don't mention it, it doesn't happen," she says. "Our daughter is seven, and it's like my husband still doesn't know the flow. If I happen to be doing something for myself near her bedtime, unless prompted, he won't get her ready for bed. And having to prompt — and prompt — raises my stress level."

After my chat with Smock, I start toting up all the invisible work I do as I go about my day. It's maddening. If Tom takes our daughter to swim lessons, I remind them when it's time to go, pack her bag, empty her bag when they return, dry her wet clothes, and give her a snack and a bath while Tom collapses on the couch. Invisible work stays hidden until it's illuminated — even Smock wasn't aware that her own mother did virtually everything in their household until she was in graduate school. "Looking back, I think, 'Oh my god, how could she have done her job teaching all day, and then come home to a second job and handled every-thing?' No wonder she would go to the bedroom and lie down for a while. How could it have been so invisible to *me*, even?" I ask Smock which jobs her father did around the house and she laughs. "My dad did car stuff, and stuff with the dog," she says. "Oh, and he liked to put wallpaper up."

....

For all my complaints that I want Tom to be more involved, he counters that I jump in and micromanage when he does — for instance, I would hurriedly check after he had changed a loaded diaper for what is colorfully known in my circle of moms as "butt rust." I must admit that when it comes to kid-related tasks, I feel I do a more conscientious job.

You can't have it both ways, says Chris Routly, a blogger from Portland, Oregon, and full-time caregiver dad (a term he prefers to *stay-at-home dad*). He says that he understands why women are hesitant to hand over power in an area where they have traditionally held more control. "But if we are going to have equality in parenting, it is going to mean that women are going to be mindful of letting go of that," says the father of two, who wears a "Dads Don't Babysit" T-shirt and posts impressive shots of the Ninjago cake he baked for his son's birthday on Instagram. "We're all figuring it out as we go along, so I think this idea that women have this built-in superpower where they just know how to take care of children is a lie. We need to do away with it."

He is right. There have been plenty of times I've waved Tom away when he tries to get involved, because I get a distinct thrill out of being in charge, as I capably knock down one kid-related task after another. Pediatric dentist appointment — check! Permission slips signed — check! I enjoy the constant buzz of organizing, researching, scheduling — a point I bond over with feminist icon Caitlin Moran, mother of two and author of *How to Be a Woman*.

Give a mother a sleeping child for an hour, and she can achieve ten times more than a childless person, she tells me when we meet before her book reading in Philadelphia. "Motherhood is really like being in an action movie that goes on for your whole life — but with all the boring, everyday bits left in," she says. "Mothers have to do a poo in four parts because a child will cry, and then they try and finish off but the child needs them again! A new mother will work far harder, more creatively, and more effectively than people who don't have children — because she has to."

But I can pinpoint the precise moment that my careful, complex balancing act blew up in my face. It occurred when Sylvie was in preschool. She was running a fever, so I kept her home. She was thrilled, and happily binge-watched *Martha Speaks* in her pajamas while I prepared for my phone interview with Jennifer Hudson for the cover story of a major magazine. I informed Tom that I would tend to Sylvie all day except from 5 to 6 p.m., when I had to chat with Jennifer. "I just need that hour," I told him, as I, ever the household manager, arranged a snack tray for Sylvie and pulled out a board game for them to play.

At 4:45, Tom and Sylvie were peacefully immersed in a game of *Enchanted Forest* as I crept upstairs to our office, where I had attached my tape recorder to the phone. Jennifer, whom I had interviewed a few times before, was delightful, as usual — charming and down to earth.

When I do phone interviews, I am intently focused so that I can quickly cover all the questions I need to get to during my allotted time — generally forty-five minutes to an hour. We had just moved on to dieting tips when Sylvie suddenly appeared next to me.

Poo, she breathed. At three, she was in the midst of potty training, and preferred that I finish the job. We had one bathroom, and it was downstairs.

I waved her away. *Where's Daddy?* I whispered.

"— my biggest thing is banana pudding, but it's the devil!" said Jennifer. "So no one is allowed to bring it into my house."

Poo.

"I'll say, 'It's not on my Weight Watchers radar,' " said Jennifer. I laughed too heartily while frantically waving Sylvie away. *Have Daddy do it,* I mouthed. "It's not tolerated! It will be thrown away! Because I can't control myself. So why put it in my domain?"

"Exactly!" I nearly screamed, as sweat pooled in my bra.

I have to poo. I have to poo now.

Desperately, I took off my shoe and threw it downstairs to catch Tom's attention.

Daddy will do it, I whispered.

Poo. Poo. Poo. Poo. Poo.

Finally I asked the Academy Award and Grammy–winning star if she could hold for "just a quick sec."

I grabbed Sylvie's hand and raced downstairs, passing Tom on the couch. His blank eyes were bathed in the soft glow of his smartphone. He quickly knotted his forehead in a feigned look of earnest importance, as if he was attending to some pressing work matter. But I knew exactly what he was doing. He was playing SocialChess with some guy in the Philippines. I was just playing for a minute, he tells me later. During our fight.

Of course, when parents battle repeatedly, no one emerges unscathed — including, depressingly, babies.

Even when they are asleep, infants as young as six months react negatively to angry, argumentative voices, as University of Oregon researchers discovered by measuring brain activity of babies in the presence of steadily rising voices. Babies raised by unhappily married parents have been shown to have a host of developmental problems, from delayed speech and potty training to a reduced ability to self-soothe.

The longer marital fighting goes on, the worse it is for kids. At ages three to six, say the Gottmans, children assume they are the cause of the fight. By ages six to eight, they tend to side (as my daughter does) with one parent. Notre Dame University psychologist

E. Mark Cummings found that kindergartners whose parents fought frequently were more likely to struggle with depression, anxiety, and behavior issues by the time they reached seventh grade. Cummings likened children to emotional Geiger counters who pay close attention to their parents' emotions to ascertain how safe they are in their family. He cautioned that he was not recommending that parents never fight — if kids are never exposed to conflict, they might not develop the coping skills to handle it themselves. They just have to work it out in a fair and healthy way. You know, like grown-ups.

There is no way around it: the quality of your marriage is closely tied to the bond you have with your child. Consider the surprising finding from psychologists at Southern Methodist University that when parents battle, it is the *father's* relationship with his kids that takes a major hit. They found that the day after a parental skirmish, most moms were able to compartmentalize and reported a quick recovery, and even an improved relationship with their child. But fathers had a much greater tendency to let the negative marital tension spill over into the rest of the family. Insidiously, the conflict from these parental fights would resurface on the first or even second day after the fight, in the form of friction between father and child.

When I tell Alan Kazdin, a Yale University psychology professor and director of the Yale Parenting Center, that Sylvie jumps between us when we fight, his reaction is sobering. "Well, it puts children in a horrible situation, because they see their stability being threatened," he says. As I describe the escalating tension between Tom and me, Kazdin drops his professional demeanor. "Look," he breaks in gently. "You're not asking for my opinion, but

I'm going to give it. You sound like a nice person. Life is unpre-
dictably short, and you and the person you have chosen to be with
for the rest of your life are arguing about housework. It's not worth
it." He pauses. "Am I lecturing too much?"

Not at all, I tell him.

"Then I'll tell you that you don't want that in your life," he
says. "And that's better for your child, too."

Enough. It is time to set the bar higher — for myself, for our
daughter, and for our marriage. It is impossible to stuff the genie
back into the bottle after you have children, and go back to the
way you used to be. Life has changed, and we have to change with
it. Denying this reality courts misery, and even disaster. It is
alarming that I no longer think it is insane to tell myself, "When
we're not fighting, we get along great!" I want to fully enjoy the
family I have been yearning for all my life, and to take active
notice of the many good things that my husband does. Our home
should be a place of safety and comfort for all of us.

Since I make a living delving into research, why not try it on
my own relationship? I decide to plunge into self-help books and
speak directly to those who make scientific findings. I will quiz
psychologists, parenting experts, neuroscientists, and fellow parents. I'll try anything. I will bring — okay, drag — Tom to couples
therapists. We will test every strategy we can find to restore harmony to our marriage and, by extension, our family life.

Sylvie has just turned six. There is still time to fix this.

Mothers, Fathers, Issues

The weekend after I craft my plan to mutually draw down our hostilities, Tom, Sylvie, and I are at my parents' house in New Jersey, joined by my two younger sisters and their families. Dinah, a book editor, is the sort of generous, kind person who says troublesome tasks are no trouble and always totes a treat in her purse — for the adults. Her husband, Patrick, a boisterous, burly Marine veteran and school chef, can be counted on to get silly if an unhappy child needs distracting.

Heather, the youngest, loyal and thoughtful, was the most sought-after babysitter in our neighborhood and is now a beloved elementary school teacher whose students hang on her like baby possums. Standing nearby is her husband, Rob, a chef — a tattooed cool guy on the outside, inwardly a sweetly easygoing dad prone to halting, sentimental family announcements after a beer or two.

As usual, we are all bunched in the kitchen. Various nieces and nephews wander in, rummage through my parents' fridge or pantry, then furtively race-walk out of the kitchen with elaborately casual expressions, clutching jars of expired Marshmallow Fluff and boxes of ancient Pop-Tarts.

My parents' pantry doubles as a food museum, because my

father, ever alert to scams "they" won't tell you about, claims that expiration dates are "bunk." Dad is a retired J. C. Penney manager whose name happens to be J. C.; his father, J. C. Senior, was also a J. C. Penney manager who once hosted the Great Man himself for lunch. I trust I need not mention where my cousin Penny worked.

Along with the unreliability of food expiration dates, my father will bring up at least a few of the following topics at every family gathering: the hidden costs buried in phone bills ("*Consumer Reports* did a big feature on it — I have it on file"), the ten-day forecast, tarps, People Are Nuts and They're Only Getting Worse, the superiority of Costco gin (he funnels it into a Beefeater bottle, claiming guests can't tell the difference), the mandatory retiree-dad family genealogy project he's "definitely going to get to one of these days," and fluctuating gas prices.

After you arrive at my parents' house, the first thing my father will inquire about is the traffic ("How was Route 80? Bad? Well, they're doing construction — it's terrible."). Of course he hopes we have had an easy ride from "the City," but it's so much more exciting when he can offer theories about the traffic jam we have endured. Then, after a decent interval of niceties, my dad, an exemplar of preparedness, will reliably bring up a disturbing news story and relate it to our own safety. "You probably read about that family in West Orange? A real shame." *Mournful head shake.* "Of course, it wouldn't have happened if they just had a radon detector/proper snow tires/an emergency survival rescue blanket/electrical outlet covers."

My father has one setting, and it is Dad Mode. He sees everything through a fatherly lens. If a child clamors for an expensive toy, he will helpfully offer that *the money would be better spent buying stock in said toy company.* If he is standing in front of any man-made wonder — the Parthenon, the Taj Mahal — he can be relied upon to *immediately speculate on the cost of maintenance.* When my father beheld the Château de Versailles, his imagination skipped past the Sun King's dazzling vision and landed squarely on the palace's heating bills ("Just look at all those windows! Guaranteed they're leaching heat.").

Viewing the world through a Dad lens means turning any request from a child into a *useful, practical action.* Like my father, Tom has now adopted this habit with our daughter.

SYLVIE: Daddy, can we wrestle?

TOM: How about wrestling into those pajamas?

•••••••••••

SYLVIE: I wish I could be invisible and spy on people!

TOM: Why don't you work on making that sandwich
    disappear?

For fathers like mine, the world teems with danger, so they are mindful at all times of an *emergency escape plan.* The first thing my father does at a movie theater, aside from pulling out a bag of microwave popcorn that he has made at home ("I just saved myself five dollars"), is to find a seat closest to the emergency exits and scan the room for sprinklers. ("You laugh, but you won't laugh when your lungs are full of smoke and you can't find a means of egress.") The trunk of his car is a mobile panic room, loaded with flares, blankets, and energy bars. On airplanes, there is no need to remind my father that "the nearest emergency exit may be behind you." He already knows.

My dad has been married for fifty-four years to my mother; at this point they are entwined like the braided ficus tree that grows in their living room. All phone conversations are conducted jointly. If my father answers the phone, he will order me not to say anything until my mother can run upstairs and pick up the extension; we wait in silence until we hear her voice. They share an email account as well, prompting me to address the both of them as a general "you," as in "Do you want ham for Easter brunch?"

My mother, Judy, a classic steel magnolia, is a former head cheerleader and beauty pageant winner who reigned as 1960's Oil Queen of Citronelle, Alabama (as crude oil was one of the area's natural resources, a small oil derrick was affixed to her crown). My mother is regal to this day, sending waiters scurrying with the command that her coffee be *scalding hot,* please. She is always beautifully put together: makeup is applied directly after waking, and never once have I seen her slop around the house in pajamas, even if she is sick.

My mother introduced many whimsical Southern phrases to the baffled kids in our New Jersey suburb, among them the threat to "slap me upside the wall." She raised her three girls with Southern propriety; we were instructed to answer the phone with "Dunn residence, Jancee speaking"; after dinner we were told to announce, "I enjoyed it; excuse me, please." Her grandkids are astonished to hear these historical facts about their fun, silly Gran, who sprays whipped cream into their open mouths and will happily draw a mustache and goatee on her face with Magic Marker ("Ooh, kids, here comes the UPS man! Let's freak him out!").

When it's time for the grandchildren to leave after a visit, they can hardly wait for my mother to produce what she calls Gran's Bag of Swag. She dumps it out with a flourish: Technicolor cheese balls, beef jerky, econo-size slabs of licorice, tubs of taffy. There's everything but a jar of corn syrup for swigging. My sisters and I call it Gran's Bag of Petroleum and Animal By-Products.

"Gran sure loves her Scotch," Sylvie likes to say admiringly. Before dinner, her favorite ritual is to sit placidly between my parents on their couch, her with a cup of milk, them with sizable tumblers of Scotch, all mechanically and contentedly munching Goldfish crackers.

....

While Tom looks on in what I hope is assent, I tell the elders of our extended clan about my venture. It immediately sets off an impassioned discussion. Heather's voice rises above the din as she describes her most recent fight with Rob. It was a Saturday morning before their sons' daylong soccer tournament, and the two boys were rampaging through the house. Laundry moldered in the hamper, the kitchen counter and stovetop were coated with a gritty film of pancake batter, and a stack of bills teetered on the kitchen table.

"That's when Rob decided to watch a movie on his iPad," Heather says. "He just plopped down on the couch, doo-de-doo." (*Doo-de-doo* is the universal sound effect for a happy-go-lucky person.)

As with everything that happens in my family — people who can generate gigabytes of "reply all" email on topics such as *should Dinah get quartz countertops?* — Heather's tale prompts an energetic round-robin:

MY FATHER: Heather, why can't you give Rob a break?

MY MOTHER: But when are they supposed to get everything done? These things don't happen on their own! You have to plan them.

MY FATHER: We raised three girls and managed to get things done, but we still had plenty of time to relax.

MY MOTHER (HOTLY): "We"? You were gone on business trips half the time! I was the one who managed to get things done! Make no mistake! *Note: my mother is getting angry about events that took place nearly a half century ago.*

ROB: My feeling is, do we have to be working all the time? The laundry can wait until the next day. I swear, I feel like I'm an employee at a big-box store, and I have to be jumping up and straightening the merchandise at all times or I'm going to be fired. Can't we just rest on a Saturday? Even for a few hours?

PATRICK: Not for nothing, but I think that's reasonable.

ROB: Honestly, I'm just so beat sometimes that doing chores is the last thing I'm thinking about.

DINAH: On the other hand, it's not like the laundry disappears when you put it off. It's just added to your chore list the next day — a list that has just gotten bigger.

TOM: I think that women might get bothered by different things. For me, the laundry is ready when the bag is too heavy to carry, or there is literally nothing to wear. She gets anxious when the bag is two-thirds full.

ME: No, the laundry is "ready" for you to do when it turns to mulch. Or it actually liquidates. Or, if enough time passes, it forms into shale.

TOM: Jancee will leave a bag of trash by the door, and I don't
see it.

HEATHER: Rob doesn't see it, either!

TOM: It's top-down processing, where you see what the brain
has been primed to see. There's a famous example of this
sort of bitterly fought football game, and each team's fans
thought the other team played unfairly. Neither saw the
same objective game. Or that famous image of the duck
and the rabbit — some see a duck, some see a rabbit. And
I'm never primed to see garbage. *Note: Tom writes about
science and technology, so he frequently talks like this.*

DINAH: But do you feel like you get some sort of pass just
because you didn't see it?

ROB: It sounds like *The Matrix.* Our wives want us to take the
red pill so we can escape from the Matrix and into the real
world. But we like the blue pill world.

TOM (CACKLING): "Do you believe in fate, Neo?"

MY MOTHER: Maybe you should just put the bag of garbage in
your bed.

Everyone resumes talking at once; my father mumbles something
about fixing a pipe and quietly escapes to the basement.

* * *

Our debate, which continues at an animated pitch through dinner
and dessert, inspires me to ask the new mothers and fathers I know to
share the most inflammatory parenting issues they have with their
mates. Then I enlist experts to help me decode their behavior to see if

32

there is any sort of gender-based psychological, social, or even evolutionary explanation. Perhaps the knowledge that certain behaviors are in some sense hardwired in your spouse — rather than a conscious choice to stick it to you — will help dial down the frustration.

Of course, it's slippery to generalize, to reach for easy Mars/Venus stereotypes and downplay the overwhelming role culture has in "naturalizing" gender differences. Nevertheless, after some raucous conversations I have with parents on the playground, at school pickup, and on social media (I focus primarily on straight couples, about which there is a much larger body of research), I notice that a few domestically divisive issues come up with striking frequency. The most common problems are the ones none of us seem to have solved — and the ones for which we mostly desperately need answers.

Why doesn't my husband wake up at night when the baby cries? If I hear the smallest whimper, I shoot out of bed like a Delta Force commando given the "go" signal for a nighttime raid. Meanwhile, my husband snores peacefully. Unless he's faking it. He's faking it, right?

This is not an idle playground gripe. The American Time Use Survey found that mothers in dual-earning households are three times as likely to have their sleep interrupted by children as fathers are.

As it happens, men really might be oblivious. Researchers from the UK's Mindlab International measured subconscious brain activity in sleeping men and women and found that while a baby's crying was the number one nighttime sound most likely to wake up a woman, it didn't even figure into the male *top ten*—lagging behind car alarms. And strong wind.

They theorized that these differing sensitivities might have an evolutionary basis: women were more attuned to potential threats to their offspring, while men were more responsive to distur-bances that posed larger threats to the whole clan. And women, as biological anthropologist Helen Fisher points out to me, not only have a keener sense of hearing, but they are better at seeing in the dark (while men are better at seeing in the light). Knowing all of this might make it at least a little easier to haul yourself out of bed when your baby starts to sob.

Then again, it could just be selective hearing. As my friend Jenny, mother of two, says, "I feel like most men seem to possess a remarkable self-preserving ability to compartmentalize tasks and ignore excess stimuli—the kind often produced by young chil-dren." She recalls one weekend in which she went to the bedroom for a brief lie-down, which was thwarted when she overheard her husband ignore twenty attention-seeking pleas of *Dad. Dad. Dad. Dad. Dad.* In exasperation she yelled, "Don't you *hear the kid?*"

"Sometimes," he answered.

> *Why does my husband need a constant escape hatch from our family—the garage, his gizmos, the basement, his sudden obsession with training for the New York Marathon?*

The writer Alan Richman put it best: "Men don't want to be alone, they just want to be left alone." Indeed, UCLA researchers found that a father in a room by himself was the "person-space configuration observed most frequently" in their close study of thirty-two families at home. It may also explain why many fathers manage to finish the Sunday paper while their wives do not—they aren't constantly leaping up to refill the umpteenth bowl of Cheerios. Fisher says there is brain evidence that when women are under stress (say, a new baby has colic), they are inclined to "tend and befriend" (become more empathetic and social), while men under stress are apt to withdraw.

Try this experiment during any major holiday, particularly Thanksgiving: drive past your local car wash, and note the colossal line of dads who suddenly feel an overwhelming urge to get the Premium Deluxe wash, full wax, and, why not, the Showroom Finish interior and exterior detailing package.

But even if they're home, they can use their gizmos as a way to be physically present yet still effectively check out. In the Judd Apatow movie *This Is 40*, many parents laughed in recognition during the scene in which Paul Rudd's character sits on the toilet, doing crosswords on his iPad, when his wife, played by Leslie Mann, yanks open the door of his particular person-space configuration. "This is the fourth time you've gone to the bathroom today," she says. "Why is your instinct to escape?"

"It is my instinct to come into the bathroom when I need to go to the bathroom," he says.

She narrows her eyes. "Then why don't I smell anything?"

"Because I shoved an Altoid up my ass before I came in here," he snaps as she grabs his device and stalks off. "Don't press *enter!*" he calls from the john. "I'm not sure I want to make that move!"

When Tom disappears for a long run, or bolts for the door, announcing over his shoulder that he has to "take care of a few things," I've often rationalized to myself that like most men, he needs his alone time. But is this anything more than some story men — and the culture at large — tell themselves about what it is to be male? Could there be some sort of evolutionary reason why men feel the need to escape — perhaps to scan the horizon for predators? I contact Joseph Henrich, a professor of human evolutionary biology at Harvard University, to puzzle it out with me. At first, he's too distracted by the news that Tom took up long-distance cycling after our daughter was born. "Wow," he says. "I have three kids, and I don't remember a bike trip, or trip of any kind, being an option. I would have gone kayaking."

Then he snaps into gear. "Well, cross-culturally and historically, there has been a great deal of variation in male parental investment, especially in babies," he begins. "So I cannot think of any evolutionary approaches that might illuminate this." He speculates that perhaps now that men are more involved as fathers, their lives change in a much more dramatic way after parenthood than those of previous generations. "So I'm thinking this kind of male sojourn might be a reaction to the life transition that now occurs for men when a baby arrives," he says.

Helen Fisher offers another take. "I would think that when your husband bikes upstate he is, number one, trying to get away from the stress of a job that he doesn't feel skilled at and trying to preserve his own autonomic nervous system; two, he feels, even unconsciously, the need to build up his testosterone again because it plunges after the baby is born. And thirdly, now he's a father, maybe he has the drive to stay fit and remain healthy and be good at his job, so he can be there to raise his kid and get her through college."

When she puts it that way, Tom sounds almost noble. I repeat Dr. Fisher's evolutionary defense to Tom, which he of course enthusiastically confirms.

My wife gets mad at me for not helping with the kids. But when I try to pitch in, she just ends up doing everything herself. I can't win.

Psychologists have a name for this widespread behavior — *maternal gatekeeping* — in which mothers can swing open the gate to encourage fatherly participation, or clang it resolutely shut by controlling or limiting Dad's interactions with the kids. The latter behavior can range from making all decisions about school without consulting the father, to criticizing what he serves for lunch ("Hello, where are the vegetables?"), to protesting when he's roughhousing with the kids ("Easy, let's not send them to the emergency room!").

In some cases, mothers are not even consciously aware that they are doing this — but even nonverbal cues of disapproval such as eye-rolling or heavy sighing can put off a hesitant father. The result is a self-reinforcing loop: as she criticizes or takes over, he grows more and more uncertain of his abilities.

Maternal gatekeeping, in fact, can start as soon as pregnancy, says Ohio State's Sarah Schoppe-Sullivan. She found in her research that by the third trimester, some mothers had already made a decision to keep the gate firmly closed if the fathers-to-be reported that they didn't feel confident about their parenting skills (despite the fact that before the baby is born, those skills are all theoretical). In another exercise, she had new parents change a baby's clothes; one mother showed the father exactly what to do, down to pointing out the positions of the snaps on the infant's outfit — and visibly grimaced when the father tried to play with the baby.

Schoppe-Sullivan says that a mother's encouragement makes a big difference in how much fathers participate in childcare. "Fathers have less confidence in their parenting than mothers do at the time of the child's birth," she tells me, "and this often sets up an 'expert-apprentice' dynamic in which fathers are looking to mothers for validation of their parenting."

Chris Routly, blogger and president of the National At-Home Dad Network, is one of the estimated 1.4 million (and rising) stay-at-home fathers in the United States. (Some chafe at this term and offer alternatives such as "domestic first responder.") Routly has seen firsthand how men can be crowded out of the equation before the baby is even born. "Women have baby showers thrown for them, they join classes, they have multiple doctors, they get advice from friends and family," he says. "So by the time that baby is born, she has been prepared as much as she can be." But there is very little preparation for fathers, he says. "They start out on a very unequal footing."

Schoppe-Sullivan says fathers should be encouraged to spend time alone with their infants without maternal meddling. "Mothers can also become more conscious of their reactions to fathers' parenting," she says, "and bite their tongues regarding small stuff, like whether or not the baby's clothes match."

38

I must admit that I'm frequently guilty of gatekeeping. When, for instance, I asked Tom to help Sylvie with a book report for her homework, I made myself go into the bedroom with a book so that I wouldn't interfere. Unfortunately for Tom, I could still hear them talking as they sat at the kitchen table.

TOM: Okay, right. So who is the main character in *Clifford and the Big Storm*?

SYLVIE: Clifford.

TOM: Yes. Great. Write that on this line here. And what did Clifford do?

SYLVIE: Well, he went to the beach with the girl, Emily Elizabeth? To see her grandma? And he built a castle in the sand, but it was so funny because he's so big that the castle looked like a real castle.

TOM (GHOST VOICE): How about that.

ME (CALLING FROM THE BEDROOM): Tom, are you on your phone?

TOM (SOUND OF HIM HASTILY STASHING AWAY HIS PHONE): No! So, okay, write that down: *Clifford built a large castle.* Then what happened?

SYLVIE: Then there was a storm, and guess what? He rescued two puppies! And at the end he made a big pile of sand in front of Grandma's house so nothing happened to it in the storm.

TOM: Great, write that down. Okay, I think we're done here.

ME (READING THE SAME PARAGRAPH THREE TIMES AND FINALLY CALLING): Tom? Her teacher said she has to write about how the character develops and what lessons he learns. It's not just supposed to be "and then this happened."

TOM: But Clifford's character doesn't really develop. There is nothing described here except the plot mechanics.

ME (THROWING DOWN THE BOOK AND MARCHING INTO THE KITCHEN): He learned that saving Grandma's house was a good impulse and you should help people, or whatever! You know, teachable moments and all that crap!

TOM: But if you parse the text, he doesn't actually learn anything, it's very external in that he...

ME (GRABBING THE BOOK REPORT AND SHOOING TOM AWAY): Oh, for Christ's sake!

Looking back over that little exchange, I see that I was being ridiculous. My daughter wasn't writing her Harvard dissertation. Most of her homework involves shakily coloring in triangles, or guessing which frog isn't like the others. (And, for the record, Tom pretty much taught Sylvie to read by age three, with nightly story marathons and a constant *Clockwork Orange* barrage of sight words.)

I swear that my husband does a — literally — crappy job of changing a diaper on purpose, hoping I'll just take over and he can wriggle out of it.

Ah, yes: the deliberately inept job. On the rare occasion that Tom changed an erupting diaper, I would, inevitably, hear this from the baby's room:

"Oh, no! It's oozing out the sides. Do I wipe it? Where's the diaper cream? Oh, never mind. Wait, this is ointment. Is ointment like diaper cream? Should I wrap this diaper in something before I put it in the Diaper Genie? Because it's pretty messy. Oh no, her face is turning red. Her arms are really flapping. It's sort of... okay, this is really alarming. Can you just — can you just come in here and help me hold her still?"

When I'd run in to assist, the relief on his face was almost comical.

The idea that men aren't inherently skilled at housework and childcare is perpetuated by both males and females. Clare Lyonette of the University of Warwick in the UK says that when she and her colleagues did a study on the division of labor between parents of young children, they discovered that while the women were frustrated at doing the bulk of the housework, they were mollified by their belief in what Lyonette calls "the myth of male incompetence" — that men were lousy at it, anyway.

"It's definitely a myth, but women excuse their men from doing more by saying this, and men do the same," she says. "But as my coauthor used to say, 'Pushing a Hoover around isn't exactly rocket science.'"

Delving further, Lyonette and her colleagues uncovered an intriguing twist in the research: the men they studied who had lower incomes were more likely to help their partners with housework than the higher earners. (As Lyonette tartly put it at the time, the wealthier guys were "reluctant to lift a finger and appear to simply throw money at the issue by hiring a cleaner instead.")

But no matter what the men earned, those who did contribute tended to choose more "visible" domestic tasks. Why? "Because people can see them doing them — food shopping, cooking the Sunday roast," she tells me, "whereas nobody wants to do the cleaning." There are numerous Instagram shots of fathers' homemade pancakes for the kids, but not so many of that meticulously reorganized closet.

Feminist writer Caitlin Moran says that men who say, "You're the expert" on childcare and running a load of laundry need to be shamed. "When they say, 'I'm scared I'm going to shrink the clothes so you must do the washing,'" she tells me, "I recommend you just laugh at them and go, 'Seriously? You're a man with a degree, you drive a car, you hold a job, you've climbed a mountain, and you tell me you don't know how to operate a washing machine? Go on! Go do it!'"

Portland dad Routly agrees. "The truth is, we men treat these things like 'Oh, I can't — it's just too hard for me,' because that's an easy excuse to get out of it," he says. "Changing diapers is not pleasant, but it's a skill you learn with experience. And in the larger scope of things, when you're changing your baby's diaper for years, you build a level of intimacy. When your kid has peed into your mouth, there's a level of connection with that child. Whereas if anybody else in your life did that, you'd probably cut off all contact."

Routly and many stay-at-home fathers in his network say that they are living proof that gender is largely immaterial when it comes to caregiving — and an Israeli study backs them up. While women have long been assumed to be hardwired to nurture, protect, and worry about their children, researchers studied fathers who were primary caregivers of their firstborn, and found that certain neural pathways in their brains were actually being reshaped. In particular, the amygdala-centered network, which handles strong emotion, vigilance, and attention, was activated, which configured the dads' brains in a similar way that pregnancy and childbirth do for mothers. The research suggests that the neural circuitry that powers the so-called maternal instinct can be developed by fathers.

Stay-at-home dads even complain about the same things that mothers traditionally do, says Routly. "A lot of the gripes women have about their husbands have more to do with the roles that each is playing in their family, and less to do with gender," he says. "Stay-at-home dads complain just as much about 'Why can't my wife load a dishwasher properly?' My wife will come home from work and leave her Snapware containers from her lunch on the counter, rather than put them in the dishwasher."

"Tom does the same thing, just leaves everything *near* the dishwasher," I say.

"Right?" he says. "And it's like, 'Why can't she just put it in the dishwasher?'"

"Exactly!" I cry, wishing that he lived in Brooklyn and we could meet for playdates.

Why is my wife so impatient if I don't rush to do something the second she asks? If I say, "I'll get to it soon," she flips out.

That's an easy one, says New York psychotherapist Jean Fitzpatrick. "Women tend to be the ones who do the time-associated tasks that involve deadlines all through the day, like preschool pickup or night feeding," she tells me. "Her entire day is programmed in that way — to respond instantly. So women will get furious when they say to their male partners, 'Listen, can you fix this thing that broke in the bathroom?' And he'll be like, 'Why are you bugging me?'"

My husband didn't do a thing all weekend to help with our baby son, and I work all week just like he does. By Sunday night, I was fuming, but I swear that he didn't even notice. How could he be so oblivious when I'm glaring at him?

This seemingly willful obliviousness is one of the commonest complaints that I hear. A study of heterosexual couples led by Shiri Cohen, a couples therapist and psychology instructor at Harvard Medical School, revealed that women reported feeling much happier when their male partners understood that they were angry or upset. "This research bore out what I see every day with couples," Cohen tells me. "When the man can register his wife's negative feelings, and communicate that on some level, the wife feels better, because she knows that 'Oh, he gets how I'm feeling.'" She points out that, conversely, men do not derive the same satisfaction in knowing that their wives are upset. "Research shows that men tend to retreat from what feels like conflict to them, because they tend to physiologically get much more negatively aroused," she said, "so conflict feels way more intense for them."

What's even more intriguing is that key to the women's satisfaction was the perception that their mates were simply *making an effort* to understand where their angriness was coming from—

rather than reading their emotions perfectly. "It kind of gives people a sense of encouragement that we don't have to be 100 percent perfect and tuned in to our partner for them to know we care about them," says Cohen.

If you both happen to be sleep deprived from a new baby, there is also the distinct possibility that his brain truly can't discern that you're angry—one study measured brain activity in sleep-deprived people and found that their brains were fuzzily incapable of distinguishing between threatening and friendly faces.

But even if your mate seems oblivious, he may be detecting your wrath on a subconscious level. A University of Southern California study that observed married couples over several days found that if a mother was stressed, the father's levels of the stress hormone cortisol would also rise—that, in effect, families "sync up" stress levels. Specifically, mothers drove the fathers' cortisol changes, while, in a dismaying trickle-down effect, fathers drove changes in their kids' cortisol.

"When I'm counseling couples," says Cohen, "I've noticed a pattern: if I ask a broad question like 'How are you doing?' or 'How was the week?' the husband always looks at the wife to see what she's going to say. So it's like men sort of expect that women are the ones who are taking the temperature in the relationship." Or, as my mother often pronounces, *If Mama ain't happy, nobody's happy.*

Why does my wife get so tense if the house looks less than perfect? Who cares?

Because women still fear being judged, says San Francisco psychologist Joshua Coleman. "If little Shaun shows up to preschool with torn jeans and peanut butter on his face, people don't think, 'What is his father thinking?'" he points out. "They're saying, 'What is his mother thinking?'" (I cringe to recall how often, in similar circumstances, I have silently impugned a mother myself.)

Mothering and keeping house are, like it or not, still more central to women's identities, so if the house is dirty, women are typically more fearful that they'll be blamed. "Which is still the legacy of these roles that we've inherited," Coleman says. "So I think because generally it doesn't mean as much to men, they have more immunity to those sorts of things. A clean house means much more to my wife. When I leave in the morning, I don't give a shit if the cereal is all over the place."

I do — especially before playdates, which provide thousands of opportunities for judgment. Until I had a child, I had never been inside half of my friends' New York apartments, most of which were so cramped that it was easier to meet at a restaurant or bar. Now that my friends and I constantly host playdates, we all make panicked sweeps beforehand to hide things that might raise eyebrows: the towels blooming with bleached-out stains from adult acne medication, the video game consoles (stash those behind the austere Swedish wooden educational toys), the catalog of foot supports and "comfort insoles," the tube of Aquaphor on your bedside table that you use as cuticle conditioner but could easily be misconstrued as lube.

Rivers of ink have been spilled over the impossible standards of perfection to which mothers hold themselves. One study of working parents found that women reported greater feelings of inadequacy when describing their family life: 30 percent said they were failing to meet the standards they wanted, as opposed to 17 percent of men.

Brené Brown, author and research professor at the University of Houston Graduate College of Social Work, calls herself a recovering perfectionist. "Perfectionism is so destructive," she tells me. "Never once in the twelve years I interviewed CEOs and award-winning athletes did I ever hear someone say, 'I achieved everything I have today because I am a perfectionist.' Never! What I hear people say is 'My success is very much based on my ability to keep perfectionism at bay.'"

However, that awareness, she added, doesn't stop her from occasionally lurching awake at five in the morning "in a dead panic, like, 'Oh, my God, I am such a loser, I can't believe I didn't email back that person about my son's school project.'"

> *I* suspect that my husband deliberately takes his time when I ask him to do something, so I won't ask him to do something else.

"You are correct," says every man, ever.

"If I finish up quickly, Dinah has plenty of other jobs lined up," says my brother-in-law Patrick. "So I've gotta be honest, I take my time."

"There's something called Zipf's law," chimes in Tom, "named for a linguist, who said people naturally economize to do the least amount of work they can over time. It's why most of us only use a small number of words in daily life — why reach for the obscure ones? Also, yes, I'm afraid you'll ask me to do something else."

> *When we're trying to get our three kids into bed at night, I've done fifty things in the time it takes my husband to put away Legos. It makes me crazy.*

During school mornings, I, too, am a hurricane, while Tom waits by the door jingling his keys, genuinely puzzled that I'm "never on time." (Key-jingling is the soundtrack of my life. Tom's tolerance for playgrounds tops out at one hour; then out come the keys. My father is similar: if we visit a museum, an hour and fifteen minutes is his absolute limit before he goes outside to sit on a bench and people-watch. "I've seen all there is to see," he announced recently after a brisk stroll through the priceless treasures in the Met Museum.) Tom also tends to do one thing at a time; if I throw more tasks at him, I watch his eyes grow blank as his circuits overload.

The old stereotype that women are better multitaskers might actually be true, according to a University of Pennsylvania study. Scientists found stronger neural connectivity in men from front to back and within one hemisphere, suggesting that their brains are built to "ease connectivity between perception and coordinated action" — that is, to perform a single task. In women, meanwhile, the wiring runs between the left and right hemispheres, suggesting it "facilitate[s] communication between the analytical and intuition" — so women have better memory and social cognition skills, making them better equipped for multitasking and creating solutions that can work within a group.

A study conducted by UK psychologists found that in some cases, women may indeed be better multitaskers. In one test designed to mimic everyday life, a group of women and men had eight minutes to finish a series of tasks, such as deciding how they would search for a lost key in a field. (I have actually done this: Tom once dropped his keys in a field during a bike race in Red Hook.)

As it wasn't actually possible to finish everything in eight minutes, the exercise compelled the participants to quickly prioritize, use time wisely, and stay calm with a ticking deadline. Women aced the key search task in particular by drawing a map of the field and showing how they would methodically go around it in concentric rectangles — which is exactly what I did in order to find Tom's keys. "That's a highly productive strategy for finding a lost object," study coauthor Keith Laws told the BBC, "whereas some men didn't even search the whole field in any particular manner, which is just bizarre."

The women, he said, tended to plan out a strategy in the beginning, whereas men jumped into the "field" too quickly. One theory the researchers floated as to why women might be more skilled at multitasking is that in earlier times, they became adept at doing many things at once as they tended to the clan — a prehistoric "struggle to juggle" — while men were out doing more so-called linear tasks, such as chasing down dinner.

If my wife is fuming that I stand there while she empties the dishwasher, why doesn't she just say "Help me empty the dishwasher" instead of banging pots and pans around?

In general, says leading communication scholar Julia T. Wood, men are more direct in speech than women within the context of relationships. "Some men may assume that if a female partner has a grievance, she will state it forthrightly," she says, "and may not perceive the banging pans as a statement of anger." Nonverbal cues, she adds, "operate largely on the relationship level of meaning—which some men are not especially adept at interpreting." (Indeed, a large survey of divorced people over age forty commissioned by AARP found that 26 percent of men who were served divorce papers *didn't see it coming.*)

Biological anthropologist Helen Fisher says that the ability to read facial expressions and body postures is better in the average woman than in the average man. From an evolutionary perspective, she says, "Women for millions of years had to raise the most helpless babies on the planet, and for the longest period of time. And because the babies don't talk for a while, the mothers need to know what the problems are—so women are better at reading emotions in the face, tone of voice, and all kinds of body postures, because of their long, *long* evolutionary job of raising babies."

In fact, she goes on, men are better at detecting emotions such as anger in the eyes of other *men* than they are in women. In hunter-gatherer times, men had to protect their group, "so it would be adaptive for a man to recognize anger in another man because those that didn't, did not notice the blow coming, and died out, and perhaps the group died out. So there was probably positive selection for the kind of man who could read anger in another man: you could lose your life by not noticing anger in a man's eyes, but you probably don't lose your life by not noticing anger in a woman. You're just gonna sleep on the couch." In other words, that maddening thousand-mile stare on your husband's face when he's at brunch with you and the kids may be grounded in evolution.

New York psychotherapist Jean Fitzpatrick says that in her practice, she has seen that "very often, for some reason, women think that guys are going to just pitch in and contribute, and if they don't, then they're deliberately choosing not to pitch in. Or they don't care. So they go to 'Well, he doesn't really care about me.' And instead, it would be really helpful to say, 'Here's what I need from you right now.'"

Brené Brown calls this tendency to project a motive onto someone without actually knowing the facts "the story I'm making up." In her book *Rising Strong*, she describes a scene in which it's nearing dinnertime, her two kids are hungry, and her husband, Steve, opens the refrigerator and announces, "We have *no* groceries. Not even lunch meat." She immediately snarls at him, saying that she's doing the best she can and that he could do the shopping, too.

Then she had a moment of clarity. She apologized and told him, "The story I'm making up is that you were blaming me for not having groceries, that I was screwing up." Steve told her that he was actually frustrated because he was planning to shop the day before but didn't have time.

I realize I do this all the time with Tom. If I'm doing five chores at once while he's relaxing with a game of computer chess, my mind constructs a story in which he's thinking, "I've suckered my wife into doing everything, and it feels fantastic! I'm king of the woooorld!"

When in fact he's thinking, "Do I castle on the queen side or the king side?" Which is slightly less diabolical.

> *Why is it that my husband feels perfectly happy to plop down on the couch while I'm running around after our three kids and cooking dinner at the same time?*

Often, men simply feel more entitled to take leisure time. A University of Southern California study of married couples found that at the end of a workday, women's stress levels went down if their husbands pitched in with housework. No surprise there — but the mind-boiling part is that men's stress levels fell if they kicked back with some sort of leisure activity — *but only if their wives kept busy doing household tasks at the same time* (an effect I term While You're Up, I'll Take Another Cold One).

When study author Darby Saxbe started looking at the data, she says, "We sort of thought it would probably be all the more relaxing to have leisure time if you have a spouse that's doing that leisure *with* you," she tells me. "So it was kind of surprising that we found the opposite effect — that the more leisure time dads had and the less leisure time wives had, the more men's cortisol levels dropped."

The somewhat dispiriting conclusion: a man's biological adaptation to stress is healthier when his wife has to suffer the consequences.

• •

Now that I have gathered some background information, it is time to move on to the tougher work: our fighting. Tom initially resists when I propose couples therapy. "I don't know," he says, shifting in his chair. "I guess I've always viewed couples therapy as a rearranging the deck chairs on the *Titanic* sort of thing." But he is more convinced when I tell him, calmly but resignedly, that if our situation does not change, I am afraid we will not stay together. When he goes away on business, I add, things at home are so much easier and more peaceful that I sometimes wonder if this would be a better situation for all of us. He looks stricken. For him, my subdued demeanor is much more alarming than my usual yelling.

He thinks for a minute and clears his throat. "I suppose I can see where having new sets of tools handy could be useful," he ventures, "especially when our old ones no longer seem to be working." Because he is a naturally curious person, I am also able to sell therapy as an unusual new experience for us to try.

He complies, but admits he still dreads the idea. And when I fill him in on the therapist we are seeing first, his dread promptly turns to panic.

"Get off Your Ass and Help Out!": Our Harrowing Encounter with the Man from Boston

There is this amazing guy from Boston, a friend confided in me. *You have this long, excruciating session with him where he drills down to your problems really fast, then sets you both straight. It's not cheap. And he's no bullshit, so you need to have a very, very thick skin. But he stopped us from getting divorced.*

I frequently write about relationships for magazines, so I have long known about Terry Real. A family therapist and founder of the Relational Life Institute in Boston, Real is a vociferous advocate of moving men and women beyond tired traditional gender roles. Famously blunt, he's an East Coast version of Dr. Phil, sans mustache and Texas twang. Real's specialty is working with couples on the brink of divorce whom no one else has been able to help, sort of a Memorial Sloan Kettering for marriage. Clients, among them celebrities and CEOs, fly to Boston from all over the country for his dramatic relationship overhauls — and pay $800 an hour for the privilege. I reason that a bracing session with him would be the perfect jump start.

Suffice it to say that neither of us is looking forward to it. We aren't alone in dreading couples therapy. Even therapists do: an article in the trade magazine *Psychotherapy Networker* revealed that many therapists are traumatized by the sometimes-vicious battles between couples, and infinitely prefer individual sessions. But it can be life-changing to learn how to talk to each other in an effective way — a survey of counselors found that the main reason couples get divorced is not infidelity, or money troubles, but "communication problems."

Our squabbling is not just affecting our marital health, but very likely our physical health, too. One study found that if a married couple's method of fighting was harsh or controlling in tone, it was just as powerful a predictor for risk of heart disease as whether a person smoked or had high cholesterol. Researchers at Ohio State University, meanwhile, found that married couples' wounds actually healed more slowly when they had hostile arguments compared with so-called low-hostile couples. The stress from a fallout, they discovered, drove up blood levels of hormones that interfere with the delivery of proteins called cytokines, which aid the immune system during injuries.

Conversely, an avalanche of research shows that happy marriages can boost your health and wellbeing. People in positive long-term relationships have lower rates of heart disease, live longer, and are less likely to develop cancer. Swedish researchers even found that being married at midlife is linked with a lower risk for dementia.

I'd like for us to be a long-lived, low-hostile couple.

Terry Real books up months in advance, so I quickly secure an eye-wateringly expensive five-hour session. Soon afterward, I receive a note from his assistant:

> The office is a large, olive-green Victorian-type building. Come on in and have a seat, and Terry will come and get you when it's time for your session. Dress for the session is extremely informal. Terry dresses comfortably and invites you to do the same. You're going to have a long, hard-working day. Feel free to call me if you're anxious.

We are not sure what to do with Sylvie during our session: even though she has just turned six, we don't have a regular babysitter. Tom and I, committed homebodies, rarely go out and are quite content being a trio. (It is not lost on me that our lack of dates is probably part of the reason we are in this mess.)

Still, a couples therapy session is perhaps not the ideal place for a child. But my folks are out of town; Tom's live in Chicago. Both of my sisters offer to take her for two nights, but because she had never spent the night at their houses, Tom and I worry: what if she can't handle it for some reason, and we have to cut short our pricey session? Real has a strict cancellation policy.

I phone Real's assistant (well, she did say to call if I was anxious) and ask if we can bring Sylvie and stick her in another room.

"I guess so," she says hesitantly. "We had a client bring his dog once. But many clients cry and raise their voices. I'm just concerned about your daughter hearing that."

"Oh, I'll bring headphones," I say breezily. "We'll load up the iPad with cartoons, and she'll watch until her eyes bleed. I just need to position her near an electrical outlet in case it needs charging."

I can detect the hope in her voice when she tells me to let her know if anything changes and we are able to get childcare.

Finally, the day arrives. We drive from New York to Boston and, after a restive night in a hotel, are dressed and ready to go an hour in advance. We make a tense drive to the large, olive-green Victorian-type building, Sylvie happily clutching an armful of stuffed animals and a loaded iPad.

We arrange a makeshift nest for her on a sofa, and Tom assembles her gizmo, while I produce a large bag of cookies, candy, and chips. (Later, Sylvie will proclaim her parents' therapy session "the best day ever.")

Tom and I seat ourselves and wait, leafing distractedly through the magazines on the coffee table. Is Real on the premises? A sign on the wall reads "Children Learn What They Live." "Tom," I whisper. "You will be open to this, right? I mean, if we're going to do this, we should really jump in."

"Yes, I'm open," he whispers back, although his demeanor is that of a cat about to be stuffed into a carrier for a trip to the vet. Time for your shots!

"Don't worry," I whisper. Why are we whispering? I squeeze his hand. "I think if we can —"

Just then, the office door swings open and we leap up, almost knocking heads. The Man from Boston.

"Hi," he says, extending his hand. Tall and attractive, with penetrating blue eyes, Real looks to be in his early sixties and possesses a droll warmth that puts us slightly more at ease. He leads us to a wood-paneled office done in soothing greens, browns, and blues.

He shuts the door and we settle in, fussing with our seating arrangements. Then he looks at us unblinkingly over his reading glasses. "I always start with the same question," he begins. "This is a lot of money and you've come a long way. What are your hopes? What would a grand slam look like?"

For the first half hour, we explain our situation: At least a few times a week, we fight about childcare, housework, and money, often in front of our child. I yell at Tom, and he shuts me out and ignores me; it is grinding us down and worrying our daughter.

"Sylvie jumps to my defense, and I'm often the one who did something wrong," adds Tom, turning to me. "Maybe that's because you're more, uh..." — he searches for a word that will not offend — "vocal?"

Real looks at me. "See, Sylvie will side with him as a way of ameliorating your anger. She's pleading his case to you — 'Mom, don't be mad at him.' But it does set up an alliance. And yeah, it's gotta stop. This is not a good thing." He stops talking and peers at me. "You look sad."

To my profound discomfort, sudden tears are coursing down my cheeks. "I want to be kinder to Tom," I say, snuffling. "But I also want him to do more work around the house and not leave it all to me." I rub my eyes. "I wore mascara, how stupid was I?"

Real pushes a box of tissues toward me. Then he deftly dissects our family and psychological histories, teasing out key issues (I grew up in a very controlled household; Tom was a latchkey kid whose life lacked structure). He moves on to questions about our romantic history with each other, then asks me to walk him through a fight.

I tell him that Tom has just taken a bike trip through the Italian countryside for ten days on a magazine assignment. When he came home, he was jet lagged, so for the ensuing two days, I was once again a single parent as he slept all day. So when he was awake, I yelled.

Real nods. "I got news for ya," he says. "I'm on your side."

I stop in the midst of blowing my nose. "Wait, what? You are?"

Real glares at Tom over his reading glasses. "You want to go away for ten days, having the time of your life, biking through the countryside and having pasta at night? You come home, you're there for the kid, and *your wife's off her feet.*"

"But —" Tom puts in weakly.

"— I tell you this as somebody who had little kids myself," Real barrels on. "Okay? I was on the road a ton and I had to do it, too. I talk to men all the time and say, 'If you're away from your wife and kids, working, even if it's wall to wall work and it's not pleasurable, and you come home and you're dog tired, *too bad.* If anything, you have to be super thoughtful, because it's *really hard* to be home with the kids alone."

My triumph must be visible on my face, because Real stops me with a sharp look. "Not that you have a right to behave the way you behaved," he barks. "If he goes away on a trip, don't give it to him and then piss on it on the way out the door. I call that 'peeing on the gift'! Either let him do it and be okay about it, or don't!" To my relief, his head swivels back to Tom. "How do you feel about what I said?"

"Well," Tom says, shifting in his seat, "I guess I haven't heard this before. I mean, guys talk, but…"

Terry waves him away. "Guys, first of all, get together and they guy it. They reinforce this entitlement in one another: 'Wow, I would never put up with that — are you kidding me?' Meanwhile, they go home and they damn well do put up with it! But you wouldn't know about it! And then women do the big victim thing with each other — how woefully lacking their husbands are. The point being, I'm not surprised you haven't heard this before because no one will tell you. What else do you fight about?"

"Um, the fact that I tend to, maybe, be self-absorbed about taking time for me," says Tom. All of a sudden, I feel protective of him, and jump in to add that with Sylvie, he is utterly unselfish, kind, and attentive. No matter what her request — Scrabble, an after-dinner trip to the park, a tea party with her dolls — he cannot say no.

"You sound like a wonderful father," Real tells him. "So, if I were to ask Jancee if your self-absorption leans into selfishness with her, what do you think she would say?"

Tom furrows his brow. "Well, is 'selfish' more volitional, would you say? Whereas in the case of being self-absorbed, the person may be inclined toward acting selfish, but not know that —"

Real cuts him off. "Selfish would be more behavioral: insensitive, putting yourself first, not giving. Is that you?"

Tom, now so squeamish that I pity him again, agrees that it is.

Real asks me my most pressing issue and I tell him it's my temper. "I hate myself after I yell," I say.

Real shrugs. "Well, that's useless."

"And I think I get too defensive too quickly, because I'm being yelled at," says Tom. "If I think it's not a major issue, I almost just want to provoke her. So I shut down."

"I will say this," says Real. "Volatile women generally don't feel heard. So you get into: Can you hear me now? *WHAT ABOUT NOW?* That's not going to get you heard. The reciprocal piece of this, Tom, is your walling off and passive aggression. It's a way of expressing your anger by what you *don't* do. And it's provocative; it actually escalates things."

We jostle for approval from our stern new father. "In the end, I don't know why I don't just do the dishes," Tom admits. "Because I don't care that much about them. I don't know why I wall her off. Maybe it's some kind of relationship jujitsu? As they say, 'Use your enemy's strength against them.'"

Real nods. "You don't like being told what to do. You don't like being controlled and attacked. Listen, there's too much hostility and it's not good for Sylvie, especially in a small space like that."

I drift off for a minute. If only our modest Brooklyn apartment had a walk-in closet, like the one in New Jersey governor Chris Christie's house. Christie told the author of his biography that he and his wife, Mary Pat, vowed never to fight in front of their four children, as his parents did when he was a boy. So, to escape the kids (and the state troopers who drive them places), they head to Mary Pat's large closet, shut the door, and hash it out.

"— and you're falling into roles where Jancee's the aggressor, Tom is seen as the poor victim, and Sylvie's the peacemaker, and this is how shit gets passed down through generations," Real is saying. "Tom, the coalition between you and your daughter against Jancee is a really bad dynamic, particularly because you're so nurturing with Sylvie."

I tell Real that we almost never fought before we became parents, and he laughs. "Listen, you put a kid in the mix and then there's this negotiation. I remember counting the minutes when my wife was at the gym and I was stuck with the kids. Like, 'Where the fuck is she?' And 'I have work to do.' I know that tussle. That's normal, to some degree. But then throw in your anger and resentment" — he points to me — "and your selfishness and preciousness" — the finger moves to Tom — "and the more angry you get, the more selfish and withdrawn you get. It needs to be nipped in the bud. It's a toxic, self-reinforcing loop that begins to eat away at everything that's good between the two of you." He shakes his head. "You do this pattern for fifteen, twenty years and you turn into the couples I see who are at the end of this, who are about to leave. Forty-three percent of couples divorce." (In fact, while the national divorce rate has remained steady since the 1980s, it has doubled for those over fifty — when parenting duties are winding down, or over.)

Sylvie knocks on the door with a request for Tom to fix the iPad. When she leaves, Real asks us why we didn't get a babysitter, and I explain that we couldn't find anybody. Then I confess that we didn't try very hard, either.

"She's easy, so we mostly bring her everywhere," I say. "She's nice to be around. I don't crave time apart from her."

Real is aghast. "It's not a craving to be away from *her* — it's a craving to be alone with *him!* What do you do to cherish each other as a couple?"

Not much, we say, exchanging guilty looks.

"Get a babysitter!" he explodes.

Back to our toxic, self-reinforcing loop. "I feel like I do so much for Tom," I begin. "I bake for him, I —"

"Yeah, yeah, you're very cherishing," Real says. "We get it."

"But before Sylvie was born, I did all the cooking," Tom interjects. "Now Jancee does. How did *that* happen?" He mimes bewilderment and laughs in a strangled, high-pitched sort of way.

Real leans in. "Whoa, whoa, whoa. What?" I can see him gathering force; it is weirdly exciting.

"Also, I am in charge of Sylvie every day after school," I put in.

"That's what I wanted to do. But if I have a deadline and ask occasionally for Tom to take over, he usually refuses. He guards his time."

Tom nods. "My instinctive reaction is no," he admits.

Real frowns. "But she's the after-school mom and the cook and the cleaner-upper," he says. "That would be fine if she didn't work, but not if you're both working. What I see happening with guys is 'Don't mess with me — I need sleep and R&R so I can fight the dragons for my family.' But she's fighting the dragons now, too." In the old days, he goes on, if a man was a good provider, had a steady hand, and didn't beat anyone, he was a good husband. "And what most men I work with don't get is that their relationship job description has changed," he says. "What I hear over and over again from women is 'I don't feel like I have a real partner.' But what most men *really* think is if their partners would just simmer down and get off their backs, things would be fine."

Real sits back in his chair and chuckles. "Listen, my wife is a no-bullshit gal. And when the kids were little, I'd be due to give a lecture the next day to a thousand people and nervous as hell. And one of the kids would inevitably wake up in the night, and Belinda, who's a psychotherapist like me, would have woken up three times already. And she'd say, 'Go see what he wants.' And I'd say, "I've got this lecture tomorrow — I can't…" And she'd say, 'So you'll give your lecture tired. Go deal with the kid.' And that was a bit of a revelation."

He leans forward. "Tom, what you're not getting, and this is true for most men I see, is that it is in your interest to move beyond your knee-jerk selfishness and entitlement and to take good care of your wife, so she isn't such a raving lunatic all the time." He shakes his head. "The idea that withdrawal is going to work is nuts. You're a sweet guy; I can see you have a sweet soul. But you have to do more. You have it in you; you know how to reach outside yourself with Sylvie. You could be in the chair and be dog tired, and she goes, 'Daddy,' and you get out of the chair and see what she wants."

Real looks steadily at Tom over his glasses. "When your work is done for the day, why wouldn't you split everything fifty-fifty? It's not fair. You know that. Tonight you cook; tomorrow she cooks. Tonight you put Sylvie to bed; tomorrow she puts Sylvie to bed. Show up and participate."

"But I think men have a problem with fifty-fifty," I put in.

"We're not talking about men, we're talking about Tom," he snaps. "Don't turn him into a class!" He asks Tom if he has a problem with splitting down the middle.

"Well, entropy takes over sometimes, and I...," Tom begins.

"Look, I know what you're talking about," Real breaks in. "The inertia, the laziness. But it's also entitlement. And it's dumb. Because it's short-term success and long-term resentment. It's in your interest to give! Learn to be a family man! Because your wife is *pissed off!*"

I watch as Tom's face slowly turns gray and put my hand on his arm: *Don't retract like a gastropod. Don't do it.*

Because Real is not done: "And part of being a family man is to help out when it's needed! If your wife is overburdened, and doing all the cooking and cleaning, get off your ass and help out!"

I try, without success, to hide my exultation. Why didn't we go to couples therapy sooner?

"You're right," says Tom meekly. "And I don't want Sylvie picking up my passivity. Now she says, 'In a minute' like I do when Jancee asks her to do something."

Real snorts. "Well, she's learning from her passive-aggressive father! She watches how you handle her. It's like that sign in my waiting room: children learn what they live." He lists three reasons why men tend to stonewall: They feel that they need to fix the woman's negative experience, and when they can't, they're caught in a "frustrated freak-out." They feel entitled ("like, 'I don't need this shit'"). And no one educated them on how to handle feelings. "Boys are taught to dampen emotions at the age of three or four," he says.

And this suppression continues through adulthood. Psychotherapist John Gottman found that during fights, men are more likely than women to experience diffuse physiological arousal, or DPA, as the body responds to the stress with a "fight or flight" response. This reaction makes a person feel "flooded," or overwhelmed: the heart beats uncomfortably fast, blood pressure soars, and people have trouble processing information, solving problems, or even listening (if a subject's heart was beating over 100 beats a minute, with some rocketing alarmingly to 168, Gottman found they were literally not able to hear the other person). Not only do men tend to experience DPA more than women, but their heart rate stays escalated for a longer period of time, and takes longer to return to normal.

So it could very well be that while Tom may resemble an impassive Easter Island statue during one of our showdowns, he's an emotional typhoon on the inside. (This turns out to be true: out of curiosity, I later measure his heart rate after a mild post-Real tiff, and it had zoomed from his usual 60 to 102.)

Real asks Tom if he tends to suppress his emotions during conflict, and he nods. "I think it's easier to have a release when, say, you're driving and someone cuts you off and you flip out. Or I tear up at the absolute worst, crappiest movies on airplanes."

Real laughs. "Men who won't cry at a funeral will cry at the friendly dinosaur movie." Then he gets serious again. "So, the best way to make your wife feel heard is to lean into it and disarm her, rather than stonewall her and have a three-hour fight. There are easy ways to do this. It works to say, 'You're unhappy; let me hear what you're talking about,' instead of going away. Or, "Oh, that must feel bad. I can see why you feel like that." Or, 'What can I say or do right now to make you feel better?' Those are phrases you're going to have to learn how to speak. Then she feels heard, and they render you a nicer guy to live with."

"I will do the work," says Tom solemnly. "It seems selfish to impose this on Sylvie." He turns to me and says quickly, "And because I care about you."

Real leans back. "Good," he says. "Your job walking out of here is to be more giving — physically, with helping around the house, and emotionally. I want you to open your heart, share more, listen better, cherish more. Verbally cherishing your wife with compliments, for example, is a good thing for her, good for Sylvie to see, and a good thing for Sylvie to expect from her guy or gal when she grows up."

Compliments and sweet words are no small thing. University of Michigan psychologist Terri Orbuch has studied divorced people for decades. As they looked back on their broken marriages, many told her that one of their biggest regrets was that they had not given their mate more of what Orbuch terms "affective affirmation": kissing, giving compliments such as "I would still choose you" or "You're a great parent," saying "I love you," and making small gestures of affection such as filling your partner's gas tank. Orbuch has called the neglect of these simple acts an "overlooked relationship-killer."

I snap back into focus as Real looks at me. "I'm telling you point-blank that this is a good guy, and I'd be shocked if he didn't come through for you," he is saying. "So, relax. Trust him."

Well, I think, *that was worth the money. It's definitely helpful that Terry is a man. What is it, five o'clock? Must be around quitting time. Maybe Italian for dinner?* I reach into my purse for my phone so I can check the time.

Then Real turns my way.

"Now," he says, "let's talk about your temper."

Uh-oh.

• •

Real has me shamefacedly repeat the invective I fling at Tom: *asshole, dick, I hate you.*

He nods. "You're verbally abusive."

I frown. "Well, I wouldn't say that, I mean, I —"

"Yes. You are. And it may get results, intermittently. That's the seduction of the dark path." He fastens his unblinking gaze on me. "But the idea that you can haul off and be abusive to your partner and somehow get a pass, that you can't control it, or whatever you tell yourself to rationalize it, is nuts. Also, your whole 'angry victim' role is going to get worse. You are extremely comfortable with your self-righteous indignation."

67

He then tells me, in stark terms, that it's time for me to climb off the cross. "Stop playing the martyr," he says. "Just say, 'Hey, sweetheart, I want you to know that I just cooked dinner, and you're doing the dishes.' If you're in a constant state of Self-Righteous Angry Victim, you're fucked. It's over. You're not a victim. So knock it off."

He isn't through. "More importantly, you need to take verbal abuse off the table," he says. "You can say, 'I'm angry.' But you don't say, 'You're an asshole.' You don't yell and scream. You don't humiliate or demean. They're off the table. You are verbally abusive. You can buy a book called *The Verbally Abusive Relationship* by Patricia Evans. You're in it."

I try for levity. "But isn't what I do just 'venting'?"

He doesn't play along. "It's not venting," he says levelly. "Get it? And you're yelling at your *daughter*, by the way, when you do that—just so you know. There's no differentiation for a six-year-old. And you've proved that you can stop it. Do you do this to Sylvie?"

"No."

"Right. Do you ever find her behavior trying?"

"Yes."

"So if you have the discipline to stop doing it *directly* to her, you can stop doing it *indirectly* to her," he says. "There is a very small group of people who truly can't control themselves—and, by and large, they're in mental institutions, or in jail." He leans forward. "Humiliating and ridiculing have no place whatsoever in a healthy relationship. There's a world of difference between assertively standing up for yourself and aggressively putting him down. As crazy at it might seem, arguing or complaining can actually feel safer to most of us than simply and directly making a request. So, starting today, you have to tell him what he could do to make you feel better by using the phrase 'What I'd like you to do now is...' Okay? Rather than just pounding him into the ground."

I ask Real if we can hash out any differences in front of our daughter. He shakes his head, telling me that for the time being, it must take place behind closed doors. "She's only six," he says. "She's too in the middle. She's seen you fight enough to last for a while."

Then he lays out a plan. The next time my temper engulfs me, I must immediately take a time-out and move to another room. "If you stand there and open your mouth, all kinds of crap may come out, and you may not be able to control that," he says. "But you can turn on your heel and leave — that, you can control. You don't even need to talk — just make the *T* sign and go. Anything you need to do to stop your temper, you do it. It's the number one priority."

He considers for a moment and then holds up his hand. "Here is exactly what I want you to do during your time-out," he says. "Go to another part of the house, shut the door, and take out a picture of Sylvie that you're going to keep nearby. I want you to say this to her picture. Ready?" I nod humbly. *"I know that what I'm about to do is going to cause you harm, but right now, my anger is more important to me than you are."*

The soothing blues and browns of his office waver as I am again overcome with tears. "Oh!" I sob. "Oh, this is awful."

I hear a loud sniff and look over at Tom. He is crying, too.

Then Real takes out a tissue, removes his glasses, and gingerly dabs his eyes.

As we drive back to the hotel, Sylvie is chattering happily; we are silent and shell-shocked. Tom quickly orders room service ("Right, what kinds of bourbon do you have?"), then we talk quietly as Sylvie snores on a nearby cot. We are being solicitous and tender with each other, holding hands as we hash out the day.

Real has told us the truth. We agree that having a third party forensically examine our problems with brutal candor is strangely exhilarating. Freeing, even. We promise each other that we will try hard to do what he recommends.

"Things are going to be different," I say. "I really feel like —" I sit up. "Tom?"

He has fallen into a deep sleep. It is 8:20.

* * *

I know that holding Sylvie's picture and repeating Real's terrible mantra will go a long way toward dousing the flames of my temper. But what if I need extra help — an additional behavioral Taser that would quickly get me back to baseline?

For days after we return from Boston, I ruminate. Then one morning, as I am halfheartedly doing the elliptical at the gym, the television cuts from a morning talk show to an unfolding hostage crisis at a Texas bank. The gunman is distraught, but within a few tense minutes, a negotiator has quickly calmed him down and persuaded him to surrender his gun. This sparks an idea: would it be possible to use the same methods to swiftly pacify a livid spouse? Do negotiators follow a formula? If Tom had those sorts of skills in his back pocket, they might be handy to pull out when my face starts to turn dark purple.

Back at the apartment, I research hostage negotiators. Soon I come across Gary Noesner, a thirty-year veteran of the Federal Bureau of Investigation and chief of the FBI's Crisis Negotiation Unit for a decade. Noesner spent his career reasoning with highly agitated people in life-or-death hostage situations, kidnappings, prison riots, and right-wing militia standoffs.

I promptly phone him up. Noesner, a father of three married for over forty years, is as affable and even-keeled as you would expect. Crisis intervention, he tells me, generally involves an intense effort within a relatively short period of time to lower physiological arousal and restore a person's ability to think more rationally — and its strategies, he tells me, could definitely apply to marriages. Noesner designed the FBI's conflict-resolving Behavioral Change Stairway Model, five steps that include active listening, showing empathy, building rapport, and gaining influence — which leads, finally, to the fifth step: behavioral change.

Noesner tells me that the harder we push — our usual impulse in a disagreement — the more likely we are to be met with resistance. "I always tell police officers, when you get a barricaded subject, if we do things like make loud noises or try to agitate him to get compliance, it typically creates the opposite effect," he says. "It's a universal human trait that people want to be shown respect, so negotiators must avoid intimidating, demeaning, lecturing, criticizing, and evaluating subjects." (All the things, ironically, I tend to do in my marriage.)

Noesner gamely sketches out a plan, based on FBI protocols, for Tom to de-escalate a crisis when his wife becomes a highly agitated individual.

First, he says, contain the situation. "When we show up in law enforcement to a dangerous, evolving situation, we know we have to contain it so it doesn't get worse or spread beyond its current confines," Noesner tells me. In a relationship, he says, don't allow the specific issue that's prompted the conflict to overflow into digging up dirt from ten years ago.

Next up: employ the seven active listening skills taught by the FBI. Do you want your mate to change? Then pay genuine attention to what he or she is saying. "Despite the popular notion that listening is a passive behavior, abundant clinical evidence suggests that active listening is an effective way to induce behavioral change in others," says Noesner. And when you actively listen to your partner, he adds, they tend to listen to *themselves* more carefully, and clarify their own scattered thoughts and feelings. They also grow less defensive and oppositional, and more open to solving problems.

As you're actively listening, put your own swirling thoughts on hold, adds Christopher Voss, the FBI's former lead international hostage negotiator and now the chief executive of the advisory firm Black Swan Group. "No one can listen and think about what they want to say at the same time," Voss tells me. "It truly is an either/or. Hearing the other side out is the only way you can quiet the voice in the other person's mind. A full two-thirds of people in negotiations are more interested in being heard than in making the deal." He thinks for a minute. "Also, just as an aside, if you let them go first, it gives them the illusion of control."

Active listening consists of the following seven techniques:

Paraphrasing

This is simply restating the person's message in your own words. "In law enforcement, I'll hear, 'You damn cops, you no-good sons of bitches,'" says Noesner. "And I'll say, 'It sounds like you really are suspect about why we're here and what we're doing.' 'You're damn right — you just want to kill me.' 'You're concerned we're going to hurt you, is that what I'm hearing?' I don't tell them they're right or wrong, I just paraphrase the way they feel. It's a way to say, 'I get it. I understand.'"

This technique quickly communicates that you comprehend the person's perspective, which is immediately disarming. "It's powerful stuff," Noesner says. "And tone is everything. You want your voice to convey sincerity and genuineness and come across as nonthreatening. I tell officers, do *not* do the military cop voice." (Which probably doesn't fly in relationships, either.)

Emotion Labeling

This technique helps a keyed-up person identify their emotions, some of which they may not even be aware they're experiencing. Don't use definitive language in case you miss your mark; use phrases such as "You sound as though" and "You seem as if." (A husband could say, for example, "You sound as though you are angry that I have no idea who our child's pediatrician is.") Naming and validating the person's feelings instead of minimizing them — or, worse, ignoring them — can take the person from a purely emotional, reactive frame of mind to a more rational state.

A brain imaging study at UCLA's Social Cognitive Neuroscience Laboratory appears to back this idea. Scientists found that the act of identifying our feelings makes anger or sadness less intense. In one experiment, they showed people a photo of an angry or fearful face and then measured their brain activity with an fMRI. They found heightened activity in the amygdala, which acts as the body's alarm system to trigger the "fight or flight" response if it senses danger. But when they had people *say* it was an angry face, rather than simply seeing it, the mere act of putting feelings into words caused their amygdala to calm down.

People want to be understood, Noesner says, "particularly when we're dealing with agitated individuals. When you say, 'I can see you're very, very angry over what happened,' they say, 'Yes! I am!'" This exchange takes the wind out of their sails, he says, because "it reduces their need to continue to demonstrate what you have already acknowledged clearly."

Concentrating on the other person's emotions also keeps your own blood pressure from soaring, adds Voss. "We have research that says the more you're focused on the other person's emotions, the more you're away from your own. It automatically makes you rational."

Offering Minimal Encouragements

As the person is talking, use short phrases to convey interest and concern: *Yes. Okay. I see.* "You're not really interrupting, you're just saying, 'Okay, I'm still tracking with you,'" says Noesner. "It's a little thing that lets them know you're along for the ride. And it's also hard to argue with somebody who is saying, 'Mm-hm. Yep. Yep.'"

Mirroring

Repeating the last few words of the other person's message builds rapport and allows them to vent. If a hijacker concludes a rant by saying, "and I'm angry," a negotiator will simply say, "And you're angry."

Asking Open-Ended Questions

The goal is to avoid "yes or no" questions, advises Noesner. "Instead, just say, 'Can you tell me more about that?' Or, 'I didn't understand what you just said and I'd like to; could you help me by explaining that further?'" Open-ended questions convey that you're sincerely interested and de-escalate violence by helping people collect themselves.

Using "I" Messages

The use of "I" statements personalizes the negotiator or, in law enforcement phraseology, lets you "drop the cop." An "I" message is also a way to express how you feel in a nonprovocative way without being pulled into an argument. For instance, a negotiator might say to a hostage taker, "I'm trying to understand what you're saying, but when you scream at me, it's hard for me to comprehend."

"So instead of saying, 'Don't scream at me,'" says Noesner, "you're kind of putting it notionally on your shoulders, like, 'I'm having trouble understanding — my bad.' But you're still telling the person why, so it's sort of a roundabout way to get them to quit behaving in a certain way."

Allowing Effective Pauses

Remaining silent at the right times and deliberately using pauses is hard to do, but it's particularly helpful during highly charged emotional outbursts, says Noesner. Why? Because when the person fails to get a response, they often calm down to verify that the negotiators are still listening. Eventually, even the most overwrought people will find it difficult to sustain a one-sided argument.

After the person has been calmed through active listening, it's time to move through the FBI behavioral staircase: showing empathy, building rapport, and establishing influence (in which you work collaboratively to develop "nonviolent problem-solving alternatives"). Your subject is then primed for the final step: behavioral change (hostage taker surrenders his assault rifle, wife stops yelling).

••••••••••••••••••••••••••••••

Two weeks after I consult the crisis negotiators and school Tom on their techniques, he creates a prime opportunity to try them out.

Sylvie has just started a new after-school art class, and because I am meeting with my *Vogue* editor for a rare drink in Manhattan, we arrange for Tom to pick up Sylvie from class at 5 p.m.

I have just settled into a booth with my editor when my phone rings. It is the proprietor of the art class. "Um, your daughter is still here," she tells me, "and we are closing soon." She had called our backup contact — a mom friend from Sylvie's preschool — but as it happened, the mother was at an urgent care facility dealing with her daughter's sudden heart palpitations.

I text Tom: *WHERE THE F R U?* No reply. Usually he gets back to me quickly, so I am certain that he is on his bike somewhere. The beauty of cycling at high speed and for long hours is that you can't text (one cycling buddy of his, a father of two, learned that the party was over when he returned from an epic ride to find that his wife had pointedly left her wedding ring on the kitchen table).

I text another mom and don't hear back. I flash my editor what

I hope is a reassuring smile, but I know it's more like a demented grimace that shows all my molars. I reach a third mom, who tells me she can't help because she's at her son's soccer practice. However, her babysitter is in our neighborhood park with her daughter, and she will ask her to pick up Sylvie. As my editor waits, I send a fourth text to Tom, who does not respond. Then I call the art class and convince them to allow Sylvie to leave with the babysitter, who isn't on their emergency contact list. After that, I burble apologies, postpone our meeting, and race home to relieve the babysitter before she leaves work at 6 (stopping first to pick up some chocolate as a thank-you).

At 6:30, Tom bursts into our apartment, his bike uniform soaked. "The park was empty today—it was so great!" he says with a grin. Then he stops, suddenly wary.

I stand motionless, chest heaving, eyes unnaturally bright.

"What?" he says guardedly.

I make the time-out sign and run, a move I will soon call Exit the Dragon (when smoke starts curling out of my nose, I retreat to the bedroom to roll a stone over the door). I take Sylvie's picture out of the bedside table and tell it, *I know that what I'm about to do is going to cause you harm, but right now, my anger is more important to me than you are.* My pulse slows. Slightly.

Tom follows me into the bedroom and closes the door. "Unreal," I whisper furiously, so Sylvie can't hear me from her room, where she is singing and drawing pictures. "What did I tell you this morning? *Please pick her up at 5.* Then I followed up with an email! Do you know how long it took me to pick out an outfit before this meeting so that I wouldn't look like I was trying too hard?" One of my eyelids starts twitching. I can see him watching it with fascination, which makes me angrier, which prompts it to spasm more crazily. My shoulders sag. "I can't count on you."

He runs over and stands next to me. "You think I'm unreliable," he paraphrases. "You don't like...uh, you don't like feeling panicky in a business meeting. You feel overwhelmed, like you have to do everything."

I nod, and tell him it's especially annoying to take the extra step — no, *steps* — of reminding him. "I'm not your mother," I hiss.

"Mm-hm," he says mechanically, looking into my eyes. "Go on." I know full well he is "offering minimal encouragement," but it is still sort of endearing, mostly because he's never uttered the phrase "go on" to me in our entire married life.

"And," I remind him, "you *still* didn't show!"

He nods gravely. "Still didn't show," he mirrors. I can sense him trying to remember the next step, which works inadvertently as an effective pause. I deflate just a bit.

"I know how you feel," he says. "I'd be frustrated, too." *A double "I message,"* I think. *Well played.*

"I normally am good about picking her up, so why don't we figure out ways that I'll absolutely remember?" he asks, open-endedly and collaboratively. And stiltedly, but I don't care too much: his patter may be scripted, but like the wives in Shiri Cohen's study, I appreciate any sort of effort. He is absentminded, not evil (although his absentmindedness is rather chronic — he has walked halfway to the subway carrying the morning's garbage, and daubed his toothbrush with Preparation H). I tell him later that if I hadn't been so mad, I would have laughed at his baffled, what-did-I-do expression when he burst through the door.

We construct a plan for his phone to issue a spate of reminders before all school pickups.

A week later, Tom's crisis negotiation skills are required yet again. It is a school morning, and he is sleeping in after a late night of binge-watching a Swedish crime series. I am up at 6 a.m. with our daughter, making her breakfast and lunch, supervising her homework, ordering a replacement water bottle after she somehow lost hers at school, filling out a form for a class trip, and baking carrot muffins for Tom.

Tom rouses himself fifteen minutes before she is due at school. As I am helping Sylvie get dressed and brush her teeth, he waits by the door to take her, absorbed in his phone. As she pulls on her coat, she reminds me that she must take in a dozen paper towel tubes we have been saving for a school art project.

"Where did I put them?" I say as she and I ransack her closet. "Oh, Lord, you can't get marked down as late again." Because I am often scrambling as we leave the house, one of the first phrases that Sylvie learned as a toddler was *Oh, Lord,* which she pronounced as *Oh, Yord.*

Tom is still standing in the front hallway, tapping on his phone. "Why wasn't this done earlier?" he calls.

Yord, give me strength.

When Tom returns from school, he steps into the swirling eddies of a tropical low-pressure system massing toward Category 5.

"You didn't lift a finger this morning!" I seethe.

I explain, as calmly as I can, that mothers have a particular pet peeve about feeling judged and inadequate, especially when the hundred things they do with smooth efficiency pass without comment. Tom is genuinely surprised and aggrieved that I am upset. He explains that he was just figuring out how we could have done something better — or, as he nerdishly terms it, "counterfactual troubleshooting." He thinks for a minute. "You were frustrated that I didn't help," he paraphrases. "You feel like...you feel like you are doing everything by yourself."

"'Why wasn't this done earlier?' Like I'm an employee?"

"Like an employee," he mirrors. "Mm-hm."

"I know what you're doing," I remind him. Although it is sort of funny. "Why didn't you jump in and help us find the paper towel rolls?" He pauses here, which gives me a second to reflect on the fact that I am raging about paper towel rolls.

"I...feel embarrassed that I didn't help," he says. Bull's-eye! My anger slowly ebbs away as I wait for the open-ended question. "Why don't you tell me what things I can take over in the morning?" he asks.

I know Tom's recitations aren't entirely sincere, but the FBI's techniques do calm me — if they work on armed hijackers and violent militia leaders, it's not surprising that they are effective on an angry wife. And maybe with enough practice, his questions will move from scripted to genuine. As Noesner and Voss tell me repeatedly, people just want to be heard — and in order to actively listen, you must pay real attention. You can't fake a paraphrase — if you do, you have failed to contain the situation with the agitated and potentially dangerous individual.

"Also, Sylvie was not marked down for being late," Tom points out as normalcy resumes. "A nanny showed me a side door, and I had Sylvie sneak in."

"You're the best," I say.

I am pleased with our new techniques, but aware that we have a way to go. We are now armed with methods to calm my temper, but the real work is to tackle the much larger, underlying problem: how we got into this situation in the first place. Under the guidance of some of the most eminent couples therapists in the country, we will try to learn how to quickly identify what is bothering us, conserve the energy our child has sapped by choosing the right battles, fight fairly, divvy up our household work, and tackle problems efficiently.

It's a daunting plan, so I decide to begin our next phase gently, with something called the Zero Negativity Challenge, a thirty-day program developed by Dallas couples therapists Harville Hendrix and his wife, Helen LaKelly Hunt.

I show Tom the calendar I have ordered from the Hendrix-Hunt "Couplehood Store" — complete with smiley face and frowning stickers — and explain the goal put forward by the plan: zero put-downs, comments, or negative behaviors for thirty days.

Tom studies it and shakes his head. "This is stupid," he says. "It's never going to work."

"Nice going," I say, slapping a frownie sticker on Day One.

Rage Against the Washing Machine: How to Divvy Up Chores

H. and I have been in a fight for two days and haven't been talking. The silence is amazing.

—ANONYMOUS, FROM THE "CONFESSIONAL" SECTION OF THE

MOTHERHOOD BLOG *SCARY MOMMY*

One evening I swing by my sister Dinah's house in the New Jersey suburbs. Her two daughters have had late sports practice and have just finished their dinner of hurriedly microwaved pizza bagels. Dinah, who commutes from Manhattan, has arrived home at her usual hour of 7 p.m.; her husband, Patrick, finishes his shift in food service in the afternoon, so he handles school pickup. In their cozy yellow kitchen bright with family photographs and kids' artwork, Dinah is eating a bowl of cereal, still in her work clothes, as the girls retreat to their rooms. I am helping myself to some Girl Scout Thin Mints I have excavated from their pantry.

Dinah and Patrick listen, eyes round, as I tell them about our harrowing trip to have our hair blown back by Terry Real.

"Wait, you paid a lot of money to get yelled at?" says Patrick, sitting down at the kitchen table and brushing aside a pile of manuscripts that Dinah has brought home. Jokey and gregarious, Patrick likes to hold forth on his twin passions: the New York Giants and smoked meats of all varieties.

As I work my way through five more cookies, I explain that Tom and I don't want to waste our waning years together enmeshed in a petty war. "You get to be in midlife, and you realize your time is finite," I say, dispensing my trademark oldest-sibling wisdom with a world-weary air.

Patrick gawps at me. "You guys could have just taken that money and gone to the Bahamas together!"

"Yes, but then we would have come back to the same problems," I say. I've always viewed couples therapy as a costly last stop before divorce court, I tell them, but our communication had become so muddled and highly charged that we were deadlocked. Terry Real identified our problems and provided a plan to break that deadlock. Instead of attacking each other, he had us attack, together, the polarizing cycle in which we had become trapped.

Caught in the laser beams of Real's penetrating gaze, I went on, we had no choice but to share our true, unguarded feelings (a process therapists call "empathic joining") instead of taking our usual shots at each other. When Real guided us to some common emotional ground, we were able to at last begin to open up lines of communication that had been closed for a long while.

"Terry shook up Tom so badly that he started doing dishes the night we came home," I say to Dinah. "He just silently got up and grabbed a sponge." And with Real's new shaming exercise involving Sylvie's photo, I report, I haven't raised my voice in two weeks! I pause to think. "Although yesterday I sent Tom an all-caps text that was perhaps a little forceful." *(HOME. NOW.)*

Patrick shrugs. "I guess we're lucky, because at this point, we don't really fight," he says. "I mean, we've been married for almost twenty years, so we've pretty much worked a lot of this stuff out."

Dinah looks at him wryly, her cereal spoon paused in midair. "Well, I wouldn't say that," she says. "Here's something I resent: we both live here, and there are basic things that just need to happen in our house. They don't get done by magical elves. Like, the place needs to be vacuumed."

"I knew you were going to bring up the vacuuming," he breaks in. "Okay, look, I forgot. But I spent the afternoon being a taxi service! I picked up the kids from school, picked up their friends, then drove one to soccer and one to basketball."

"I know, and I appreciate that," says Dinah, getting up to extract a container of yogurt from the fridge, which completes her improvised dinner — "but I have to say that I am really, really tired of having to ask you to do things."

He sighs. "All right, I admit that I don't like being told what to do. But here's another thing: what's the big deal about having to ask? Obviously there's a mental block with men, so we have to be asked! So just ask! Ask us!"

She shakes her head. "But you just said you don't like being told what to do. You see the bind this puts me in, right? After a while, I don't feel like asking, because you make it clear that you don't like being told what to do, and I figure it's easier to just do things myself."

He holds up his hands. "You're right. Look, Dinah, I love you, but I do think women in general have a higher standard." He turns to me. "I can watch TV for two hours and not check on the kids, but Dinah feels the need to entertain them. I wish I could be as doting as she is, but I'm not. As a parent, you're never supposed to put yourself first. You can do the most outrageous thing, but if you say it's for the kids, then it's okay." True, I say. He points to Dinah. "She gets the girls ready, packs the lunches, works eight hours in the city, comes home and puts the kids to bed, and then works some more. I think she does too much and wears herself out."

Dinah sits down at the table with a sigh and eats her yogurt. "Yes, but especially by me working all the time and leaving early and coming home late, I feel like I'm caring for the girls when I do all the extra things I do, like leave them breakfast on the table. I mean, Claire's thirteen — she can make breakfast herself. But that's my way of telling her I love her while I'm running for the train. And I also like being efficient. You know? I like being needed."

I ask Patrick if he feels guilty when he doesn't do his fair share of things around the house. He sheepishly admits that he does. "Oh, definitely," he says, glancing uneasily at his wife. "I mean, I can still sleep at night, but yes. I gotta admit, I'm lazy." I think about the fricasseeing Patrick would receive if he divulged this in front of Terry Real.

"Do you do anything without Dinah having to remind you?" I ask.

"I do the grocery shopping," he points out.

Dinah laughs. "Well, yeah. You care more about the food."

"I make dinner two or three nights a week." He ticks off his jobs on his fingers. "I do the cat litter. I feed the cat. I water the cat."

She raises her eyebrows. "You water the cat," she repeats, deadpan.

They continue Not Fighting as I get up and ransack their pantry for more cookies.

In study after study, research indicates that — surprise! — when men take on their fair share of household responsibilities, their partners are happier and less prone to depression, disputes are fewer, and divorce rates are lower. The day-to-day labor of keeping a household running is a remarkably significant issue for couples: a Pew Research Center survey found that sharing household chores ranked third in importance on a list of nine items associated with successful marriages. This put it ahead of pretty vital basics like good housing, common interests, and "adequate income" (which ranks at number *four*).

This rather amazing finding surprised even the Pew researchers, who said that in seventeen years of polling, no item on the list has risen in importance nearly as much. In other words, this issue is about more than laundry: it's a direct depiction of the sense of fairness, or unfairness, that exists within a relationship. It touches on so many significant, and interrelated, issues: gender roles, money, respect, values, intimacy, tradition.

Yet many women either don't bother persisting (and, like Dinah, stoically do chores themselves), do not ask forcefully enough, or — like me — somehow do not feel justified in urging their spouses to raise their game. As Real pointed out to me during the one-on-one part of our session, I somehow skipped over the crucial step of simply asking Tom, clearly and calmly, for what I wanted, and rocketed straight to anger and frustration. Why was I so reluctant to elucidate my needs?

"As women, we sometimes have trouble asking for help," says my friend Jenny. "Maybe we really do want to do it all, or don't want to admit we can't. Or we think our husbands should intuitively know what help we need, and if they don't we're annoyed. But doing everything ourselves isn't heroic — it's toxic."

Jenny is right. Part of my hesitation is that I feel the pull of traditional societal expectations more than I'd like to admit — starting with the baseless but tickling fear that if I'm too "demanding," my husband will leave me. (For many women, "standing up for yourself" still carries the stigma of "being a pain in the ass.")

And for hundreds of years, a woman's central identity has revolved around being a good wife, mother, and housekeeper. My role model growing up was my mother, who stayed home with three daughters and capably ran the house, joining the working world only when we were almost in college. Most of my friends, whether they are employed or not, do the vast majority of household work and childcare. As the saying goes, you can't be what you can't see.

My taking on all the household work started slowly. When our baby was born, Tom took three weeks off from work — which, as a self-employed writer, he was able to finesse. During that mostly harmonious time, he gingerly bathed our daughter, burped her, and laundered her onesies, carefully spraying stains with spot remover. He played with her for hours, and took her for long morning walks in the stroller he had fastidiously researched, measuring out turning ratios in our apartment, agonizing over cup-holder placement, squinting at folding configurations on web pages. He spent more time on the stroller in total than he had when he bought the family car, as if our daughter's very future depended on some perfect arrangement of ergonomics.

And we had diligently set aside a portion of our incomes so that I would be able to stay home full-time with her. As it took much longer than we anticipated for me to get pregnant, the only upside was that we had a decent-size nest egg by the time the baby arrived—enough for me to be a stay-at-home mom for at least two years. Of course, we had to be careful not to live extravagantly. Occasionally, for quick cash, I'd knock off a few magazine assignments that I hurriedly wrote (or, to paraphrase Truman Capote, typed) while the baby slept—a health story on vitamins here, a celebrity interview there. During that sweet, carefree time, I vowed to profile only the celebrities who were sane and smart, a modest list that included Julianne Moore and Nigella Lawson (who supplied me with a mantra I have now adopted: *I believe in moderation, in moderation*).

Tom, meanwhile, left each morning to write at the New York Public Library's Reading Room while I tended to the baby. Normally, he handled the cooking, but since I had time during the day to prep for meals, I completely took over kitchen duty. Soon I was doing everything domestic, and he was slipping away for longer times on nights and weekends, but I was so contentedly ensconced in our little nest that I was unconcerned.

Then one pleasingly drowsy afternoon, I received a call from Cyndi Lauper's manager: Would I be interested in cowriting her autobiography? Cyndi had apparently retained fond memories of a late and rowdy night that we spent together in Las Vegas when I was a reporter for *Rolling Stone* (and regularly stayed up past 9). It was as fun as you'd expect: so often a celebrity's image is completely at odds with the real person—comedians are dark and brooding; America's sweethearts are unhinged nightmares—but Cyndi is irrefutably the adorably kooky and down-to-earth gal from Queens her fans know and love.

Our daughter had just turned two, and our savings were nearly gone. After much deliberation with Tom, we decided that this opportunity was too good to pass up. We hired a nanny for three days a week, whereupon I would meet Cyndi in her apartment on the Upper West Side for interview sessions. Her manager instructed me to wear exercise clothes and bring my tape recorder, so that I could conduct my interviews while we did a vigorous walk together in Central Park.

Well, my exercise clothes stayed pristine. Day after day, Cyndi, clad in gym gear, would mutter, "Oh, to hell with it, let's just stay here." She'd make a cappuccino to take down to her doorman and brew us some tea. Then we'd sit in her vintage-style kitchen (which looks exactly like the set in the "Girls Just Want to Have Fun" video) and eat, and gab.

Often, it was hard to get her to focus — life with Cyndi was a constant 1930s screwball comedy — but her digressions were so entertaining that I didn't mind.

CYNDI (PICKING AT A COFFEE CAKE): I'm so fuckin' fat.

ME: In what universe? No, you are not. *Note: she is not.*

CYNDI: Am so. How do you stay so skinny?

ME: I'm actually not that skinny. I have a big behind that I can never get rid of.

CYNDI: Lessee. *I stand up to show her.* Pull your pants tight so I can see the outline. *She inspects my behind.* Eh, it's not so bad. *Then her gaze travels up to my face.*

CYNDI: C'mere. You know what, doll? Not for nothin', but your face looks a little dry. I'm going to spray you.

ME: With what? I'm not sure I —

CYNDI: Just c'mere. *She extracts a bottle from her purse and proceeds to spray my face with some concoction that burns. She does this a dozen times; it is like being in a car wash.*

ME: What is it?

CYNDI: An activator.

ME: What does it activate?

CYNDI (SHRUGGING): Who knows?

After spending the day with Cyndi, I'd race home, relieve the nanny, play with Sylvie until bedtime, and then transcribe and write up my interview after she had fallen asleep. I found that one benefit of dealing with the famous is that it is excellent practice for handling a toddler. Celebrities are used to being the center of attention, have little impulse control, are prone to meltdowns, and can be aggravating — until they give you a dazzling smile, and all is forgiven.

But as Sylvie started to walk and talk, and our family life grew busier and more complicated, it was as if I suddenly woke up and noticed that I was doing all the donkeywork. Even Tom's small transgressions began to grate on my nerves, such as his near-daily habit of asking me to help find his keys, prompting me to inquire if he had checked up his ass. (As Roseanne Barr used to say, men think the uterus is a tracking device.) This tic, once somewhat endearing, was less so after I had spent the day scouring various playgrounds for our daughter's lost stuffed lamb. A turning point had arrived in our marriage. We began to quarrel, and never stopped. But Tom was still, understandably, reluctant to change his habits. Why alter the status quo that works decidedly in his favor?

But equality, as *Lean In*'s Sheryl Sandberg has stated, is not a zero-sum game. Beyond the most immediate and obvious benefit — that I will cease being, as Real memorably put it, a "raving lunatic" — there are so many others. A Cornell study found that couples with young kids who split housework more evenly reported better and more frequent sex than when the woman took on most of the chores. (As study author Sharon Sassler noted drily, "Perhaps if more men realized that sexual frequency was higher when the domestic load was more equitably shared, they would grab that Swiffer more often.") Children benefit, too, in surprising ways: research has shown that when men share housework and childcare, their kids do better in school and are less likely to see a child psychiatrist or be put on behavioral medication.

And girls with more involved dads develop greater self-esteem. I inform Tom that fathers who regularly do household chores, according to a University of British Columbia study, have daughters who are more likely to aspire to less stereotypically feminine careers, instead voicing an ambition to be an astronaut, professional soccer player, or geologist. When girls see fathers pulling their own weight, they receive a direct message that they are not — and should not be — destined to shoulder all the tedious work by themselves.

"What she hears from us is 'Girls rule,'" I say, driving the point home as Tom flinches, "but in our house, what she sees is 'Girls clean.'" We can repeat all the empowering slogans we want, but as the author James Baldwin once wrote, "Children have never been very good at listening to their elders, but they have never failed to imitate them."

At the moment, my daughter wants to be a clown in the circus when she grows up, but I'd like her to feel confident that she has a shot at being a CEO if the whole clown thing doesn't work out.

It is time to make some changes around our housework. I conscript a flotilla of experts to help me begin.

••••••••••••••••••••••••••••

The first order of business, advises psychologist Joshua Coleman, author of *The Lazy Husband: How to Get Men to Do More Parenting and Housework,* is to change my language. Your husband isn't "helping," he tells me, nor is he "doing me a favor." "You are both parenting," he says pointedly, "and this is an even exchange of services."

Then have what psychologists call an "intentional conversation," in which you are extremely clear about your need for change and your wishes going forward. "Most men are actually willing to negotiate and compromise, but they expect the woman to be direct," says Coleman, who cheerfully admits to being a reformed "lazy husband" himself. "Men often do best if they know exactly what to do." Do not use moralistic or shaming language, he continues, which only brings on defensiveness.

A useful mantra is *affectionate though unmovable.* Coleman says that women who get the most compliance from men are those who are comfortably assertive in their expectations of their participation — as though it's a done deal, and you're merely figuring out how to get there. If you're hesitant, vague about what you want, or guilt-ridden, he says, you set yourself up to be at the mercy of your spouse's goodwill — not very twenty-first century. (Or, as Oprah Winfrey says, "You teach people how to treat you.") "And stay in the game longer," Coleman coaches me. "So many women tell me, 'Well, I asked and he said no.'" He laughs. "That was just round one!"

And so one evening, after our daughter has gone to bed, I ask Tom if I may have a quick word. He eyes me like I'm a clipboard-wielding Greenpeace canvasser asking for a moment of his time. "This cannot be good," he says warily. "It's like a telephone ringing in the middle of the night." But he sets aside his newspaper.

I've been counseled that I need to begin my "intentional conversation" with a statement of appreciation, so I take a breath. "I really appreciate how hard you work and how much time you spend with Sylvie. However, even though we work equal hours, I am doing almost all the housework and childcare" *(state the problem in a neutral way)*. "This has made me exhausted, unhappy, and resentful. Our current system is not working. When you have a child, your household has to function at a higher level, because there are so many more moving parts.

"You have told me that you feel guilty sometimes that I am doing almost everything. If you would just do your bit, instead of ignoring me or giving me attitude like a teenager" — *(oops, "shaming language")* — "I mean, instead of fighting me, you wouldn't feel guilty, I would be happier, our child would be better adjusted, and our lives would be more peaceful. Don't you want peace? Who doesn't love peace? Instead of wasting your energy by taking a stand, why not just channel that energy into doing what needs to be done? If you are afraid I will assign you even more jobs once you have finished, you have my solemn vow that I will not. Nor am I asking for fifty-fifty, even though Caitlin Moran tells me I should."

Then *appeal to his sense of fair play.* If you're a stay-at-home mom, says Dallas psychologist Ann Dunnewold, an expert in women's issues, inform him that you work just like he does — and in many ways it's tougher, because he is at least surrounded by adults all day, while you are with needy children. Most adults, at least outside of the company holiday party, are not going to vomit on you, grope you, or have spontaneous crying fits.

"My husband says that I 'have it easy' because I stay at home with the kids all week," says my friend Sarah. "He has the balls to tell me, 'You're at the park in the sunshine while I'm at the office.' I tell him, 'If it's so easy to be at the park with three kids under six, why don't you do it on the weekends?' Because it's work, that's why! Our two-year-old thinks it's funny to run into the middle of the road! I'm on high alert *all the time*."

Make no mistake: raising babies, as biological anthropologist Helen Fisher tells me, is humankind's hardest job. Dunnewold tells clients who are stay-at-home moms that they are working seven days a week if their mates do not pitch in on weekends. "Listen, federal labor law dictates that in an eight-hour shift, we have two twenty-minute breaks and a half hour for lunch," she said. "If you're sleeping for eight hours, you have two eight-hour shifts. That adds up to two hours, twenty minutes, per day that you need to be off. So how are you getting that?" When you put it in numbers like that, she tells me, these are points that often make sense to men. "Did he have an hour for lunch? Probably. Did he go to the gym on the way home from work? So you say, 'Let's look at the hours we have during the week and try to make this equitable.' And equitable doesn't mean equal — it just means fair."

My friend Jenny, also a stay-at-home mother, uses similar business logic on her husband. "A lot of working folks can appreciate analogies to the workplace, a domain where they might feel more comfortably on top of things," she says. "I tell friends to embrace the view that home life *is* a functioning business, albeit a weird twenty-four-hour diner/daycare/hospital type of business."

Moving on: *request, don't demand.* Most of us respond better to a request," says Gary Chapman, the pastor and marriage counselor whose book *The Five Love Languages* has sold ten million copies. "You can say, 'When you vacuumed the floor yesterday, it was like heaven,'" Chapman tells me in his honeyed South Carolina drawl. "Then if you say, 'Now, if it's possible, I'd really like for you to get the hairs out of the sink when you finish in the bathroom,' and he's feeling loved by you, he's far more likely to say, 'Okay, yeah, I'll do that.' You know?" The craving to be valued, he adds, is not a male impulse, but a human one.

Of course, this advice isn't exactly new: Jesus mentioned it during his Sermon on the Mount, when he told people to treat others as they wish to be treated. In 1937's *How to Win Friends and Influence People,* Dale Carnegie wrote that people respond to appreciation and kindness and resent criticism and displays of temper. Yet clearly we still need to be told this, again and again.

Coleman agrees with Chapman. "I understand that you're annoyed to use positive reinforcement, but in many cases, it probably ain't gonna happen any other way, and we have to start somewhere," he says with a sigh. "It's strategic to be friendly, and complimentary."

And my request is more likely to be fulfilled if one magic word is used: *because.* Harvard psychologist Ellen Langer found that people are more willing to comply with an appeal if you simply provide a reason — any reason. Langer observed a group of people waiting in line to use a copy machine (mind, this was an earlier era). When someone asked to cut in line but supplied a reason, even when it didn't make much sense ("Can I use the copy machine first *because* I need to make a copy?"), nearly everyone acquiesced. The word *because* appears to be the behavioral cue, so even if your reason sounds slightly bonkers *(Please clean up your mess because it's messy),* it can still get results.

What's not effective is to announce, "Here's what we're doing today," Coleman goes on, because, as mentioned earlier, males are socialized to assert their independence. Instead, he advises me to present the tasks in the spirit of negotiation. "Say, 'Here's a list of five things that need to get done — you can pick three.'"

Having to deploy multiple strategies is, frankly, irritating, but the reality is that even though men are doing more housework than previous generations, asking them to scrub the bathroom remains a tough sell. Society is much more apt to celebrate engaged fathers: witness how many male celebrities have made being an involved dad part of their image. They pose for paparazzi wearing infant carriers; they post loving shots of their children on social media. Nowadays, it's cool to be a hands-on father. "I'm literally an Uber driver now," soccer star David Beckham mock-lamented on a talk show of his post-retirement. "I have four drop-offs at four different schools."

But while dads may enthusiastically display the huevos rancheros they whipped up for the family breakfast on Instagram, they're not quite as likely to post shots of the family laundry they just folded — because it's still not cool for a man to be seen doing housework. A University of New Hampshire study found that only 2.1 percent of commercials featured men doing work around the house.

So how do you persuade them? Coleman compares the process to game theory: "What are you willing to trade off, and how are you willing to use your power?" he posits. Tell your spouse that changing his behavior will directly benefit him because you will be happier and more relaxed. Make trades with items of value to him that are sometimes hard for you to give him: time alone, sleeping late, spending time with friends of his that you aren't wild about, like the college buddy who still goes by the nickname Toilet Seat.

Coleman points out that a tradable item of value for me was Tom's lengthy bike rides. "Tell him, 'I'm willing to do this for you' — the phrase 'do this for you' makes it clear that this is a favor, and not something he's entitled to — 'but I want you to do more when you're around, and here are some things you can do that would make me feel much better.'" Calm. Specific. Business-like. Assuming it's a done deal.

Fired up, I approach Tom with Chapman's and Coleman's scripts. "What now?" he asks resignedly as he sets his book aside.

"I love that you checked Sylvie's homework this morning," I say. "And when you went out to get us bagels, it was like heaven."

He regards his new wife quizzically.

"Now, I'm wondering, if it's possible, if you can take Sylvie to a birthday party at the bowling alley this weekend. Because I don't feel like it." I smile at him. "Please," I add.

Normally, I happily take our daughter to birthday parties. Some people moan about them, but I love the overexcited kids, the balloons, the face painting, and, especially, the supermarket sheet cake encrusted with sprinkles. When it is brought out to a chorus of "Happy Birthday," I always give Sylvie a penetrating look that says *Now, you know what to get for Mommy, right?* She will nod discreetly, and telegraph back *Corner piece, which has the most frosting.*

But I'm terrible at bowling, I tell Tom. "And you've never once taken her to a birthday party by yourse —" *Whoops, too negative.* "And it would be a fun thing for Sylvie to have her dad take her to a birthday party alone." *Yes. Better.*

He shrugs. "Okay."

"And if you want to go on a long bike ride on Sunday, I'm willing to do this for you, if you'll take us to lunch afterward. I would look forward to that."

I brace myself for pushback, but he nods. "All right."

It is as simple as that. As a friend of mine says, "If you don't ask, you're probably not going to get. So I negotiate my fitness time, book a class and prepay it, so it's locked in. I make a plan with a friend and get it on the calendar. I've learned to be protective of my time, just as my husband is."

Once you have a child, says New York psychologist Guy Winch, whom we will meet later, *everything* has to be up for renegotiation. "You both are managers of the household, and should have regular discussions, every two weeks minimum, about how things are going, and brainstorm about what needs to be done, and track and tweak accordingly," he says. I say that this seems a little chilly and transactional. "If it feels transactional and not the organic way these things are supposed to develop, there *is* no organic way these things are supposed to develop," he counters.

"Couples should negotiate all the time, and it requires communication and coordination."

We take his advice. Every Saturday morning, when we are feeling relaxed after a late breakfast, we start building in a fifteen-minute managerial meeting. Managerial meetings aren't exactly sexy, or fun. Sometimes they feel collaborative, but other times they feel distancing and lawyerly as we briskly run through what needs to be done. But I see now that our hectic daily life is never, ever going to sort itself out organically, as I once envisioned. Within a few weeks, our meetings become a necessity.

As Winch puts it, "Each spouse has his or her own needs, and the marriage has its own needs. The relationship is a third entity. So you're thinking not 'What would be good for her?' or 'What would be good for him?' but 'What would be good for the marriage?' And this invites a more cooperative, teamwork kind of attempt at resolution."

One Saturday, we trade a three-hour chunk of time — a bike ride for him (which he is desperate to do) and a stint at the gym and coffee with a friend for me. I keep in mind what Ann Dunnewold told me: when a mother takes care of herself, children absorb important lessons. "Both boys and girls learn that mothers have needs, too, which is also very important if they have children of their own," she says. If you must conquer guilt, she adds, tell yourself, 'When I take time for myself, I come back and I'm more the mother I want to be. More patient. Less reactive.'"

After my gym and coffee date wrap up, I still have a half hour of free time. I fight the urge to pop by the grocery store, mindful that a woman's free time is likely to be "contaminated," as one study put it, by other things, such as taking care of kids or housework.

Instead, I force myself to sit in the park. Had I contaminated my time with food shopping, I would have missed the sight of a squirrel perched on a fence jauntily eating an entire ice cream cone. I sit, dreamily musing: *Is that chocolate chip? Those could definitely be chips. I suppose it might also be rum raisin. Do ice cream places still sell rum raisin? Is he going to eat the cone, too? Whoops, yep, there he goes.*

Next, take a page from same-sex couples and *allocate jobs according to preference.* A survey commissioned by the Families and Work Institute, a nonprofit that tracks workplace information, found that same-sex couples were much more likely to evenly share household and childcare responsibilities — and tended to divide chores based on personal preference. This may have stemmed from the fact, the researchers speculated, that same-sex couples have already broken out of social norms and thus could divvy up more innovatively, while straight couples tended to backslide into traditional gender roles — as Tom and I did.

But it's still unrealistic to demand a fifty-fifty split, says Dunnewold. "The hard-core feminist position would be, 'Absolutely, it should be fifty-fifty,'" she says. "Well, I'm a feminist, too, but that might not necessarily work if, for instance, you're breastfeeding. You've got to jockey with what works for you."

With that in mind, Tom and I sit down at the kitchen table and make a list of the chores we actually like and the ones we can't stand. I start by saying that I like to grocery shop. I am the type of shopper who methodically examines every new product on the shelves: *Ooh, look at these sriracha-flavored potato chips! Hello, is that dark chocolate banana–flavored peanut butter?* I could easily spend hours at a supermarket. Eventually they would find me at closing time encased in ice in Frozen Appetizers and Snacks.

When I do the food shopping, I've noticed that more men are joining me in the aisles — as it happens, a record 41 percent say they are the primary grocery shoppers in their households, according to the NPD Group, a market research company (although bear in mind that this is self-reported information). Another study found that millennial dads were significantly more likely to shop at least four times a week. Male shoppers have been shown to be drawn to bold flavors such as chipotle, as well as high-protein offerings. Accordingly, companies have gone after these "manfluencers" — an actual trademarked term from Chicago's Midan Marketing — with a slew of products such as "brogurt," Greek yogurt packed with extra protein.

Tom, with his aversion to crowds and fluorescent lighting, dreads the grocery store. So I take over that duty, along with registering our daughter for classes, commandeering playdates and doctor's appointments, and cooking, provided I can get one day off from kitchen duty a week. I also derive a demented satisfaction out of vacuuming and dusting, and do not recoil from cleaning the bathroom, as Tom does. Tom enjoys supervising homework, all things car and computer related, paying bills, taking our daughter to swim class ("I find the smell of chlorine strangely satisfying"), household errands, and Swiffering. He volunteers to do the dishes and laundry, a task I loathe since the laundry room is on our building's ground floor and we have to haul a bulging bag downstairs. Every one of our jobs is well defined, which eliminates our usual debate on who is working more hours per week and thus deserves fewer chores.

Clarity is vital when it comes to parceling out household work, as research from the UCLA Center on Everyday Lives of Families found. The couples in their study who "lacked clarity on *what, when,* and *how* household responsibilities would be carried out often said they felt drained and rushed and had difficulty communicating their dissatisfaction," researchers wrote.

Those drained respondents negotiated their responsibilities anew every day, starting from scratch — as Tom and I had been doing. This cracked system trapped the participants in an exhausting cycle of "requests and avoidance of these requests." Conversely, spouses who knew exactly what to do around the house didn't spend as much time negotiating responsibilities and didn't tend to monitor and criticize each other. Not surprisingly, "their daily lives seemed to flow more smoothly."

Moving on, the experts said I should consider *loosening my standards.* Maybe our less-frazzled husbands are on to something here. Why, for instance, did I put needless pressure on myself to stay up until midnight making Pinterest-worthy ladybug cupcakes for my child's fifth birthday, painstakingly piping on a bristling army of tiny antennae? Why, for that matter, did I bother making homemade vanilla cupcakes when most kids just lick off the frosting and toss the uneaten cake into the trash?

Because making those cupcakes was about my ego. I was eager to dazzle the kids, the teacher, and my fellow moms. If I *really* wanted my child's birthday to be the biggest hit in kindergarten, all I had to do was squeeze a dollop of neon frosting from a tube into a cupcake wrapper, top it with sprinkles, and serve.

Nor do I need to make every moment of my child's life a developmentally significant enrichment activity. Joshua Coleman often hears complaints from mothers who say that their husband's idea of a meaningful encounter with the kids is to let them crawl around underneath his feet while he watches TV. Coleman answers that kids don't require focused, minute-to-minute attention in order for them to grow and learn — that in fact they can learn from crawling around on the floor at Dad's feet.

Lily, a friend of a friend, says she tries not to obsess about her husband's quality time with the kids. "I would get resentful when I'd get home from brunch with a girlfriend, and the house is a mess, my husband is watching TV, the kids are playing together in another part of the house, and it seems clear he hasn't really been engaged with them at all," she says. "But now I'm trying hard to simply go through a quick checklist when I return. House still standing? Check. Kids unhurt? Check. Dog not lost? Check. All's well that ends well."

I realize that I sometimes condemn Tom as being an uninvolved parent, when he is just engaged in a different way. My idea of involvement is to plan an elaborate art project; Tom's is to tote Sylvie with him when he buys bike tires ("She knows the different valves and air pressures," he says proudly). I used to get annoyed when he started pulling our daughter into his world of computer chess, protesting that we had agreed to limit her screen time. But then he taught her to play — and now she regularly beats him. Unlike me, Tom has always tried to include Sylvie in his pursuits, rather than the other way around — something I want to start doing, too. He says this is less some carefully thought-out, progressive parenting strategy than sheer self-interest.

"I am also, at heart, trying to win her over, and prove to her that her father is an endless source of fun activities," he says. "And there's an added wonder in seeing those things you have always enjoyed suddenly encountered through the eyes of your child, which somehow awakens you again to the pleasure and power of those things. But the virtuous circle here is that I acquire a partner in crime — a riding buddy, a bird-watcher and a stargazer, a willing soccer goalie. Instead of dutifully filling in my Dad hours, I'm doing things I want to be doing anyway, which makes me want to do them longer, which allows us to spend more time together, which only leads to more shared interests, which brings us closer together. Not that I still don't have to go to the damned bouncy castle once in a while."

In a similar vein, I have to train myself to *let some things go*. When I phone New York professional organizer Julie Morgenstern, consultant for *Fortune* 500 companies, who has ordered the closets of Oprah Winfrey, among others, I divulge a pet peeve: that while Tom has taken over laundry duty, he typically waits to do it until the bag has swelled to the size and shape of a manatee. "Right," she says. "So my question to you is, if he waits that long, what does it cost you, other than your obsessive need to not have it pile up? What's it actually costing you?" I tell her that because he is a cyclist and has a constant churn of exercise clothes, the bag is perpetually off-gassing, causing me olfactory distress. Also, at a certain point I run out of underwear.

"Right. So those to me would be legitimate reasons. Whereas if you're thinking, 'I hate to see something pile up when it could be getting done,' that's emotional. If it's just annoying you, no one's gonna get motivated — unless you stop having sex with him because there's too much laundry." Asking myself what something costs me has headed off many fights, because often the answer is "Not too much, actually." If his disorder is hidden behind a cabinet and I can't see it, if his pile of periodicals is not physically blocking my way, it's not "costing" me a thing. Let it go.

My more freewheeling new attitude should probably include *whittling away nonessential chores*. Do the kids' meals need to be home-cooked when they'd much rather bolt down microwaved chicken fingers? (One friend's sons request them "extra rubbery," so she obligingly blasts them for an additional minute.) Does the house have to be spic and span? Do the kids need to be bathed every night, or even every other night?

And must we be compulsively busy every second of the day, briskly doing something "useful"? Nonstop activity can be addictive, but it's a mistake, warns the University of Houston's Brené Brown, a mom of two. "One of the most insidious and probably profoundly dangerous coping mechanisms that we have absolutely glommed on to as a culture is staying busy," she tells me. "And the whole unconscious idea behind it is 'If I stay busy enough, I will never know the truth of how absolutely pissed off I am, how resentful I am, how exhausted I am from juggling everything.'"

Brown remembers that when she was waitressing in college, she was told to consolidate — do as much as you can at once, carry as much as you are able, make as few trips as possible. "And I realized that I was consolidating in my life," she says. "I'd stop at a red light and think, 'Oh my God, I have thirty seconds, let me check my email.' I was constantly so proud of everything I could do."

Now Brown is careful to build calm "white space" into her life — by regularly saying no, and ruthlessly paring down her schedule. "When I stop at a red light, I don't check anything," she tells me. "And I lock down nonnegotiable off-the-grid time. We schedule so many things, even fun things, that they all become a hassle to cross off our list."

After a while, she says, as your body starts getting used to the quietude, it's less tolerant of anxiety. "It's like 'Uh-uh, I got used to being calm and sleeping through the night,'" she says. "It's like when you give up sugar and then go and eat a candy bar and it makes you physically sick."

And so I eye my schedule, thinning out my daughter's after-school activities and my weekend engagements. Do I need to volunteer for every field trip? No. Are we required to attend birthday parties of classmates my daughter barely knows? We are not. A helpful way to discern if the kids are actually close is to ask my six-year-old, 'Do you know this child's favorite color? How about their pet's name? How many teeth have they lost?'" Good friends are in possession of this vital information.

Next, *eliminate every instance of what psychologists call "decision fatigue."* Put everything you possibly can on autopilot, says Julie Morgenstern. "Make the same five quick dinners every week," she says. "On the other nights, you can get creative or order out." Most kids, she points out, are not clamoring for beef bourguignon — they much prefer Taco Tuesday and Pizza Friday. (I must admit that I, too, get a little excited for Taco Tuesday.)

Those who make a regular rotation of dishes with everyday ingredients, by the way, have been dubbed by the food company Campbell's as Familiar Taste Pleasers, according to their internal research. My brother-in-law Patrick, a trained chef, is usually a Passionate Kitchen Master (adventurous, confident), but on the nights when his kids have sports, he is a pizza bagel–microwaving

Uninvolved Quick Fixer. My favorite term is the one Campbell's devised to describe time-crunched new parents who have the desire, but not the time, to make new foods: the Constrained Wishful Eater.

As for certain pernicious chores, I must accept that *my spouse is not going to be good at some things.* Therefore, I should *quit banging my head against the wall.* Gary Chapman remembers that early in his marriage, it irritated him that his wife, Karolyn, as he puts it, "loaded the dishwasher like she was playing Frisbee. I'm very organized, and we battled over that a long time." He sighs. "Finally I realized that she was just not wired to do that. She was never going to be able to do it, and I just had to accept that. Because otherwise, if you don't ultimately find a resolution, you can fight about those things for thirty years."

Loading dishwashers, it turns out, is one of the most fraught of all household tasks. According to dishwasher manufacturer Bosch, more than 40 percent of US couples say they argue about the "right" way to do it.

Just as there are specific categories of home cooks, internal research at GE Appliances has uncovered three dishwasher-loading personality types. One group was deemed Protectors, says Jennifer Adam, the company's Consumer Research and Ideation Manager. Protectors, she tells me, are focused on safety and sanitization — loading utensils with the handles up, so the fork tines aren't touched when you unload, and hand-washing any dish that didn't get clean in the dishwasher. Curators, the most exacting loaders, want to be impressive to others — they meticulously organize plates by size. Finally, there are Organizers: they just want to load and unload everything as quickly as possible. (I learned that I fall into this category when Adam shared some statements that GE uses to identify Organizers: *I need to get dishes done and out of the way so that I don't feel tense* and *When I see dirty dishes in the sink, I realize that I'm running behind.*)

Adam, a mother of two, confesses that in her own life, her husband loads the dishwasher and she reloads it. "My husband worked here at [GE's] Appliance Park," she says, "and he still loads it wrong."

One could argue that "wrong" is a relative term, but Tom really does load it wrong: he often puts glasses in sideways or upside down. Nor is he wired, I realize, to make beds — his most careful effort makes it look like someone's been sleeping — and having violent nightmares — on top of the covers. I will be much happier if I abandon all hope that he will ever do either of those things.

•••••••••••••••••••••••••••••

My next effort is to *lay off the scorekeeping.* One Saturday during our negotiating meeting, Tom asks if he can play soccer for a few hours in the morning with friends. I tell him that's fine. Afterward, he showers, makes himself a sandwich, and then slinks off to the bedroom in the furtive way that my cat used to do when she was looking for a place to quietly throw up.

I follow him into the bedroom.

ME (HANDS ON HIPS): Don't tell me you're going to take a nap.

TOM: Just for half an hour. I'm worn out after that game. It was really hot.

ME: Well, we have things to do. You said you'd help Sylvie with
    her school project.
TOM: It can wait!
ME: Nope.

After he hauls himself up to help our daughter cut out "special places, objects, or activities" from magazines and glue them onto construction paper, I feel ashamed. Of course the homework could have waited — I generated a false deadline, because I was so annoyed with his single-guy weekend bubble. I had already allotted three hours for him, and a nap would have pushed it to four or possibly five. But my scorekeeping is petty, and also pointless: our daughter was reading quietly. I was making biscuits. Why couldn't he take a nap? Keeping score to prove a point is a silly waste of energy. I apologize, enjoying the new sensation of being calm and reasonable.

Finally, many experts tell me that the best — some say only — way to teach one's husband to learn the ropes and appreciate the volume of work you do is often the technique that is least used: *leave the damn house.* Many husbands I know, mine included, have never spent more than a day alone with their offspring. This is my fault as much as his: Tom has offered to take our daughter for the weekend, but I have been reluctant to arrange a getaway with my sisters or friends. Again, part of this is ego: will they survive without me?

Please, snorts couples therapist Esther Perel. "One important intervention for my clients who are mothers that overmanage — who are overwrought *not* by difficult life circumstances but by the culture of perfection that has captured parenthood — is that I tell them to go away for the weekend," she says. I admit to her that I am that over-managing mother. "Then go away alone, go with your friends, go away with someone you haven't seen in ages!" she says. "Your child won't die! Your husband is not a nincompoop! You need to realize that you have an identity that is bigger than just motherhood, and trusting that your child will be okay in the hands of others creates a more humble presence for you. And you're not allowed to prepare all their meals and freeze them."

University of Michigan sociologist Pamela Smock agrees. "Make him learn to be competent. Make him learn to share household managing. Look at it this way: the kids can bond with their father." This is one of many instances in which giving up control can actually give you more control over your relationship.

Since we have had a child, I have never spent a single night away from home. I start slowly and book an overnight visit with a high school friend who lives a quick train ride away in Connecticut. But as the day grows closer, I worry that I'll spend the whole night... worrying. I ask a friend who has just returned from a trip with her college girlfriends how she refrained from fretting when she left her husband alone with their infant son. "Simple," she says. "Limit your contact. I told my husband, 'I don't want to hear from you unless there is a fire, flood, or blood. No emails—only texts of our son looking happy, well fed, and alive.'" She had a carefree, booze-soaked rendezvous, and nothing caught on fire in her absence.

Leaving the house for a night is unnerving; my daughter cries oceans of tears. Because I can usually be found approximately three feet away from her at all times, I have unwittingly engineered my departure to be a catastrophic event. "Please don't go," she weeps, clinging to me.

But by the time I am on the train to Connecticut, I receive a text from Tom with a photo of the two of them gleefully drinking milkshakes. That night, my friend and I stay up late talking like the teenage friends we once were. I come home rejuvenated, and our daughter pelts into my arms bursting with news: *Daddy taught me to jump rope! We saw a rat in the park, and it was almost a foot long! Daddy flipped pancakes and one of them stuck on the ceiling! See? We kept it there for you!*

•••••••••••••••••••••••••••

Finally, if compliments and courtesy and clear lists don't work, it's time to *play hardball.* Tell him if he doesn't pitch in, you'll cease cooking dinner or doing the laundry. "Or stop doing chores that you know he'll do if you don't," says Coleman. "Like, if you pay the bills and he can't tolerate the bills being late, tell him, firmly but politely, that you can't do it anymore and it's his responsibility. Say, 'This is what's on my plate, and this is what I'll be taking off of my plate.'" But it has to be a threat that affects your spouse, he warns. "It can't be, 'Well, I'll show you, I'm not going to clean the toilet as frequently.' Because he'll just scrape off the mold and go."

I covertly monitor Tom to see if there is anything he can't tolerate neglecting. I observe him for a week before it hits me: if our daughter is capering around our apartment past her bedtime, well into her third wind, he starts to fibrillate. "It's bedtime," he'll say, *to me* (another habit we most definitely have to fix). *Aha,* I think. *He is positively twitching to read books and play computer chess! A motive!*

So I announce, firmly but politely, that I am taking bedtime duty off my plate. "But she wants to hear you tell a bedtime story," he protests. I reply that if he gets her into pajamas and bed and

111

oversees teeth brushing, I'll finish with a bedtime story. Which is the same every night: a narrative-in-progress about a boy I grew up with in Pittsburgh who was extremely naughty. Sylvie revels in nightly tales of his misdeeds: how he set fire to the curtains in his living room, how he would climb to his roof and throw things at neighborhood children. "What happened to him when he became a grown-up?" she asked me breathlessly one night. Apparently, he is in jail, I told her, for posing as a doctor. Sylvie was so exhilarated by this thrilling news that she had trouble sleeping.

And so Tom takes over bedtime duty. He is not the pushover I am, endlessly fetching water and stuffed animals; he puts her to bed with prison discipline: Lights out! Some nights, he even gets her to bed early — a valuable skill we would never have uncovered otherwise.

I am not at all confident that our new division of labor will be sustainable, but because we are still rattled by Terry Real's diatribe, it is at least the right time to attempt something new. I also know our routine might take a while to stick: contrary to the conventional wisdom that it takes twenty-one days to form a habit, UK psychologist Phillippa Lally found that it takes, on average, sixty-six days. I convince Tom to at least try it out for a few months.

On to fighting without screeching.

Rules of Fight Club

It is late afternoon. Our daughter is at dance class; Tom and I are standing in the kitchen. He is making coffee while I rummage through my recipe file.

> ME: How does pasta Bolognese sound for dinner? I'll have to get started now, because it simmers for a few hours. I can stop by the butcher on the way to pick up Sylvie from class.
>
> TOM (LOOKING AT CEILING): Um. Well, I mean, it sounds okay, but we've just had a lot of meat lately? So I'm just not feeling like... *His eyes flick to me just long enough to register that I am suddenly as motionless and acutely focused as a meerkat who has sighted a jackal on the horizon.* Then again, who doesn't love pasta Bolognese? As a matter of fact, that sounds —
>
> ME: No, no! Let's not have it then, if you're not sure about a plate full of homemade Bolognese sauce that takes hours to make! Feeling doubts about it, are you? *Addresses imaginary staff.* Emperor Nero decrees that there shall be no meat tonight! Make it known! Never mind that if

someone plunked down that pasta in front of me, I'd weep tears of joy! *I open a kitchen cabinet, pull out a takeout menu, and slap it down in front of him.* There you go! Dinner is served!

Later that night, Tom mournfully eats a congealed mound of General Tso's chicken for dinner, ordered deliberately to convey that he *has no problem whatsoever* with meat, while I hate-munch a peanut butter sandwich; both of us, losers.

Tom and I have clearly lost the ability to argue like grown-ups, rather than two toddlers in a sandbox. Who better to help us than the king and queen of couples research, John and Julie Gottman? After over four decades of studies, the Gottmans can assess five minutes of a marital argument and predict with over 90 percent accuracy who will stay married and who will divorce within a few years. The Gottmans categorize couples as *masters* and *disasters*. Masters look purposefully for things they can appreciate and respect about their partner; disasters monitor their mates for what they are doing wrong so they can criticize them. Intent on being a relationship master, I order a stack of their books.

As I delve into their research, I find some of their suggested dialogue a little corny ("It is wonderful to see how much you enjoy basketball. I feel that way about sailing. I would like to share some of that with you, too!"). But it's undeniable that their blueprint for successful arguing, adopted by countless therapists, has proven amazingly effective.

John Gottman identified four behaviors lethal to relationships, which he calls "the four horsemen of the apocalypse." One is criticism (hurling insults such as "dickbag," using phrases like

"You never..." or "You always..."). The next is defensiveness: counterattacking, whining, denying responsibility. During arguments, we are so busy forming a rebuttal, the Gottmans found, that we're not listening, so we tend to repeat ourselves in what they call the "summarizing yourself syndrome." (Although my sister Heather disputes this as a syndrome: "I summarize myself because Rob is not listening the first six times," she says. "He just cues up a mental streaming video and plays it in his head until he sees that my lips have stopped moving.")

The third horseman is stonewalling, defined as freezing out your mate and creating what the Gottmans call a Pursuer/Distancer pattern, in which the Pursuer, feeling ignored, grows more aggressive — that would be me — while the Distancer shuts down or flees. Some 85 percent of stonewallers, they found, are men.

This dynamic has even managed to slip the bonds of Earth — sort of. In 2014, the Mars Society erected a dome on an uninhabited Canadian island to simulate the lives of astronauts on a mission to Mars. Over the course of a hundred days, researchers studied the crew as they interacted. Crew members could leave the dome only during an extra-vehicular activity (EVA) — excursions taken by foot or by ATV while wearing imitation spacesuits. When conflicts arose among the crew, the females often used "task coping" (or finding a way to deal with the problem), while the men tended to use "avoidance coping" — such as suddenly deciding it was high time to don fake spacesuits and head out for an EVA.

Stonewalling seems passive, but its effects are profound. In 1975, psychology professor Edward Tronick devised an experiment called the Still Face. A parent sits across from their infant and plays with the baby, who happily gurgles and coos. Then the parent is instructed to turn away and return with a still, or frozen, face and not to react to the baby at all.

Videos of this simple two-minute experiment are tough to watch: the baby, at first confused, reaches for Mom or Dad and tries in vain to get their attention. Then the baby turns away, looking sad and hopeless, before trying again, growing increasingly fussy and upset until he is fully panicked and crying. Is this outcome so different for adults?

The fourth and worst behavior, and the Gottmans' strongest predictor of divorce, is contempt, which they term "sulfuric acid for love": cynicism, attacking your mate's character ("You're selfish") rather than the problems your mate has caused, eye-rolling, mockery, and — uh-oh — sarcasm.

When I fight with my husband, sarcasm is my particular lingua franca. Penny Pexman, a psychology professor at the University of Calgary who has been studying sarcasm's effects for almost two decades, says that not only does sarcasm create a barrier to conversational intimacy, but when parents use it on each other in front of young children, the kids get confused and upset.

"People may think that kids don't understand, but the problem is they will at age four or five," Pexman tells me. "And the evidence suggests that they know you don't mean what you're saying, but they don't get the whole context of *why* you would talk that way to your mate. For them, it's cruel to not be direct."

During our arguments, all these horsemen have come riding roughshod — sometimes all four at once. But we are not necessarily doomed to divorce. The Gottmans' formula for relearning how to fight is a straightforward one.

To begin: when an issue arises, instead of pouncing on your mate with criticism, use what the Gottmans call a "softened startup." *Start with an "I" statement rather than "you"* — instead of "You never get up with the baby, which makes me want to stab you," try "I feel so much better and less tired when we take turns getting up at night with the baby."

"This is one of the things I think is super important during conflicts," Julie Gottman tells me. "You describe *yourself,* and your own feelings about some particular situation that you're upset about. You don't describe your partner. You get into trouble describing your partner — because usually you're going to be doing that with criticism or contempt. And then that only creates defensiveness, and sabotages your being listened to." For me, taking a moment to identify my rampaging emotions uncomfortably mimics a book my daughter loved in preschool called *The Way I Feel* — but it has proven to be the best way to cool my anger.

Next, *talk about your feelings.* Psychologist Darby Saxbe says that couples therapists work to uncover the "soft" emotions — like fear, shame, and sadness — that often lurk behind the "hard" anger and defensiveness that couples wear into battle like armor. She says it's important to try to locate the deeper feelings behind your reaction: What are you really feeling? Are you hurt? Are you rushing to blame yourself before anyone else can? What are your assumptions versus the actual facts? When I lash out at Tom, I realize, my soft emotions are often that I am hurt that he doesn't sense that I need a hand, and embarrassed that he seems to think I'm somehow better suited to do the grunt work.

Talking about your feelings is also, frankly, strategic. For instance, one afternoon I ask Tom to stop by the grocery for milk, bread, and juice boxes. He promptly returns with a bachelor party fiesta of beer, salsa and chips, and olives. (This forgetfulness is something of a family characteristic. When I tell my sister Heather about it later, she says that is nothing. "The morning I gave birth to Travis, Rob nicely volunteered to go to the bakery to get me breakfast," she said. "I told him, 'Anything but a cranberry muffin.' In five minutes, he triumphantly returns with a cranberry muffin.")

How, then, is talking about your emotions strategic? Normally, I would pull out my usual accusation that Tom lives in a single-guy bubble — but if I do, he will just tell me I am wrong. Instead, I say, "I feel depressed that you didn't remember to get basics like milk and bread at the store." Well, he can't challenge or question my feelings, can he? I feel depressed. And this sort of confession engenders sympathy: rather than argue, he is abashed. More so when I have him return to the store.

Moving on, *describe what is happening without judgment or blaming,* focusing on the specific issue rather than the person ("The house is a mess, and the kids are running wild"). Then — once again — *state clearly what you need.* As Julie Gottman puts it, "Describe what you *do* need, as opposed to what you *don't* need." (A prime example being "I don't need this shit.") *Admit your role* by finding some contribution you made to the problem ("I was already cranky because I just stepped on a Lego with bare feet").

As you both (hopefully) calm down, *find a compromise.* Ask each other: What do we agree about? What are our areas of flexibility? My friend Michael says that when he and his wife clash over an issue, they have learned to ask a simple question: Why is this important to you? "It seems so obvious," he says, "but it really helps cut through the clutter." And sometimes, if you're honest, the issue is important to you...because you want to win the argument.

Finally, *repair* the situation with a few words, jokes, or gestures that get you back on the same team. "When we repair," Julie Gottman tells me, "we apologize, explain what was so difficult or frustrating for us that led us to that behavior, ask for forgiveness, and listen to our partner as they say what impact your behavior had on them." (Phrases to use: *Let me try again. How can I make this better? Can I take that back?*)

I try out my new script on Tom:

I felt sad *(hidden soft emotion)* when I offered to make you spaghetti Bolognese and you turned up your nose — I mean, when you said you did not want spaghetti Bolognese. Cooking is how I express that I care, so I suppose I also felt rejected. *(Describe what is happening without blame.)* I wish that you were more enthusiastic when I offer to make you a dinner that takes a lot of work. *(State your need clearly.)* It would help if you start off by telling me how much you appreciate the nice dinners I make. Then I will be less likely to fly off the handle when you turn something down. *(Accepting influence.)* That said, I should not have called you a dickbag. And it is true that lately we have eaten a fair amount of bacon. Also, I forgot about the pulled pork sandwiches we had at that barbecue place in Red Hook, which were quite tasty but the size of a human head. *(Compromise that is perhaps a little sarcastic, but baby steps.)* If you are so concerned with meat intake, how about offering to make us a vegetarian dinner instead? *(Repair.)* How can I make this better? Not throw menus at you? Maybe not throw things in general? Right. That's probably a good start.

Sometimes, of course, resolution is not so tidy. If you're dead-locked, the Gottmans highly advise taking a break. In one study, they interrupted squabbling couples and told them that they needed to adjust their equipment. They asked them not to talk about whatever issue they were wrangling over, but to read maga-zines for half an hour. When the couples resumed their discus-sion, their interactions were more positive and productive. Half an hour, the Gottmans found, is also about how long it takes for the chemicals released during "fight or flight" to exit the body.

Eminent New York family therapist Laura Markham lists for me the many ways to take a break: walk around the block, leave the room and take deep breaths, listen to music, remind yourself, "My partner is a good person and so am I" (even if I have just hol-lered at him that he's a useless piece of crap).

"Go to the bathroom and splash water on your face," she says. "Breathe deeply, and say a little mantra that restores your calm, like 'This is not an emergency... this too shall pass.' Research shows that the more calmly we speak, the more calm we feel, and the more calmly others respond to us."

This technique, by the way, is useful to employ before sending an angry text to your spouse. Technology may make us feel conve-niently detached from the consequences of lashing out, but if you're furiously typing a message to your husband and get hit by a bus, you do not want your final earthly communication to read *U FORGOT 2 ORDER DIAPERS AGEN ASS HOL.*

Another way to break the tension quickly is to announce, "This calls for a coffee." Tom, whose java intake rivals Balzac's, can always be distracted with this offer, which doubles as both a time-out and a collaborative activity. (Alternatively, if you are having an evening tiff, try "This calls for a glass of wine.")

When the skirmish is over and you have made a decent repair, *do not ruminate* (something of a pastime of mine, one that some studies show is more common among women in general). Happiness researcher Sonja Lyubomirsky observes in her book *The How of Happiness* that research demonstrates ruminating makes sadness worse, messes with your ability to solve problems, saps motivation, and interferes with concentration. "Moreover," she writes, "although people have a strong sense that they are gaining insight into themselves and their problems during their ruminations, this is rarely the case. What they do gain is a distorted, pessimistic perspective on their lives."

With this in mind, I tell Tom that if he makes an effort to deal with me during a conflict and not retreat, I promise not to obsess about an issue that we have talked through already. Nor will I — another hobby of mine — bring it up in bed when we're about to turn out the light.

•••••••••••••••••••••••••••

Moving on to your children: if, despite your best intentions, you have a blowout in front of the kids, *do damage control immediately.*

Therapist Ann Dunnewold says that if you're hashing things out fairly, it's actually good for kids to see, because they learn that people can be mad at each other but still love each other. "The two things can coexist," she says. "But it's got to be fair — it's got to be

'I'm really upset right now that you said that to me. How do we solve this?' rather than 'You stupid idiot.' But it's good for kids to see that we're human beings, and sometimes we have strong feelings that take a toll on us, and we have to work to recover; we have to work to apologize. So that when kids have strong feelings of their own, they don't feel like they just wrecked something."

Because if you're calling your spouse a stupid idiot, your child assumes that this is how you deal with a dispute. As Texas family therapist Carl Pickhardt puts it, "If you're yelling and calling names, your kid thinks, 'If I get in a disagreement, the way to resolve it is to speak more forcefully, more loudly, and to say harsher things to get my way.' I grew up seeing people pop off, but you can change that with your own kids, which is what I did. Take responsibility, recognize your choices, and then start practicing that behavior."

Markham advises me to draw from the same patience I use with my daughter. "I'm sure you've been frustrated when she wants to go to the playground and you want to go to the store," she says. "I'm sure you've been ready to scream sometimes, right? But you have, through self-control and hard work, summoned all your patience, listened to her side of things, and tried to work out a win-win solution. But none of those included screaming at your child as a way to resolve the conflict. And I would submit to you — and this is an aspiration, not an expectation — that it's completely possible to have a relationship with your partner that does not include screaming."

It may be possible, but at the moment, it's not probable. Two days after talking to Markham, Tom informs me as we sit down to dinner that he has landed a last-minute assignment to bike through California wine country for a week and will leave in two days. Then he adds that he has signed our daughter up for a chess class after school without my knowledge.

"Absolutely not," I said. "She's in two after-school classes already."

"I knew you would say that," he says. "But we both have a ton of work lately. Besides, I already paid."

"Why didn't you consult me?" I say, my voice rising. As our argument kindles into a brushfire, I remember Terry Real's command to fight behind closed doors — but the doors in our small apartment are cheap and porous. I run for the iPad and Sylvie's low-noise headphones. "Put these on and play Minecraft," I command. I drag Tom into the bedroom and shut the door.

The fight quickly bleeds into other issues. He accuses me of being crazy, which makes me crazier. I begin to cry. "She's going to come in here, so we have to take a time-out," Tom breaks in.

I hastily dry my tears. "You're right," I say. If the motivation to stop fighting still originates in the affection we share for our daughter and not for each other, so be it. When Sylvie bounds in a moment later, we are calm. But just in case, I repeat the script Markham had given me to tell our child in case I lose my cool. *I'm so sorry. No one deserves to get yelled at, including your dad. I try hard to control myself, and sometimes I don't do a good job, but I'm working on it. I want you to know I really love your dad and I'll always work things out with him.* I give Tom a hug (a real one) and Sylvie laughs and tries to wriggle between us in a ploy she calls the "sardine can."

No damage done, at least as far as I can tell. Later, when I have sufficiently cooled off, I confess to Tom the "soft emotions" behind my outburst: when he goes on extended bike trips, I miss him. Also, I am, frankly, jealous that he gets paid to pedal through vineyard-covered valleys while I am in the midst of writing a health story on the importance of dietary fiber. And I don't want to put Sylvie in another class because I feel guilty that I am working so much. I don't want to miss any time with her, I explain, even a few hours after school. The bittersweet part about having an only child is that every milestone is the first and last. (When I dropped her off on the first day of kindergarten, I cried so hard that her new teacher had to comfort *me*. Eventually, my carrying on upset the other children, some of whom began to cry themselves — so I was gently asked to leave.)

Then I wander into Sylvie's room. I have a few questions that Pickhardt advised me to ask her about our fighting. He tells me it's helpful, and sometimes surprising, to know how we come across to our children. I approach her as she's seated at her desk in her room, absently humming and coloring a picture of a purple frog.

ME: Honey, I have a question: how would you wish that I
    argued differently with your dad?
SYLVIE: I wish you would not yell, because Daddy looks sad.
ME: Tell me how you feel when I yell at Daddy.
SYLVIE: I sometimes like to listen and hear you yelling at
    Daddy. It's kind of fun and I like to peek out of my room
    and see Daddy looking like Grumpy Cat.
ME: What are some ways that I behave that make you feel
    unsafe and unhappy?
SYLVIE: I don't like it when you and Daddy aren't talking to
    each other and I don't know why.

One crucial step remains to help stressed new parents avoid divorce court: look for the good. This means voicing what the Gottmans call the "three *As*": affection, appreciation, and admiration.

During the quotidian moments of life, they found, couples should have a 20:1 ratio of positive to negative interactions. During times of conflict, meanwhile, the magic ratio is 5:1. Positive interactions can be the tiniest of gestures: a smile, making eye contact, nodding to show you're listening, a quick joke.

This game-changing little ratio forced me to pay attention to the tone of our daily exchanges: how often are we actually being nice to each other? For the first week I keep a loose count, I notice that a dispiriting number of our communications are administrative: What time is the birthday party? Did you buy shin guards for her soccer class? Our positive interactions are mostly confined to fond chats about Sylvie after she's gone to bed. We are fading as a twosome, like the holiday photo cards we receive from friends: once they become parents, they vanish from the frame. Only the children remain, while the parents are the Disappeared.

I have been counting as "positive" interactions such as Tom's offer to clean my computer keys by spraying them with compressed air, which is done with a gallant sort of flourish. I worriedly ask Julie Gottman if one of our many neutral interactions can be labeled as positive if we're pleasant about it. "Let's say I tell my husband, 'Here's your coffee,' but I say it in, you know, a nice tone of voice," I tell her.

She thinks for a moment. "That would be considered positive, yes," she says. I sigh with relief.

Still, our feeble ratio of positives is a warning that we have to strengthen our daily bond. One of John Gottman's best-known findings is that happily married couples frequently and consistently respond to their partner's requests for connection, which he terms "bids."

When Tom is reading the paper, for example, he occasionally comments, "Hmm, that's interesting." This is a "bid," a sometimes-subtle appeal for attention. If I reply, "Oh, what are you reading?" this response is what Gottman calls "turning toward" my partner — I have given him the encouragement he's seeking. If I ignore his bid, I am "turning away" from Tom. It can be hard to take note of these bids — especially when children seemingly lie in wait to release a volley of their own bids the moment they see you sit down. A spouse's bidding can also be brushed off as needy or annoying, but often what they want is simply a quick connection: a brief chat, a smile, a reassuring word.

In a now-famous study of newlywed couples, John Gottman found that these seemingly insignificant bidding exchanges had a huge impact on marital happiness. After a six-year follow-up, he learned that the couples who had divorced had demonstrated "turn-toward bids" only a third of the time — while those still together had "turn-toward bids" almost 90 percent of the time. "All the research shows that being able to turn toward one another, and be there for one another, is what produces happier relationships," Julie Gottman tells me.

I begin to pay attention to, and identify, bids from Tom that might have slipped by me before. As it turns out, the guy is the human version of click bait:

Staring through binoculars at our neighbor's apartment across the street: "Huh."

Examining a coin from his pocket: "Now, that's something you don't see every day."

Reading *New Scientist* magazine: "Hmm. Pretty incredible about eels."

I even detect a bid from the wild-eyed, unkempt man who makes his way toward me on an otherwise-empty F train, sits down heavily next to me, and sighs. "What a day," he announces with pronounced weariness, looking at me hopefully.

• •

After you actively look for the good things in your spouse, say the Gottmans, build a culture of appreciation by pointing them out.

It's not enough just to *think* good things, says Helen Fisher, the biological anthropologist. She tells me that giving your mate affectionate comments daily is beneficial for them, but also helps *you* by reducing cortisol, lowering blood pressure, boosting your immune system, and even reducing cholesterol levels.

How important is this habit? Researchers from the University of Georgia found that what distinguishes marriages that last from those that don't is not necessarily how often couples argue, but how they treat each other on a daily basis when they are not bickering. Expressions of gratitude were the "most consistent significant predictor of marital quality." The power of a simple thank-you, as it turns out, is considerable.

Several studies have found that expressing gratitude creates a reciprocal "cycle of virtue," so that over time, even the less expressive mate will eventually voice their appreciation more often, creating an upward spiral of good feeling. Bearing this in mind, I thank Tom whenever it occurs to me — for ordering our daughter a new striped backpack she didn't need but desperately wanted, for bringing home a half dozen chocolate bars and conducting a family taste test for fun. I feel queasily New Age advancing this "attitude of gratitude" — yet is it any less strange that I politely thank Andre our UPS guy way more often than the person I married?

My friend Jenny, mother of two, tells her husband that saying "thank you" is the ultimate cheap buy-in. "The average mom does a hell of a lot," she says. "And unlike at work or school, at home, rarely is anyone saying, 'Good job.' There are no raises, rewards, or bonuses. In fact, there are, regularly, anti-rewards: screaming, complaints, and bad attitudes. So it helps tremendously." And men need emotional high fives, too, she adds. "Saying, 'Hey, thanks for making pancakes' or 'The kid really liked it when you talked into his foot like a cell phone' — these little praise seeds could blossom into more full-blown help in the future."

Just as important as "thank you" is a simple "yes."

John Gottman claims that all his research findings can be captured in the metaphor of a saltshaker: instead of salt, fill it with all the ways you can say yes, and sprinkle them throughout your daily marital interactions: *Yes, that's a good idea. Yes, I'm totally on board. Yes, that looks fun.* Couples who make a practice of doing this, he has said, are much more likely to go the distance.

So are those who touch regularly. Even a quick squeeze on the arm seems to reduce levels of the stress hormone cortisol and triggers the release of the brain chemical oxytocin, which promotes trust. Helen Fisher says that merely touching the palm or arm of someone raises your face and body temperature (as she says, "People keep us warm").

So I make an effort to grab Tom's arm when he walks by, or sling my legs over his while we are watching a movie. Going further, I've made myself reach for his hand when a fight is looming—even if I'm so irritated that I'd rather pick up a live rodent. Soon enough, I calm down. It's hard to holler at someone when they're mere inches from you, and the familiar contours of his hand remind me that this is the person I married, not the bogeyman.

How important is touch? In 2010, scientists from UC Berkeley studied and coded every physical interaction in a single game played by each team in the National Basketball Association, from chest bumps to high fives. They found that with few exceptions, the teams who touched the most won the most (at that time, it was the Boston Celtics and the Los Angeles Lakers). Their conclusion: good teams tend to be more hands-on than bad ones.

Is there a more apt metaphor for marriage?

No affectionate gesture seems too small. In the UCLA study of families cited earlier, seemingly trivial behaviors like greeting or noticing a family member when they returned to the house was important for "nourishing parent-child and couple relationships." Acknowledging a spouse takes less than a minute, researchers said—but if this habit is neglected, over time it can "adversely affect the quality of family relationships."

Often, I have been so caught up in the swirl of domestic life that when Tom returns from being out all day, I barely look up. But how hard is it to say hello or bestow a quick kiss? I also take the advice of a friend who tells me that she and her husband try to set aside ten minutes a day to chat about anything but kids, work, or scheduling (for the first few tries, we are alarmingly short of ideas).

Admittedly, "looking for the good" requires effort. When I complain to another friend about feeling invisible at home, she tells me that she had a revelation when she was away from her husband and two children on a business trip. "I was gone for a week, and my husband said they all felt sort of adrift," she said. "He said that I was the sun, and everyone revolved around me." She laughed. "Well, of course, I loved that image. I think about it when I'm feeling annoyed."

I try to do this when Tom overlooks Terry Real's message to "cherish more" and forgets my birthday. It is a Saturday, and when it hits me that he has forgotten, I feel so dejected that I crawl back into bed. This sends Tom and Sylvie into a mild panic. She's in bed? In the daytime? Now what?

I can hear them moving around uneasily outside the door. After a while, Tom runs out to get a cake and flowers, while Sylvie draws me a series of cards that say, "I love you Mommy." Part of their discomfort, I know, arises from the fact that I'm not making my usual Saturday morning blueberry pancakes. But part of it is that, as my daughter puts it, "You weren't in your spot" — the sunny place near our terrace where I like to read. Looking at their anxious faces at the foot of the bed, it occurs to me that maybe I am the sun, too.

My sunniness has limits, however. After that little episode, I realize that some of my stress arises from wondering whether Tom will remember holidays that are meaningful to me. Two weeks before Mother's Day, I send him an email saying *This is where I would like to go for Mother's Day,* and provide a link to a restaurant reservation. Then I write, *Here are three options for presents I would love,* with links for each (this adds at least a minor element of surprise). Finally I write, *Please let me know when you have ordered, unless you want me to take to my bed again.*

Is this romantic? No. But in this way, I eliminate my stress — as therapists say, I have "stayed on my own side." I have made a direct request and communicated what I would like (he usually asks me what I want, anyway). Type in *husband forgot* on Google, and Autofill supplies *my birthday, our anniversary,* and *my birthday again.* Why not remove the worry?

Which brings me to another important point: along with seeking out the good in our partners, brain science tells us it's also beneficial to look the other way. Helen Fisher and her partners conducted brain scans of parents in long, happy relationships and discovered a trio of brain regions that become active in long-term partnerships. "One is linked with empathy," Fisher tells me, "another with controlling your own emotions, and the third with positive illusions — the ability to *overlook* what you don't like about your partner." Or, as Ben Franklin wrote in *Poor Richard's Almanack,* "Keep your eyes wide open before marriage, and half shut afterward."

Avoid Fights!

Things women should perhaps not say to their husbands (actual quotes):

Just remember that I carried her for nine months.

That's not how he likes his cereal.

There's nothing as strong as a mother's love for her children. I mean, no offense, I love you, too.

This little observation recalls a study by the Open University in the UK, in which thousands of parents were asked to name the most important person in their lives. The disparity in answers among mothers and fathers was noteworthy: two-thirds of the fathers cited their wife or partner, while well over half of the mothers named their child.

That doesn't mean you have to *tell your husband that.* Yet I have heard this on the playground more than once as a mom throws out an ethical "trolley problem" and others nod in agreement: *If there was some sort of accident and my husband and child were hanging from a cliff, I'm choosing my child. No question.*

I, too, have made this dramatic declaration. I think what we are trying to get across is that our love for our children is so fierce that we would sacrifice our own mate for them. We feel guilty — but the slightest bit heroic — saying it aloud. But given the infinitesimal possibility of this disaster occurring — particularly in Brooklyn, which is free of cliffs — why am I constructing a scenario that sends my defenseless husband hurtling into a ravine? This isn't good for anybody.

Things men should perhaps not say to their wives:

Can you unload the dishwasher more quietly? The Falcons are going to score any second now.

Where are Jack's socks? *Note: Jack is seven.*

Points to youngest child: Why is this one acting so crazy?

What do the girls want for dinner?

I told the kids, "Let's go see what Mommy's doing!"

At least I'm a better husband than Justin! *Note: Justin, a strip club enthusiast, gave his wife crabs.*

It's one thing to decide to look for the good in one another; it's surprisingly difficult to put these noble intentions into practice. Tom thinks I should just be inherently aware that he appreciates me. As he points out, "You know how I feel; why do I have to tell you?" In his more freewheeling moments, he has quoted the Slovenian "wild man of theory" Slavoj Žižek: "If you have reasons to love someone, you don't love them." But when he doesn't express appreciation, I feel taken for granted (something that is felt acutely by mothers, as your infant isn't going to send you a "sorry for the explosive diarrhea" card). Tom doesn't seem to grasp that nihilist philosophy is not necessarily the best way into a girl's heart.

As for me, while I know intellectually that I must focus on the good, out of long habit, I still reflexively focus on the irritating.

I feel we need a professional nudge to help us connect more deeply and rebuild our friendship — perhaps from a couples therapist we could visit more regularly in New York.

Tom is wary about more analysis, but, once again, he admits

he's intrigued by the idea of having our relationship examined by a third party. He resignedly goes along with it when I bribe him with a lavish Manhattan lunch after each session. I immediately think of Guy Winch, a New York psychologist in private practice whom I have interviewed for health articles. Winch has an appealingly dry sense of humor that I sense Tom might like.

On the day of our first appointment, we linger nervously by the door of Winch's office in the Flatiron district before he finally invites us in. He is trim and straight-backed, with close-cropped hair and kindly eyes.

We take a seat in his office, a serene contrast to the chaotic street scene outside his window. The couch is so soft that I fight an urge to lie down. I wonder if anyone has ever fallen asleep during a session.

Winch sits back, crosses his legs, and invites us to tell him why we have come. We once again rake over our areas of conflict, as we had for Terry Real a month prior. It takes almost the entire session.

"I don't want to nag," I say, finishing up. "I'm tired of nagging. I was class clown in high school, Dr. Winch. Okay? I'm fun!"

He nods gravely. "You were class clown." *Aha, I know what you're doing,* I think. *You're mirroring. I remember it from the hostage expert.*

I explain that we've almost stopped expressing affection for each other, because we're having trouble getting past our mutual resentment. I tell Winch about the spaghetti Bolognese episode and then interrupt myself.

"I feel stupid that I'm even talking about this," I say. "It seems so trivial."

Winch waves away my concern. "In my over twenty years of seeing couples," he says, "I have yet to see one that fights about world peace."

He tents his fingers and leans forward. "You don't feel appreciated," he paraphrases.

"Right," I say, feeling as if I am tattling on Tom. "When I have asked him to express his appreciation for taking care of him and our child, he just can't do it, even though it would mean a lot to me. He's just not Mr...."

"Effusive," Tom puts in. "Verbally. But it's hard when it's called upon. I get a kind of performance anxiety or something."

Winch nods. "A lot of men feel like a performance animal, going 'Arf, arf!' If Jancee asks for praise, you hear it as 'She's telling me what to do.' But if you could reframe it as 'She's feeling unsettled, and I can do something that will help her feel more settled,' it's much easier to think of it as her need, rather than her telling you what to do. You could even simply reach out and squeeze her hand."

Winch discreetly glances at the clock. "I want to give you some homework for our next session," he announces. He turns to me. "Jancee, I want you to make a list of all the things that Tom brings to the table as a partner, including parenting."

I make a careful notation on the pad of paper I have brought. "Positive things?"

He suppresses a smile. "Um, yes. 'Bring to the table' usually means—"

"Right," I say quickly.

"—the small gestures, the thoughtful stuff he does automatically. And try to make it detailed. And then in another column, the things that annoy you. I think it will be interesting to see the spectrum in terms of the good versus the bad. Because when you squabble about small things, they get inflated. You lose perspective and it's all about the mess in your apartment. The other stuff gets lost."

When couples have been together for a long time, he continues, they end up almost stereotyping each other — reducing their partner from a three-dimensional, complex person to a much more two-dimensional caricature. "Like that of, say, a control freak who is constantly complaining," he says, gesturing toward me. Wait, what?

"And when your perception is slanted in that way," he goes on, "you naturally register everything that reinforces those perceptions, and ignore things that don't. And over time, that becomes a really narrow misrepresentation. It's a gradual process, and you want to fight against it by reminding yourself of the complexity of the other person."

Then he assigns Tom homework of his own: he, too, is to list specific things he loves about me, as well as potential remedies for the things that are bothering me.

We have to keep each list a secret from the other.

⁕⁕⁕⁕⁕⁕⁕⁕⁕⁕⁕⁕⁕⁕⁕⁕⁕⁕⁕⁕⁕⁕

We show up early for our next session, brandishing our homework like dutiful students. Winch asks me to begin with the list of Tom's thoughtful gestures.

"Should I read them to you?" I ask.

Winch shakes his head. "No. I'd like you to read them to Tom, and see his reactions while you're reading to him."

Strangely nervous, I pull out my list and begin:

> Drives me everywhere because I'm a timid city driver and afraid of what I call the Crazies.
>
> Takes us to parks and botanical gardens on the weekends.
>
> Paid the bills for our daughter's first two years so I could stay home with her.
>
> Takes our daughter out most late afternoons to exercise, and also to piano and swimming lessons and chess tournaments.
>
> Makes me laugh constantly.
>
> Does all my annoying computer fixing, which is no small thing.
>
> Painted my parents' new house last summer, weekend after weekend in the heat —

I am suddenly overwhelmed and have to pause. "Tom," I say, touching his arm. "Every weekend in the sticky heat! On a rickety ladder! Near a wasp's nest!" Tears spill down my face. "You were so nice to my parents, and when you're kind to them, you're kind to me."

"Where was this?" breaks in Dr. Winch. "North Jersey? Wow. Not that close, either." After I regain my composure, I go on:

> He is intellectually stimulating, constantly finding interesting movies for us to watch, books to read, and places to go. While the movies are often bleak Romanian films about, say, an orphan trying to survive during Ceaușescu's dictatorship, I still appreciate the gesture.
>
> Makes me coffee every morning.

Races home from business trips to be with us.

Patiently taught our daughter to read, spell, and ride a bike.

Plays games with our daughter whenever she asks, which is at least once a day.

Can refuse our daughter nothing, including the two activities he dreads the most: the American Girl doll store and the 9 a.m. "open bounce" at the bounce house off the highway, which corrals all his nightmares under one roof—loud club music, fluorescent lighting, screaming, vomiting children, and high injury rates.

Spends weeks planning our vacations.

Is very gentle and never raises his voice.

I have to pause here. "Now I'm crying again," I say, faltering, "and I can't see my paper."

"There is a box of tissues behind you," says Winch. "Tom, do you have anything to say to that?"

Tom looks slightly uncomfortable. "It's funny that we haven't done that sort of thing before," he says.

"Few people do," Winch replies.

Tom shrugs. "I was thinking for some of them, 'Well, shouldn't anyone do that?' But I was tearing up, too, in response to Jancee. It's just a weird thing to hear in that form. It's like feedback, in a way."

"It's not 'in a way,'" says Winch, "it's as feedback as feedback gets. It's not your six-month review—but if it were, you might get a raise." He leans forward. "Look, I'll ask you this question: for most women reading that list, what would they think about that husband?"

Tom, unused to this sort of scrutiny, begins to stutter. "You know, sort of, hopefully, you know, dutiful, caring? Attentive, in certain ways, at least? Just kind of maybe more action-oriented, instead of qualities like being emotionally available? Or something?"

Winch stops him. "But I think you can read emotional availability in every line, frankly." He smiles. "To me, that list pretty much reads like you should come with spandex and a cape. You're saying, 'But there's nothing there about my flowery emotional expressiveness.' But most women would look at this list and go, 'Does he have siblings?' To me, that has so much heart. There's love and devotion all through it. You're emotionally expressive, certainly, in so many other ways than the verbal straight-on. It's so much more important to write what somebody does rather than what they say. Then you can see how they really feel."

Tom nods. "It's interesting, on social media you get so much feedback, kudos and likes, but you don't give or get it with yourself or in your relationship."

"Right," says Winch. "But being mindful is difficult. That's why this exercise will help, because you may not realize how much your actions are noted and appreciated, how much they really mean. Your wife tears up as she talks about your painting her parents' house."

Winch recommends this exercise for any couple. "It's important to clear the time, look at each other when you're reading it, and talk about how each thing makes you feel," he says. The benefits of this can last months, or years.

Couples therapist Esther Perel agrees, saying that there are few more powerful gestures than telling your partner, *I took time for you, I thought about you, I am telling you out loud.* The combination of composing something meaningful and then reading it aloud, she says, "changes everything. It adds the secret sauce."

⋅⋅⋅⋅⋅⋅⋅⋅⋅⋅⋅⋅⋅⋅⋅⋅⋅⋅⋅⋅⋅⋅⋅⋅⋅⋅

Winch then has me read the list of things that annoy me about Tom. I am a little reluctant to pollute the rosy atmosphere we have created, but I carry on.

> He just forgot my birthday, which never happened until we had a child. This is a person who regularly makes meticulous plans for bike trips and forgets nothing.

Winch looks placidly at Tom. "I say this to husbands a lot," he says. "The return on investment with cards is huge. Huge. Those few minutes to get a card and write something nice — biggest and best investment ever. Some things are hard. That's not." Tom nods meekly and I continue with my list.

> When I ask him to do something, he ignores me or says, "Later."
> He shovels in beautiful meals that I prepare, sometimes three a day, and often does not say thank you or even bring his dishes to the sink.
> He doesn't acknowledge all the extra work I do with our daughter, much of it hidden.

He gives our daughter compliments and tells her he loves her, but not me.

After we fight, he doesn't apologize or even allude to the fight. He just starts speaking in a normal voice about a new topic, which I find weird and jarring.

Winch nods slowly. "What strikes you when you hear the two lists together?"

"The contrast," I reply. "The list of good things is larger and the acts are more significant."

Then Tom pulls out his homework detailing the ways he can demonstrate how he cares for me, and nervously begins:

Consistently thanking her for meals and small things. Like I could say, "Thanks for picking up the milk."

Try to give her time to herself.

Answer her and be more communicative and try not to be reactive. Try not to fly off the handle or play weird little games, and be specific about when I'm going to do something instead of "later." It's easy to just give a time.

Recognize special events like birthdays more conscientiously.

Make our daughter's meals more often.

Take our daughter to birthday parties and appointments.

If Jancee's rushing around with our daughter getting her ready for something, I could maybe ask, "What can I do?" (Or, as my friend Jenny likes to say, the magic phrase is *I've got this.* "Preferably if you really mean it, but let's just go ahead and give you a free pass to sprinkle it into the dialogue here and there even if you're not completely sure you 'got this,'" she says. "It's aspirational, and reassuring.")

Then Tom reads the list of things he loves about me, among them:

> You make me laugh. I think it's a sign of a deeper connection, something unusual that we share; and now, if you'll notice, we have incorporated Sylvie into our mirthful existence.
> You are a wonderful mother. I just love seeing these new parts of you emerge, and I love you more for it.
> You are my best friend. There is no one else I would rather spend time with, tell things to, wake up next to, silently exchange knowing glances with. Romantic love gets all the attention, but I think this is not to be underrated.

In fifteen years of marriage, I had never heard that Tom considers me his best friend.

"There's a box of tissues behind you," Winch reminds me.

◆◆◆◆◆◆◆◆◆◆◆◆◆◆◆◆◆◆◆◆◆◆◆◆◆◆◆

And so we try to say kind words to each other. It often sounds scripted and false, but we do it. It is more difficult for Tom: Georgetown linguistics professor Deborah Tannen has famously noted the disparity in men's and women's conversational styles: women, she says, tend to use "rapport talk," in which they focus on personal experience and seek to build connections, while men favor "report talk," giving information about impersonal topics.

Tom's favorite thing to do is dispense information about impersonal topics, so I appreciate the effort it takes for him to disclose that an encounter with me and Sylvie left him feeling a bit stung. He had opened Sylvie's bedroom door to find us playing a game she invented called Unicorn Land.

"What's going on here?" he said, using his Hearty Dad voice. Sylvie, upset that he had torn the fragile web of magic she had woven, shooed him away and ordered him to shut the door behind him. I said nothing, assuming that I was sparing him the labyrinthine rules of passage to Unicorn Land, a complex intermingling of spells, passports, and secret words. But he confessed to me later that he felt shut out of this cozy family scene.

There is no doubt that being mindful of your every interaction is wearying. It requires vigilance. Communicating. Adjusting. Over the next few months, I take many time-outs in which I pull out our daughter's picture, try to steady my breathing, and wait for the initial wave of anger to pass. I dutifully recite the words Terry Real supplied: *I know that what I'm about to do is going to cause you harm, but right now, my anger is more important to me than you are.* It's been helpful to use time-outs, shape my turbulent feelings into "I" statements, state clearly what I need, and keep my voice neutral. Day by day, the more cordial we are with each other, the more harshly out of place an argument sounds.

I constantly remind myself that the more affectionate we are in front of our daughter, the more secure she will be. And teaching by example — what psychiatrists call modeling — can be used strategically to help develop a kid's own behavior, says the Yale Parenting Center's Alan Kazdin. "Modeling is so important," he tells me. How potent is it? Research has demonstrated, he says, that there are special cells in the brain called mirror neurons. When we watch someone do something, our mirror neurons become active in the brain, as if we ourselves are engaging in the same behavior we're observing. "If I'm lifting a stapler on my desk, and you're watching me, your brain would fire cells that are equivalent to your hand lifting up the stapler as well," he says. This suggests, he goes on, that *observation* of a behavior forges the same neural connections made from *practicing* that behavior — so that modeling can actually change the brain.

I tell Kazdin that I have given Sylvie many lectures on how we must treat others with respect — yet she has observed many times that I haven't treated her father with respect. "I think it's nice in some ways that parents don't really realize the responsibilities that they have," Kazdin, a father of two grown children, says sympathetically. "And that is that their behavior is being observed all the time. It's really daunting. You make one obscene gesture in traffic, and you're going to see it in your house ten times. You can say, 'I only did it once.' It doesn't matter: the mirror neurons took it right up, and it's there."

Along with being more affectionate in front of our daughter, I hit upon the idea of telling her about how the two of us met, after uncovering a small but growing body of research that suggests that when parents share family stories, their children benefit in all sorts of ways.

Psychologists from Emory University's Family Narratives Lab

found that teens with a solid knowledge of their family history have lower rates of depression and anxiety, greater coping skills, and higher levels of self-esteem. Researchers theorized that this was "perhaps because these stories provide larger narrative frameworks for understanding self and the world, and...a sense of continuity across generations in ways that promote a secure identity."

And so, to strengthen the family folklore and to show her that our relationship has endured for many years, we start telling our daughter tales of our early days together. We always begin with our first date in 1999, a century so distant to her young mind that it could figure in a Ric Burns documentary, with TLC's "No Scrubs" subbing in for the tinkly ragtime music. Soon she finishes our sentences.

"When I first met Daddy, we were set up on a blind date, and he was so shy and nervous that he—"

"—talked about how Bubble Wrap is made!" Sylvie supplies gaily. "And how he played a game called Dungeons and Dragons for hours and hours when he was little."

"Right. He sure did love Dungeons and Dragons—and I guess because he was nervous on our date, he went on for some time about it! That's not how most grown-ups chat when they go out together, so at first I thought maybe he was too odd for me. And at the time, I was working at a music magazine called *Rolling Stone,* and Daddy was worried that I was wild and stayed up too late."

"When sometimes you go to bed before me," she observes.

"Yes, I can barely make it to 8:45. Anyway, the more I talked with your dad, the more I realized that being odd is a good thing, and that he was the most interesting person I'd ever met."

After a while, Sylvie committed our stories to memory—so

that in a way, they have become her stories. *On their first date, they went to the movies, and Daddy put his arm around Mommy. Mommy knew she wanted to marry Daddy within two weeks. Mommy has seen Daddy cry only two times: when she was walking down the aisle to marry him, and the night I was born.*

TGIM: How Not to Hate Your Weekends After Kids

On a Friday after work, I call my sister Heather for a quick catch-up. She is in the car rushing from her teaching job to the grocery store; to avoid holding her cell phone while driving, she puts me on speakerphone and drops the phone in her lap.

Tonight, she informs me, she is hosting a slumber party with the triplets — three identical friends of her youngest son, who come as a package deal. "So I have to run to Price Chopper because we're out of snacks," she says, sounding muffled from the confines of her lap. "And I need spaghetti makings for dinner. Oh, and breakfast: when the boys sleep over at other people's houses, the parents make a real breakfast, so I should get bacon and eggs and all that stuff. Then I'll run home and clean the house and get the spaghetti ready."

I inquire about the rest of her weekend. On Saturday, she'll fry up the bacon and eggs for the crew of boys, ferry the triplets home, deliver both sons to other playdates, and buy birthday presents for two of the kids' friends before her son Gray's yearbook committee meeting at 3.

"Hold up," I interrupt. "That's a school project, isn't it?"

"Oh, weekends are the new weekdays, even for kids, don't you know? It's nuts." From 6 to 7:30, she continues, her older son, Travis, has soccer practice.

"Then we do a family movie night," she says. "But even that is exhausting, because by the time everyone scrambles to shower and eat dinner it's always 8:30. Rob and I put the movie on and we just want to be in bed already, and it's 10 and we're nodding off. But if we tell the kids, 'Let's finish the movie tomorrow,' they get so upset because it's supposed to be family time. So we try and stay awake."

On Sunday, she goes on, both boys have soccer tournaments from 8:30 to 3, which she and Rob divide. This time commitment — almost a full workday in itself — is a familiar reality for parents of the estimated 44 million American kids who play organized sports. Youth sports have become so highly professionalized that the travel industry built around it alone generates an estimated $7 billion annually. In response, specialty travel agencies have sprung up whose sole focus is to book hotels for traveling youth teams and their families.

The old games of kick-around in the local park have given way to sports campuses like Rocky Top Sports World in Gatlinburg, Tennessee, an 80-acre, $20 million facility that hosts "tourney-cations," in which the whole family can build their vacation around a kid's soccer tournament. Heather's town has its own sports campus, housed in a former prison, which for authentic period details still sports some of its barbed-wire perimeter — presumably to deter parents who contemplate making a break.

But Heather gets no time off for good behavior. After her kids' soccer tournaments, she drives them home for showers, homework, and dinner. When the boys are in bed, she prepares her teaching lesson plan for the following week. "Oh, and from Friday to Sunday I'm also doing at least five loads of laundry," she says. "And of course the whole time Rob and I end up fighting about who does what."

She pauses. "You know what? I almost like my workweek better, because it's more regimented. Like, I know the kids will be in bed by 7:30 reading. If I'm shopping on the weekend, it's not even fun shopping — it's shopping for their sports socks. How can two boys go through so many sports socks?"

She abruptly stops speaking.

"Heather?" I say worriedly. "What is it? Oh no, were you speeding? It's a cop. Is it a cop?"

"No," she says, sighing. "I got so distracted talking to you, I forgot to go to the grocery store and drove home."

She curses and pulls out of her driveway.

Tom and I sometimes exchange wry looks when we see child-free couples on the street. With their yoga mats tucked under their arms, they good-naturedly bicker about where they will go to brunch before a roll in the hay and a nap. "When I was single, I used to be annoyed by people with kids," Tom says as we pass a duo making out on a street corner. "Now I'm annoyed by couples."

The cruel paradox of weekends with kids can be boiled down to this: Parents want to relax. Kids do not. Those with younger children desperately contrive ways for their offspring to "run it out" as if they're training greyhounds; those with older kids spend their weekends as a taxi service. "Before I had kids, I thought of weekend time as available," says Caroline, a part-time freelancer and stay-at-home mom of two. "As a mom, you start calculating like a crazy person to save time any way you can. What if I skip the shower, then maybe I could get a coffee at the grocery store Starbucks so I could drink it and shop at the same time? I always think of those walk-in tubes at Chuck E. Cheese's where you try to catch the tickets: the tickets for parents are minutes and hours."

Making matters worse is that for many parents, work obligations have bled into the weekend. In 2014, the Organization for Economic Cooperation and Development (OECD) examined work-life balance in a number of countries by measuring the proportion of employees who toil fifty hours or more per week, against the time they devote daily to "leisure and personal care." Out of the thirty-four member countries in the OECD, the United States ranked a dismal number twenty-nine. (Denmark is number one.)

For Tom and me, weekends are a lingering source of tension. We have at least gotten better about arranging our weekdays. During the four months of our relationship shake-up, it is becoming clear that much of our friction has arisen from a lack of clear roles. Because we've sorted out what to do, I no longer expect him to read my mind, or fume that he isn't helping. Now that Tom readies our daughter for school two mornings a week, for example, I am fully off the clock. That small, sweet bit of free time when I can linger over breakfast makes an enormous difference in my day. Of course, I am still "household manager," constantly reminding Tom to do fundamental things such as feed the kid breakfast — but he does it.

If a fight brews, Tom has been effectively disarming me with his FBI training and the statements supplied by Terry Real: *Oh, that must feel bad. I can see why you feel like that. What can I say or do right now to make you feel better?* It's calculated, but who cares? If I'm emptying the dishwasher, he now jumps up and helps me unload. This largely symbolic task takes two minutes, but he's clueing in to the fact that the goodwill he engenders lasts much longer. Sometimes he even says, "Need a hand?" This golden phrase lights within me a tiny flame of warmth; he is saying, in effect, *If it were up to me, I would never do dishes and would happily eat directly out of a bag, but I care that you care.* Recalling Dr. Chapman's advice, I make myself thank Tom, and refrain from reminding him that no one thanks *me* for emptying the dishwasher. Our civility is indeed creating an upward spiral of goodwill: I am happier; Tom gets his much-needed peace.

Some of this newfound courtesy is, admittedly, a performance that we put on for our daughter — I had shown Tom the research on modeling and explained that when Sylvie witnesses me doing the vast majority of household work, she forms an expectation of her future. I break out the modeling paradigm again to persuade him to be a parent volunteer for one of Sylvie's field trips to a children's museum. Parent volunteers, I inform him, are overwhelmingly female. It would be good for our daughter and the other kids to see that dads can volunteer, too. "Plus you work from home," I say. "You don't have to deal with getting permission from a boss." When we tell Sylvie that Daddy will be coming along on the field trip, she is overjoyed.

But as the day of the field trip approaches, the backpedaling begins. "I have a lot of work to do on Thursday, so I'm going to have to cancel," Tom says breezily. "Most of the volunteers are stay-at-home moms anyway, so they have the time. I'm on deadline for three articles."

I sit down at my computer and call up the teacher's email containing details about the field trip. Of the six women chaperoning, five have full-time jobs. I point to the names. "She's a lawyer," I say. "I guess she'll work late tonight. Jessie works at a nonprofit in Manhattan. This one is an editor, this one is —"

Tom holds up his hand. "Okay, okay, I'm going," he says.

That afternoon, he returns from the trip full of funny stories about our daughter's classmates. "It's so interesting to see this part of her life that has been sort of hidden from me," he says. "At lunch, the kids had a long debate: if an invisible person eats lunch, can you see the food, or does it become invisible, too?" Tom was called upon to solve the dispute, and presumably only made the kids more confused when he told them it depended if the "mechanism of invisibility" was the man's skin ("which would act as a kind of cloaking shield, so the food would be invisible") or his whole body, in which case "a foreign substance would presumably be shown." Thankfully, he then reverted back to Dad Mode, and told the kids to make their sandwiches disappear.

As he becomes ever more involved in our child's life, his wife and daughter grow closer to him, and more appreciative. Upward spiral.

•••••••••••••••••••••••••••

Our weekends, however, still need help. When time is less structured and all family members have conflicting agendas, skirmishes tend to erupt. My friend Marea says that for stay-at-home mothers like herself, weekends are especially complicated, because they often don't feel comfortable or justified in asking their husbands to pitch in.

As a result, her weekends are no different from her weekdays. "Our daughter wakes me up early; I make breakfast and get her dressed," she says. "Sean sleeps in and then takes his time waking up, complete with a stretch session. After he's good and limber, he hops in a hot shower for twenty minutes to loosen up completely. By that time, I've made lunch and there are two stacks of dishes. My stress level might be getting up there by this point, especially when he comes out of the shower, sits on the couch, and nine times out of ten pulls out his phone, completely ignoring the kid. And he knows I'm annoyed." She sighs. "I just see this stuff as some sort of bad-boy act of defiance, and it's enraging."

Yet he won't offer to help, and she, hamstrung by her belief that he needs the entire weekend to recharge, doesn't feel empowered to ask — which means that seven days a week, the mundane work is dumped entirely on her.

I recall therapist Ann Dunnewold's advice to appeal to a man's sense of fairness. "So Sean gets weekends totally off, which means he has eight days of leisure a month," I tell Marea.

She nods. "Right."

"That's" — I do a quick calculation of sixteen waking hours times eight — "128 hours a month that he has off on weekends. How about you? What do you get?"

She blinks. "Zero."

I nod. "Uh-huh."

So why would she not rise up and insist that he do more, when she has nothing to lose except extra loads of laundry? I relay the story of Marea's hesitation to feminist writer Caitlin Moran at our rendezvous in Philadelphia, and she erupts in a most satisfying way. "Well, then there's no rest for your friend, is there?" she says, shaking her head. "Clearly she needs to negotiate. It's something I literally can't understand when I see it happening in other relationships. If you love your wife, how can you not address this issue? You have to have a conversation with your man and go, 'Fairies don't do all the work. Why are you doing this to me?'"

Moran's husband, journalist Peter Paphides, is, to no one's shock, an avid feminist. "My husband has turned his geekery toward being an excellent parent," she declares to me. "He was so proud about getting the right Tupperware for our girls' packed lunches. I constantly point out to the girls, 'You are very lucky you have an absolutely exceptional father. There are a lot of girls out there who do not have fathers like this.'" She cackles. "I did dick-move him early on, because I can't drive, and absolutely refuse to, so he's had to do all the school runs and shopping, while I just sit at home typing on Twitter, going, 'It's great not driving!' It's working out quite well for me."

Returning to Marea's dilemma, Moran does have sympathy for the classic feminist demand that housewives should be paid for their work. "There's a complete logic to that. If you put your granny in an institution and you're paying someone to care for her, it's a business transaction. But caring for your granny yourself is an unpaid thing?" She leaps up and stomps around the room in her heavy boots. "We've been told that there should be some sort of element of pride to keeping house and being a good wife and mother. There is this massive underlying belief that a woman will *never* run out of love and care and attention — that they should be able to give until they *die*. Without any point where you go, 'That's enough.' Men need to be either inspired into doing this stuff, culturally, or they need to be shamed!"

Moran continues this rant for a good twenty minutes. I must admit, it is fun to wind her up.

⁕⁕⁕⁕⁕⁕⁕⁕⁕⁕⁕⁕⁕⁕⁕⁕⁕⁕⁕⁕⁕⁕⁕⁕⁕⁕

A restful, restorative weekend with kids may not be entirely possible, but surely someone, somewhere, has found a way to elevate it beyond a bleak slog through sports, playdates, and chores.

I suddenly think of my friend Jenny. She has earned the admiration of other moms by deftly sorting out her family's weekends with forethought and planning.

We meet at our usual lunch spot, a former Cobble Hill carriage house, now a coffee shop by day and bar by night that peddles microbrews and "specialty craft drinks." Signs affixed to the space's exposed-brick walls offer homemade sausage-making workshops, a meeting of the Brooklyn Accordion Club, CSA pickup times, and a show featuring vintage electric pianos.

A very New Brooklyn clientele gathers at the large communal tables: bearded, tattooed guys with man buns eating artisanal Pop-Tarts, laptop tappers sporting bold eyewear, twenty-something creatives updating their Etsy websites, and moms like us marking time before the school run.

I race in, late from a stint as a volunteer cafeteria helper at my daughter's school, and slide onto the bench next to my friend, who, with her willowy frame and wavy red hair, resembles a contemporary version of Millais's painting of Ophelia. Both of us are wearing a variation of the Brooklyn mom uniform: striped shirt, skinny jeans, small gold earrings fashioned into an "organic" shape, Bold Lip.

I order my usual avocado toast on pepita multigrain with a house-made ginger ale; for Jenny, the triple kale salad (raw, charred, and "crispy sesame"). I quiz her on her weekend formula and she obligingly lays it out for me. She, her husband, and their two sons begin with a family meeting. "As corny as they sound, they really do work," she says. Gather everyone, she says, and go around the circle asking each family member to say one or two things they'd like to do that weekend.

"Kids as young as two can do this," she says. "Even if the idea is not feasible, such as cotton candy for dinner, try to incorporate some aspect of it — like, kids pick the restaurant for dinner. At the very least, don't shoot down an idea right away. Nobody likes that person at a meeting."

"Say out loud," she goes on, " 'This weekend I want A, B, and C' in order of importance. Assume nothing," she says. For kid activities, she and her husband alternate weekends, allowing one free pass to *Run! Save Yourself.* "That way," she says, "both parents have an opportunity to grab the easier job on offer — like staying home while the baby naps versus taking the big kid to the paint-ball birthday party." (Alternatively, Jenny and I know one set of parents who simply flip a coin when confronted with a kid-tivity that's particularly dread inducing.)

She suggests the following noninflammatory ways to commence the bargaining process:

If you want to go play basketball for a few hours this weekend, that's fine. I'll stay home with the kids. Next weekend, I'd love to catch that new art exhibit, and you can take care of the kids. Cannily, she is presenting this in the very way that psychologist Joshua

Coleman suggests: as though it's a done deal, and you just have to figure out how to get there.

You've been working a lot the past few weeks, and I've had a lot of solo-parenting time. I'm feeling burnt out and impatient with the kids. It'd be great if I could recharge my batteries with some alone time.

You know what, I miss my fun side. What are some ways you can help me rekindle that?

I've made a list of the kids' weekend activities. Do you think you could handle X, Y, and/or Z? Asking if he can "handle" it, she says, presents a little challenge no guy will want to back down from. And as Yale psychology professor Alan Kazdin points out, choice increases the likelihood of compliance. It's not the choice itself that's important, it's the feeling that the person *has* a choice that makes a difference in behavior.

When delegating, consider which child-related duties play to your husband's strong suits, she says, and which jobs you are happy to truly hand over — tasks that aren't going to summon your inner micromanager. Then give him the reins. "If he takes on the kids' swimming lessons, let him do it soup-to-nuts — the clock watching, the bag packing, all of it. There may be a week that the kid swims naked," says Jenny. "You might smell a moldy diaper in the gym bag a month later. Shut your mouth and let it go. He will eventually work out the kinks. He will. He may relish giving *you* updates on the kids for once, or gloat a little about how on top of it he is."

She is also a fan of the "after eight" bargaining chip: you'll find your spouse is much more open to the idea of you hitting the gym or grabbing a drink with friends, she says, after the kids go to sleep.

Finally, she says, "Give 'me time' freely and fully." Her husband knows not to offer her time for a relaxing bubble bath only to ignore the kids as they amble off to the bathroom to cannonball plastic penguins into Mommy's bubbles. If she tells him he's free to meet friends, she won't bring it up for the next three weeks every time she's annoyed with him.

In other words, as Terry Real so memorably put it, don't pee on the gift. "Oh, my favorite new saying," says Jenny.

⁎⁎⁎⁎⁎⁎⁎⁎⁎⁎⁎⁎⁎⁎⁎⁎⁎⁎⁎⁎⁎⁎⁎⁎⁎⁎⁎⁎

Parents tell me that their thorniest weekend problem by far is time management — so again I phone Julie Morgenstern, the New York City time management consultant. She has devised a novel approach to organizing weekends with kids that has been an instant hit with her high-powered clients. Envision your weekend, she says, as seven distinct units of time: Friday night, Saturday morning, Saturday afternoon, Saturday night, Sunday morning, Sunday afternoon, Sunday night.

"So, if you think of your weekend as seven units of time," she says, "you can dedicate each unit to various things: quality time where you reconnect, renewal time, and household stuff." She then has clients keep each unit distinct. "I'll tell families, 'Look, stop trying to do chores and errands in every available moment," she says. "On the weekend, compress it to one unit or two, maximum. So the Saturday morning unit could be devoted to housework, like 'This is when we get the house clean together as a group, compress, consolidate, get it done.' And then maybe in the afternoon you do your grocery shopping. That's two units — but if you could get it down all into one, even better."

For many families, some weekend units are quickly gobbled up by sports or birthday parties. If this is the case, she says, parents should purposefully set aside another unit or two for fun and restoration. She uses the acronym PEP: Physical activity, Escape (hobbies and activities that instantly transport you), and People (those who relax or energize you, not drain you). If you don't intentionally block out a unit for leisure, she warns, it will be consumed with another task. "Planning is exhausting, even making these damn decisions about units," she says. "But if you don't do it, you're going to squander the time. 'Free time' is not the leftover hours after everything else. Build it into your schedule, so you have something to look forward to."

This means that, as in my friend Marea's case, it's essential to get behind the idea that you need recharging time, too, or eventually you become a depleted human equivalent of *The Giving Tree*: a gnarled stump who is gradually stripped of her apples, wood, and branches by a child. (Described as a metaphor for a mother's unselfish love, *The Giving Tree* is one of those children's books that is loved and loathed in equal measure; its many Amazon detractors scorn it as "an abusive and codependent relationship" and "boy with psychopathic personality disorder uses mother-figure tree to his benefit.")

Using the seven units of time, Morgenstern sketches out a potential weekend. "So, the Friday night unit could be a potluck with other families, if you need that social connection; Saturday night and Sunday afternoon could be units for fun family outings;

while the Sunday night unit could be devoted to getting ready for the week."

I ask her: Isn't the point of a weekend *not* to be organized — to have carefree, unstructured time? "Kids really benefit from routine," Morgenstern, also the mother of one daughter, replies firmly. "A kid's world is already pretty chaotic. So if you have a rhythm not only to your weekdays but to your weekends, like 'Oh, Friday nights is when we have pizza with friends, and Sunday afternoons is when we go out and do something physical,' the routine frees everybody from having to figure out what to do with your time, and just enjoy it."

After time units are slotted, examine the weekend schedule with a ruthless eye. Morgenstern says that when we overstuff our weekends, we needlessly inject conflict into our own lives. As she says, "You shouldn't ask, 'How much can I fit in?' but 'What's going to fuel us? What is going to energize or relax us?'"

This includes sleep. "As a parent, you're working so hard, and giving, giving, giving constantly, so you have to be very thoughtful about what recharges you well — such as rest," she says. On Sunday nights, many parents are tempted to stay up late to cram in a few extra hours after the kids are finally in bed — but Morgenstern says we need to reverse our thinking. If you think of sleep as something to cap the end of the day, you may be tempted to keep the party going. But if you use her psychological trick and view sleep as the beginning of the following day, it can be easier to slip into the sheets.

Morgenstern advises sleep-deprived clients to stash away all electronics ninety minutes before bed. "Going online before bed is like drinking a Red Bull," she says bluntly. Studies show that the light from even a small device miscues the brain and promotes alertness — yet a National Sleep Foundation poll found that one in four parents reads or send emails or texts *after initially going to sleep* (and then they wonder why they're staring at the ceiling).

Comedian and mom of three Dena Blizzard tells me that her husband would disappear at night for hours to play video games in the den. "At first I thought it was just his thing to de-stress," she said. "But after a while it got out of control and he wasn't coming to bed until two in the morning." One night, he crawled shakily into bed, covered with sweat. Alarmed, Blizzard asked him what was wrong. "He said, 'I've been playing Call of Duty, all right? I lost a couple of my men and had to go back into the field. My men were down. You do not leave your men down.' I said, 'Do you have PTSD from the game? Because I can't deal with this. You're done. You're done saving people.'"

⁕⁕⁕⁕⁕⁕⁕⁕⁕⁕⁕⁕⁕⁕⁕⁕⁕⁕⁕⁕⁕⁕⁕⁕⁕⁕

There are obvious reasons why recharging for parents is crucial — you need energy to run after your children, for starters. But one researcher uncovered another reason that came as a surprise to both her and the parents she was analyzing.

In the first-ever study of what children think of their working parents, researcher Ellen Galinsky talked to more than one thousand children ages eight to eighteen about their family relationships and their parents' work lives.

She found that what parents believe their children think and what their children are actually thinking can be markedly different — the most telling example being what she calls the "one wish" question. She asked the children: If you were granted just one wish that could change the way your mother's or your father's work affects your life, what would that wish be?

She then asked adults to guess how their child would respond. Most parents guessed that their kids would wish for more time together. Not so: their most ardent wish was that their parents would be less stressed and less tired. Only 2 percent of parents got that one correct.

What surprised Galinsky further was how much those children worried about their parents — and their primary anxiety was that their parents were tired and stressed. One-third of the kids she talked to worried about their parents "often or very often," while two-thirds worried some of the time. When we are frazzled and racing from one thing to the next — when even weekends have become a strain — kids notice, and become distressed.

What often compounds working parents' tension is the pressure they put on themselves to create Memorable Moments on their few days off. But research tells us you do not need to jet to Disney World for the weekend to wow the kids. As Galinsky found, you don't even need to go to Uncle Stinky's Unlicensed Fun-Plex off the highway.

She also asked the children what they would remember the most from their childhoods and had their folks predict what the kids would say. Parents almost always guessed the five-star big event or vacation that took meticulous planning and buckets of cash. But Galinsky says that instead, kids specified the small, everyday rituals and traditions that said, "We're a family." One girl mentioned that every morning when she left for school, her father would say, "You go, tiger — you go get them." This seemingly insignificant, throwaway ritual — which brings a lump to my throat every time I think about it — was singled out as the experience this child would remember most vividly from childhood. As Galinsky discovered, those little things matter so much, more than we think they do.

··························

Taking Julie Morgenstern's and Jenny's advice into consideration, I've started creating weekend scenarios that I call Everybody Sort of Wins, based on the principles of Utilitarianism developed by English philosophers Jeremy Bentham and John Stuart Mill: everyone's happiness is of equal value, so we should bring about the greatest amount of good for the greatest number.

In every instance of weekend family time, I strategize: How can everybody sort of win? These scenarios take planning but have been extremely helpful. When I have to take Sylvie to the park one Saturday, I mitigate the tedium with a "fun" coffee (caffè mocha and, what the hell, extra whipped cream) and a highly entertaining podcast of Keith Richards on Desert Island Discs. Every time he breaks into a phlegmy cackle, I do, too, eliciting quizzical looks from other parents.

Another example: our daughter's piano teacher comes to our house every Friday afternoon. While they labor over the *Peanuts* theme song, I pile magazines and newspapers on the bed, Tom pours wine and brings in a little dish of olives and cheese, and we decompress together. This small ritual kicks off the weekend with a welcome dose of sweetness.

My friend Sarah, meanwhile, takes her daughter to a kids'

movie every Saturday morning. "She looks forward to it because it's our special ritual, and we go out for ice cream afterward," Sarah says. "I look forward to it because I bring earplugs and one of those neck pillows, and get a nice, two-hour nap. I just tell her to wake me up if she has to go to the bathroom."

If we go on a car trip, Tom will download a podcast to listen to while he drives, Sylvie watches a movie on the iPad using her special volume-limited headphones, and I read a book (happily, I am able to read in a car). Everyone is doing what he or she likes. No one is held hostage to grating kid music.

We've also started taking our daughter to Brooklyn's Green-Wood Cemetery. Tom and I love its rich history and discovering nineteenth-century names that will probably not make a comeback (Hippolite, Ebenezer, Bertha). Sylvie loves the 478 acres of mostly empty parkland studded with wild violets, and she's not quite aware yet that there are moldering bodies underneath all the "statues." ("Daddy, what does 'Ye know not the hour' mean?")

The three of us used to do most weekend activities in unison, until I thought, why? Why, for instance, were we going to the grocery store *en famille,* when it made Tom tense and Sylvie antsy? As I mentioned earlier, I happen to love grocery shopping — so now if I need to do it on the weekends, Tom drops me off and takes Sylvie to a nearby park. They kick a soccer ball around while I obsessively inspect every new granola flavor ("Ooh, coffee–dark chocolate–hazelnut? Into the cart it goes!"). *Doo-de-doo.* I text Tom when I'm done and they help load the car.

On Saturdays, Tom has started meeting a cycling friend of his with a daughter who is Sylvie's age. The girls disappear into a bedroom while the men talk about tire width and the size of their bike's rear cassette ("Did you get a 12-32?").

Father-initiated playdates are fairly rare, but they're important, particularly for daughters. Attitudes may be changing, but studies have shown that married fathers still spend more time in shared leisure activities with their sons, and children of both genders receive greater attention from their father when there is a son in the family. Once Tom found success with his cycling buddy, he began to devise father-friendly outings for other friends with daughters: an athletic editor friend, for instance, joined him at a nearby rock-climbing gym that has supervised programs for kids. The four of them then headed to an ice cream parlor for malted milkshakes. Another time, Tom and a friend took their girls to the park to kick a ball around and then to the car wash (six-year-olds think an automated car wash is big fun). The same father later met him at a social club in our neighborhood that offers hundreds of board games for walk-in play. The four of them spent a happy hour playing Pentago and eating pizza from the club's little café.

By far, Tom's greatest Everybody Wins success was a jaunt to a pinball arcade in Manhattan accompanied by a fellow pinball geek and his son, capped by a visit to a taco truck. Meanwhile, I lounged in bed and read an entire book in one shot, something I hadn't done since I was pregnant. When they returned from the playdate, I, newly refreshed, played with Sylvie while Tom had a nap.

Still, I am having difficulty applying my Everybody Wins principle to Heather's traveling sports time-suck (and I am well aware that with one child, I have an easier time of it). I ask

Morgenstern for advice. "Even with these obligations, you still have the opportunity for renewal time," she says. Return to the car between games and read a book or listen to music, she suggests. If you have a younger kid, put down your cell phone and toss around a Frisbee with him or her. Bring something festive to eat and treat it as an occasion to catch up with your husband. "Just be mindful about it rather than see it as throwaway time," she says.

A friend of mine with two kids in traveling sports says that she turns off the music for long drives to various ball fields and uses the opportunity for a real conversation with her kids. "My oldest is thirteen, and he's pulling away from me a little," she says. "It's so painful to see that I'm no longer in his inner circle. So I've just started viewing it as my way of keeping in the loop, and also see how he's interacting with his friends."

Finally, the simplest, easiest Everybody Sort of Wins: Tom now sleeps in on Saturdays, and I sleep in on Sundays. Everybody sort of nearly wins! For the most part!

After my lunch with Jenny, I receive an email from her entitled *Forgot one thing*. In it, she issues a clarion call for women: *Why are we all taking two-minute military showers on the weekends?*

Think like a man, and shower with impunity, she writes. *Feel no guilt! A man doesn't and wouldn't. Self-imposed guilt over not putting others' needs first at all times is a disease carried almost exclusively on the extra X-chromosome. Ladies, just get in there, lock the door, turn those knobs, and don't look back.*

Guess What? Your Kids Can Fold Their Own Laundry

Like many children, my daughter does not take going to bed lightly. It is an excruciatingly elaborate drawdown, full of arcane ceremonies, methodical checklists, and lawyerly negotiations. One of these myriad steps involves the exacting arrangement of stuffed animals on her bed, so that when her eyes have finally closed, she resembles a small Egyptian pharaoh surrounded by ritualistic objects.

So, we tend to get started early. One night, the living room is a debris field of Legos, puzzle pieces, and art supplies.

"Honey, it's time to clean up," I say. "Then go put on your pajamas."

"Okay," she says, as she nestles on the couch, absorbed in a book of amazing animal facts.

Ten minutes pass and still she has not moved. "Kid, it's time to clean up," I say in an I-mean-business tone. I often channel Tommy Lee Jones as an FBI agent, when he sends people scuttling with shouted commands to "secure the perimeter."

"Okay," Sylvie says absently, and remains motionless.

Oh, to hell with it, I think, sweeping up her Legos and puzzle pieces. *I can do this much more quickly. She had a long day at school. Plus, she's learning that rats don't burp and houseflies hum in the key of F. To deny her that knowledge may derail her path to a good school.* I breeze into her bedroom, fold and restock the clothes on her bedroom floor with Gap precision, and lay out her pajamas. Then I finally rouse her to brush her teeth.

My six-year-old is not a naturally shiftless person. She is not the problem here. I am.

It's an issue that's rarely addressed in the ongoing "chore wars" conversation: God forbid we ask our kids to pitch in. Numerous studies show that children today are much less likely than previous generations to help out at home. Research conducted by the cleaning products firm Vileda found that a quarter of children ages five to sixteen did not do a single thing around the house to help their parents — including make their own beds. In the UCLA study of Los Angeles households cited earlier, two-thirds of children resisted or ignored completely their parents' appeals for help.

As UCLA study director Elinor Ochs tartly noted in the British newspaper the *Guardian,* while most of the debate about housework focuses on the mother and father, the idea that "school-aged children might relieve some of the burden is off the table as a culturally possible option."

It wasn't always this way. Pioneer children were expected to haul water, make soap, and harvest the crops. In *Small Worlds: Children and Adolescents in America,* historian Elliott West describes the experience of nine-year-old Marvin Powe, who grew up in nineteenth-century New Mexico. Powe's father tells him to find and return some runaway horses that have bolted from the family ranch. They had wandered miles away, so the boy spends a week living off the land and camping with cowboys before locating the horses. He heads home just as his father reckons he should probably venture out and look for his son. I, on the other hand, have trouble persuading Sylvie to round up her My Little Pony figurines when they've escaped to the bathtub.

More recently, researchers from Wellesley College pored over eight decades of magazine advice on childcare and found that while earlier generations of kids were required to do tasks such as make the family dinner or mow the lawn, today's parents are reluctant to ask their children to do the same. (When was the last time you saw a child raking leaves, instead of a beleaguered dad? Or a landscaping crew?)

These days, a child's only real responsibility is schoolwork, according to Wellesley study author Markella Rutherford. In the rare cases when kids are asked to attempt something more strenuous, like cleaning out a garage, parents are advised to sweeten the deal with instant cash payments or "points" that can be traded in for toys or outings.

For the most part, Generation Z children (yes, that's a term, and no, I don't know what comes after that, although "Generation Alpha" is gaining traction) are responsible for only the mildest of jobs, such as feeding the dog or setting the table. Contemporary parents tend not to push it for a variety of reasons: topping the list are guilt over long working hours and reluctance to add one more item to their kids' already-crowded schedules. Some want their children to spend more time "pursuing their passions" (such as the Baby DJ School in my Brooklyn neighborhood, which promises to "introduce your little one to records, digital DJing, and funky beats!"). Others would rather outsource unpleasant household tasks (and if you pay someone to mow your lawn, why would your kids want to do what their parents won't?).

Finally, as my mother frequently reminds me, contemporary parents are less authoritarian and more egalitarian with their children. "Parents your age like to reason with their kids, like they're little adults with rational minds," my mother says, rolling her eyes. "No one wants to be the bad guy." As a kid, I had daily, weekly, and monthly chores, and if I didn't do them, I was grounded.

I fully admit that I'm less strict than my mother was. What's wrong with a little spoiling? When I leap up to get a bowl of sliced apples when my daughter requests a snack, or lay out her shoes for school, I'm showing her affection. It would be bliss if someone laid out my shoes for me. I once brought my daughter to a playdate, and her friend's mom asked me to stay for lunch. She apologized, unnecessarily, that the only clean plates she had left were some compartmentalized kids' trays with dinosaurs on them. When the mother plunked down my lunch—a turkey sandwich, a banana she had sliced into toddler-friendly chunks out of habit, and some yogurt, all portioned neatly into sections—I was so unexpectedly moved that I had to compose myself for a second. We all like to feel cared for.

But there is a difference between "cared for" and "coddled to the point of helplessness." I may not bribe my daughter to do household jobs with cash or outings, but the duties I give her are few, and sporadically enforced. She sets and clears the table when I remember to ask, and puts away her laundry when she's not happily tunneling under the warm piles of just-cleaned clothes that I've dumped on the bed.

And I'm not proud to say that the main reason I haven't had her do anything more arduous is that I haven't had the patience to teach her how to do chores, nor to remind her to do them.

....

This does not benefit either of us. Research shows that doing chores makes children thrive in countless ways, and is a proven predictor of success, says Richard Rende, associate professor of psychiatry and human behavior at Brown Medical School. "It's about raising kids who will be successful in life and work, not just in their college application process," he says. "They develop empathy, because they understand that someone might need their help. They learn about being industrious, and the importance of doing the 'dirty jobs' in life. Kids who aren't willing to do the grunt work are not going to just leap to the top of the heap. This is the recipe for the young adult who will not be entitled —'nuff said."

Nor does our child's lack of participation benefit our marriage. A relationship that caters to children and treats them as beyond the reach of chores and other daily responsibilities creates a setting in which resentments between parents gain a good, solid foothold.

Chores teach children that their contributions to the family are necessary and important, and — life lesson alert! — that people, even small ones who wear light-up shoes, need to get things done whether they feel like it or not.

Austin child psychologist Carl Pickhardt advises me to think of chores as household membership requirements. "So you explain to the child, 'Look, it takes a lot of work to run this family, and

Daddy works at it, and I work at it, and you can work at it, too, and make a really important contribution,'" he says. "And when they help, you immediately say, 'Thank you! This makes a big difference.'"

Pickhardt often hears from parents, *Oh, I'm going to wait until my kid is eight or nine, when they're old enough to really help.* "Uh, nope," he says. By the time your kid is in preadolescence, he says, being asked to help is an imposition — so you want to instill the habit of chores by the age of three. "At that age, a child sees helping the parents as an act of power, as in 'I'm doing what my parents can do, and that feels good,'" he says. "It's like when the kindergarten teacher asks who wants to help erase the chalkboard, and hands fly up all over the room."

Certainly, it is my daughter's natural impulse to help. Whenever I'm baking, she drags over a chair to the kitchen counter (prompting in me equal parts pleasure and dread). If I announce that I have to run to the drugstore, she races for her coat, jubilantly telling Tom, "Mommy has to pick up tampons!"

Developmental research shows that young children are actually wired to pitch in, says Rende. "Drop something, and they'll pick it up," he tells me. "Reach for something that's out of reach, and they'll get it for you." Interestingly, Rende says that this tendency can diminish quickly if an adult rewards them for their helping. "They don't want to be rewarded, at a deep level," he says. "It extinguishes their payoff because the payoff is inherently internal." The language you use is important, too: Rende and other researchers say it may be more effective to praise them for being "helpers" rather than give thanks for "helping." "Drop a sock from the laundry pile in front of your toddler and see if he or she tries to pick it up for you without your asking — and reinforce that now and then with 'You're a good helper,'" he says. "Raise your child to be a helper and live with a little imperfection in their 'product.' Your kid matters more than your laundry does."

And the key to locking in lasting participation down the line, he says, is to emphasize chores as a group effort by using the word "we" — "*We* need to get this done" or "*Let's* clean up the living room." "That gets across that we're all working together to help each other out," says Rende. "It's about understanding that the mind-set of 'we' rather than 'me' benefits all. Those 'we' kids will cultivate that instinct to jump in, without being asked, to help solve a problem or just get something done, to the benefit of the larger group — and will climb the ladder faster and higher because they're not just serving themselves."

Instilling these lessons during the preschool age is ideal, because the kids are easy to brainwash: parental pronouncements such as "We help each other out as a family" are received and incorporated without question. Many of our official-sounding "family rules" are ones that I hastily made up on the spot when Sylvie was three or four. All I had to do was state it in an Official Announcement voice, and it became gospel (oh, how I miss those gullible days in my benevolent dictatorship when she actually believed my declaration that toy stores were closed on weekends, and the iPad stopped working after sundown).

The Official Announcement voice, just as an aside here, works for instantly conjured-up family traditions, too. One weekend when Tom was away on assignment, I woke to the sight of Sylvie standing by my bed at 6 a.m., smiling and ready for the day to begin. I just didn't feel motivated to leave the house (or, to be honest, to put on shoes, or pants without an elastic waist). So I issued the proclamation that it was a "Lazy Saturday," and we were fully authorized to stay in our pajamas all day, make cookies, and loll around watching *The Sound of Music*. Some on-the-spot rebranding transformed my slothfulness into hallowed family custom: Sylvie still begs for Lazy Saturdays. There's no reason the Lazy Saturday approach can't be transformed into Busy Sunday.

Along with emphasizing "we" rather than "me" with household chores, Rende says that parents should try to limit their own moaning about it. "Kids don't perceive household chores as being awful when they're very young — we're training them to do that when we complain about them," he says. Adults may carp about having to wash the car, but to a four-year-old, splashing around with a bucket of water and a sponge is simply play.

Granted, involving your toddler in any household task will triple — or possibly sextuple — the length of time it takes to get done. But that can be precisely the point. My friend Amanda, a single mom, used to park her three-year-old daughter in front of the TV while she hurriedly cooked dinner after work. "I'd whip together some spaghetti so we could have quality time afterward, and do stuff like play Barbies or read a story together," she says. "But then I figured out that if I have her help make dinner, we'd have more time together. It took forever, and it seemed like every other night she spilled a can of Parmesan cheese on the floor." She laughs. "Which I also taught her to vacuum up. Anyway, now she's thirteen and we still make dinner together. Now that she's a teen and never tells me anything, I find I can pry at least some stuff out of her when she's distracted with chopping the carrots."

It's especially important to have boys lend a hand around the house. As mentioned, from an early age, boys in particular tend to assert their independence by refusing to do something they've been asked to do. A study by the educational children's magazine *Highlights* found that 73 percent of girls reported that they had chores to do, while only 65 percent of boys did.

Not only are girls more likely to be asked to help out at home, they are less likely to get paid: the national nonprofit Junior Achievement found that the pay gap between males and females starts squarely at home, with allowance: 67 percent of boys said that they received allowances, while just 59 percent of girls did. Similarly, a British study discovered that boys get paid 15 percent more for the same chores done by girls. Think about the message being given here: that when boys feed the dog or straighten their rooms, they deserve a reward, but girls are just "doing what comes naturally."

And when boys with female siblings see the grunt work being off-loaded onto their sisters, the effects can carry into midlife, according to a paper published in the *Journal of Politics*. Two economics professors analyzed decades of data on families and found that boys who grew up with sisters were more likely to leave the cleaning, cooking, and other drudgery to their wives when they reached middle age. Why? Because boys with sisters are less likely to be asked to help with chores. Boys who grew up with only brothers, meanwhile, were less likely to view housework as "women's work."

But many parents say that enlisting their sons' help can be a challenge. On one visit to my sister Heather, I see her picking up a long trail of her sons' shoes, and offhandedly ask her why she doesn't have them pitch in more.

She looks at me, agog. "Do you think I haven't asked them

175

every day since they were in preschool? I bug them a hundred times a day! You don't have boys! Every single day I tell them to make their beds, and every day they stare at me like it's the first time they've ever heard the request." She sighs. "I ask and ask and ask because I don't want them to grow up to be slobs. All my friends with boys say the same thing. But I stay on them because I just hope it will click one day."

And when it does, they will benefit. Once chores have become regularly incorporated into a kid's life, the impact can reverberate for years — even decades, according to a study from the University of Minnesota's Marty Rossmann. She found that having children take an active role in the household, starting at age three or four, directly influenced their ability to become well-adjusted young adults.

Rossmann pored over data that followed kids across four periods in their lives, ending in their mid-twenties. Those who began chores at three or four were more likely to have solid relationships with their families and friends, to be self-sufficient, and to achieve academic and early professional success.

Edie Weiner, who heads the New York consulting group the Future Hunters, which maps out future strategies for corporations, believes that we are moving from a world of "have and have-nots" into a world of "can and cannots." Chores are important, she has said, because in the coming years, career success will not be as dependent on whom you know or where you went to school (your "haves"). Instead, it will hinge much more fundamentally on what you can *do* — specifically, the ability to adapt on the fly, learn new skills, and grow.

So my zeal to "enrich" my daughter has been misguided.

While she is now able to play chess and competently swim the length of the community pool, she doesn't know how to perform basic life skills that will allow her to be a self-reliant person. I assume I'm bestowing a gift on her when I tidy her room — but what I'm really giving her is the message that she's not quite capable of doing things herself. No one wants to raise a "cannot" child whose cooking skills do not stretch beyond heating up something from the "grocerant" (a hybrid of "grocery store" and "restaurant," which offers ready-made meals, an exploding retail category). No one wants a teenager who heads off to college unable to do basic laundry. My friend's eighteen-year-old tells me that her roommate asked her, in all seriousness, which machine was the washer and which was the dryer.

Consider this gem from a C. S. Mott Children's Hospital National Poll on Children's Health: most parents surveyed agreed that their children should be ready to move from seeing a pediatrician to a regular doctor by the age of eighteen — but less than half of parents thought that their older teens, ages eighteen to nineteen years — who were old enough to drive a car and to vote — *knew how to make a doctor's appointment.*

Sylvie is already six. I have to establish a routine. Quickly.

After doing deep research — books, papers, blogs, fellow parents — I field-test various approaches to find the most effective motivators.

Squelch the ignoring.

New York psychologist Laura Markham tells me that there is a likely reason Sylvie stays rooted to her chair when I ask her to clean her room. Children, she explains, are still forming their frontal cortex, the region of the brain that manages so-called executive functions such as attention, decision making, and self-control.

"Young kids are not as good at thinking logically as you are, and they're still developing the ability to switch gears from what *they* want to what *you* want," she says. "Therefore, when she's playing, and she has to stop and go to the grocery store with you, she's upset." (Knowing that at least some of this resistance is brain-based, and not simply giving attitude, eases my frustration somewhat.)

The best way to have a child make that transition, Markham advises, is to approach with empathy ("Listen, I know you're immersed in your book, but..."). Make contact by touching your kid's shoulder and looking her in the eye (for us, this technique has been especially effective). Then make your request collaborative. "If you say, 'We have to go to the store because we need food in the house, and you know how good you feel when you open the fridge and your favorite yogurt is there,' you've given her a reason to want to cooperate," says Markham. And when she does, says Markham, her brain gets a boost. "Every time Sylvie decides that her relationship with you is more important than what she wants at the moment," she says, "she's strengthening her brain's ability to exercise self-discipline."

Describe what you see, or describe the problem.

Adele Faber and Elaine Mazlish, who wrote one of my favorite parenting guides, *How to Talk So Kids Will Listen & Listen So Kids Will Talk,* say that describing the problem gives kids a chance to decide what to do on their own. Instead of "If I have to tell you again to hang up your wet towel, I'm going to take a hostage," try

"Hon, there is a wet towel on my bed." Information, Faber tells me during a long, enlightening phone call, is a lot easier for kids to take in and process than an accusation, and describing the situation encourages cooperation and problem solving.

After describing the problem, tell your child, using neutral, nonaccusatory language, how this behavior makes you feel, which engenders empathy: "I don't like sleeping in a wet bed." "Children are entitled to hear their parents' honest feelings," says Faber.

Be specific.

In *The No-Cry Discipline Solution*, Elizabeth Pantley says that starting a sentence with a question like "Will you...? Could you...? Would you...?" makes it sound like compliance is optional (as when you end the request with "Okay?"—which I immediately stopped doing). Instead, Pantley advises, be direct, and be concise: *Please put your pajamas in the drawer. Please put your blocks in the toy box and turn off the light.* (As when I assign tasks to her father, assume there will be conformity.)

...Or use just one word.

This is one of the most life-changing tips provided by Faber and Mazlish. Think about it: How much did you loathe being lectured as a kid, and how quickly did you tune out said lecture? Why would your child be any different? Instead of windy recriminations, empty threats, and a sermon on accountability, you're much more likely to get results if you say one word. *Homework. Toothbrush. Backpack.* Point to the dog standing by the door with its legs crossed, desperately waiting to be walked, and simply say, *Dog.* Done.

"One word is wonderful for parents," Faber tells me, "because you can say it when you're calm, slightly irritated, or crazy out of your mind. And what's the worst thing that could happen? Will your kid lie on the psychiatrist's sofa in ten years and say, 'My mother yelled, *Dog*'?"

Do the jobs together, even though it takes forever and you'd much rather be watching the video your cousin just forwarded entitled You'll Never Believe What This Hamster Is Wearing.

Your child doesn't see much inherent value in household work, unless she's doing it with you — so view the work as an opportunity to bond, says Markham. "Your goal here isn't getting this job done, it's shaping a child who will take pleasure in contributing," she says. "If you make chores about fun and contributing and mastery — 'Wow, you really got this bathroom mirror to shine! How did you do that?' — that's a kid who will think, 'I'm really good at mirrors.'" The first twenty times you'll have to do the mirror together, she says, but at some point, she'll make it shine on her own.

Making the bed: small act, major results.

In a commencement speech at the University of Texas, Admiral William H. McRaven, commander of the US Special Operations Command, said that when he was training to be a Navy SEAL, he was required to make his bed every morning to square-cornered perfection — annoying at the time, but in retrospect one of the most important life lessons he ever learned.

"If you make your bed every morning, you will have accomplished the first task of the day," he told graduates. "It will give you a small sense of pride, and it will encourage you to do another task, and another, and another." Making your bed, McRaven went on, reinforces the fact that the small things in life matter. "If you can't do the little things right, you'll never be able to do the big things right. And if, by chance, you have a miserable day, you will come home to a bed that is made — that you made. And a made bed gives you encouragement that tomorrow will be better. If you want to change the world, start off by making your bed."

Don't rush to re-vacuum.

"It's so discouraging for kids to see you swoop in and correct what they've done," says my friend Aditi. "Plus it teaches them that Mom will finish the job, which you do not want." Instead, forget perfection and aim to be what Barry Schwartz, author of *The Paradox of Choice: Why More Is Less,* calls a "satisficer." It's the term, mingling "satisfy" with "suffice," invented by the Nobel Prize–winning economist Herbert Simon as a way to make a good decision rather than be paralyzed by the search for the best decision. It can apply equally well to household tasks done not quite up to four-star hotel standard. As Schwartz puts it, "Good enough is good enough."

As soon as they're old enough to hold a sponge, teach them that we always clean up our own messes.

When Sylvie spills her milk, I race over with a paper towel to take care of it. Not good. Instead, counsels Markham, "Encourage her to help by handing her a sponge as you pick one up yourself.

Similarly, when she leaves her shoes in the hallway, hand them to her and ask her to put them away, saying, 'In this house, we always clean up our own stuff.'" Once again, I make this pronouncement as if it is officially inscribed on a tablet somewhere, and Sylvie accepts it as incontrovertible fact. (I'm aware that this golden era of credulity, which commenced when she was two, will end soon, now that she is reaching six and a half. But for the time being, it still holds.)

Get everything off the floor.

"This is the best rule for having kids clean up their bedrooms," says my friend Kendra, mother of two. "It's easy to grasp, and their rooms really do look decent if the floors aren't a mess, even if they're just stuffing clothes and toys in drawers."

Find ways to easily enable their helping.

Tom hit upon the solution of buying Sylvie her own dustpan and whisk broom to help out with cleaning jobs. They are not a kid's version of these tools — he has a constant gripe about kid's versions of anything being cheap and basically useless — but simply a smaller, quality set for hard-to-reach areas. Now we can say, "Sylvie, can you get *your* broom and clean up that jar of cinnamon that you knocked over?" (although Sylvie, like most children a master of the passive voice, will report that *it* "got knocked over").

Post a written routine.

Chore charts cut down on nagging and keep your routines, per Julie Morgenstern's advice, conveniently on autopilot. "After a while, it will simply be a habit," says Markham. "Kids really do rise to meet our expectations, as long as we stay connected so they want to please us."

Write a note.

This requires more effort, but it works well for a recurring problem, says Faber. "It's different, it's fun, and it's another way to reach them." If your child strews wet towels around the house, for instance, she and Mazlish suggest posting a funny note above the towel rack saying, "Please put me back so I can dry. Thanks! Your towel."

Give options.

Pantley writes that offering your kid a choice — *Do you want to empty the dishwasher or sweep the floor?* — heads off arguments. If your calculating child proposes a third option, such as *I want to watch TV,* tell him that wasn't one of the options and repeat your original choice. If he won't pick, you choose (and going for the more odiferous one, such as scooping out the cat's litter box, will prompt a swifter decision next time).

Turn it into a game.

"My daughters are competitive with each other," says my sister Dinah. "So I'll say, 'Who can put away their stuff the fastest?' I'll put on music and we'll have a Living Room Cleanup Dance Party. Or I'll set a timer for five minutes and have them quickly put away the groceries. Well, except the eggs."

Approaching chores in a playful way, says Faber, "is magical stuff. Do anything nutty and kids become more responsive, more inventive. Often they come up with something no adult would ever dream of."

Be consistent.

"My kids know the drill," says Lysa, a mother at my kid's school. "They make their beds after they get dressed in the morning. When they come home from school, they empty their lunch bags and do their homework. When they get up from dinner, they clear the table and put their plates in the dishwasher. They have a few extra chores on Saturday, and no sports, electronics, or trips to the park until they are done." At the risk of overkill here: clarity, clarity, clarity.

And, last, separate chores from allowance.

Before Daniel Pink wrote his bestseller *Drive: The Surprising Truth About What Motivates Us,* the father of three thought that rewarding chores with an allowance was perfectly sensible. But after he immersed himself in research on motivation, he changed his mind. He, and many other experts, contend that by linking money to the completion of chores, parents turn an allowance into an "if-then" reward. This sends a message that in the absence of a payment, no self-respecting child is going to willingly empty the trash.

He promptly separated allowances from chores in the Pink household. "We did provide a very modest allowance of a few bucks a week," he tells me. "And while we didn't have assigned duties for each kid, as in, 'Eliza, you're in charge of setting the table,' we made it very clear that everyone was expected to help out around the house. And, amazingly, everyone did."

Pink contends that kids — and parents — do chores because families are built on mutual obligations. "I wouldn't expect to be paid to drive my daughter to dance class," he says. "She shouldn't

expect to be paid for emptying the dishwasher
clean plates left on Pink Family Taco Night."

Allowances, he says, are useful for teaching kid
dle small amounts of money. "But combining allo
chores," he says, "is a case where adding two good thin͙ ͜ogether
produces less, not more."

Markham agrees. "I remember being about six, and wanting
to buy this plastic horse," she says. "I got an allowance for doing
chores, so I did them long enough to buy the horse, and then
stopped. I didn't understand the need to do chores beyond getting
paid for them."

And so, once again I call a family meeting (which still feels a
little funny with three people, but I do it anyway) and explain that
in our family, we all must help out. I pull out a chore chart I have
made, and do a demonstration of Sylvie's daily and weekly tasks
so she knows exactly what to do (if she learned how to order a
Tetris app on my phone, she can master spritzing a bathroom
sink).

And now she does her chores. Does she do them perfectly? No.
Does she complete every one each week? Not always. But she does
them.

My mother, who has long grumbled that her grandchildren
don't pitch in enough, is pleased when she observes Sylvie industriously sweeping our six-by-eight-foot kitchen one afternoon. I
know a speech is coming about how she helped her mother pluck
chickens growing up in Alabama, and she does not disappoint.

"Mama wrung their necks, and I'd help pluck them," says my
mother with a faraway look, as "I Wish I Was in Dixie" plays
somewhere in her mind. Many decades have transformed this

pleasant job into a gauzy memory of gratifying hard work and mother-daughter bonding.

Sylvie wanders over. "What did you pluck?" she says.

My mother's eyes widen. "Feathers, child! Do you think chicken just falls out of a Trader Joe's bag?" But she gazes at her granddaughter approvingly as she carefully empties her dustpan into the trash. "Still, I will admit that this is a good start."

It's never too late! Age-appropriate chores.

Age 3–4

Pick up toys.

Help make the beds.

Set the table.

Stuff their dirty laundry in the hamper.

Age 4–5

Clear the table.

Put away silverware while Mom or Dad is unloading the dishwasher.

Hang up towels in the bathroom.

Take out recycling.

Weed.

Match socks and put away their own laundry.

Water indoor plants.

Age 6–7

Sweep kitchen and dining area with small broom.

Fold laundry.

Make their bed.

Organize toy cabinets.

Swiffer the floor.

Help with meals (wash vegetables, set out ingredients).

Get the mail.

Clean out the gunk in the microwave.

Wipe counters.

Age 8–9

Dust.

Empty trash in each room.

Vacuum.

Help with dinner.

Change a lightbulb.

Empty the dishwasher.

Feed and care for pets.

Clean bathroom surfaces.

Pack lunch.

Age 10–12

Do laundry.

Clean the kitchen.

Clean out the refrigerator.

Cut the grass.

Scrub the tub.

Bone of Contention

One night, my daughter's endless bedtime send-off runs even later than usual. The enterprising child had crafted a sure-fire way to detain me after I told her that old people like to talk about their childhoods. At the time, I was referring to my father, given to misty reminiscences of his upbringing in Bay City, Michigan ("Mother had warm cookies waiting for us every afternoon when we came home from school"), but my daughter categorized me, perhaps not incorrectly, as an old person, too. Just as I am about to make my escape from her bedroom, she asks for a story of my Pittsburgh girlhood.

"Tell the one about the car," she begs.

I hesitate at the door. I can never resist. "Well, there were no car seats then, and I used to ride in the front seat of our enormous light blue Buick LeSabre with my mom, while my sisters rode in the back," I begin. "When my mom took a corner quickly, which she often did, my sisters would roll and bounce against the door like marbles. And because we didn't wear seat belts, if we stopped suddenly, my mom would hold out her arm to prevent me from banging my head on the dashboard. Which didn't work so well."

"So once, she was smoking in the car," Sylvie prompts.

"Right. In the olden days, my parents loved to smoke cigarettes in the car with the windows tightly rolled up at all times. Why do you think that might be?" I like to encourage Sylvie to think critically. "Maybe so that way," I propose, "they could get the most smoke in their lungs as possible?" Sylvie agrees that this makes sense. "Anyway, once a car suddenly pulled in front of us, and my mother threw her arm in front of me." I pause for dramatic effect. "But she was holding a lit cigarette at the time!"

"And your hair almost caught on fire!" Sylvie finishes triumphantly. It is one of her most treasured bedtime stories.

After one more exciting tale of my youth — in which I play for hours with a large, unsupervised gang of children in a trash-strewn vacant lot, to Sylvie's amazement — I finally get her to sleep. Then I (quietly) clap my hands together. It is time for my Mom Party.

Your basic Mom Party lasts roughly 45 minutes to an hour before the celebrant slumps forward in a dead sleep. It has a few general components. One is food, which should be either sugary or salty (or in the case of salted caramel brownies, both). Add any sort of calming beverage — a glass or three of wine, a mug of decaf tea. Garnish with your choice of mindless entertainment: blogs that obsessively compare moisturizers, a trashy reality-TV marathon. One mom friend of mine favors a bathtub, a pile of home decorating magazines, and a joint; another likes playing Candy Crush while slowly eating a small bowl of chocolate chips she has microwaved to the consistency of hot fudge. Party attire is Festive Casual (yoga pants stretched out just the way you like them, an old T-shirt worn to translucence, maternity underwear in a fetching shade of "greige").

Humming, I head for the kitchen, extract a family-size bag of

SunChips from the pantry, and take out the magazine I swiped earlier from the gym: *Star* magazine's "Worst Celebrity Beach Bodies."

That is the moment that Tom picks to approach me in the kitchen and give me a back rub — conveniently ignoring the fact that I am holding a bag of SunChips in my hand at the time, in frolicsome Harvest Cheddar flavor, which clearly indicates Mom Party in progress. In our relationship, there is no such thing as an agenda-free back rub. (As comedian Dena Blizzard puts it, "With husbands, a back rub always leads to a front rub.")

Weary from Sylvie's extended bedtime ritual (and also eager to *Turn to Page 23 to Find Out Whose Cellulite This Is* and *Match the Man-Boob to the Celebrity*), I ask for a rain check and hurry off to the bedroom, while Tom glumly wanders into the living room to play computer chess.

It is not the first night that this particular scenario has occurred. After six months of trying to fight fairly and actively looking for the good, our interactions are decidedly calmer and happier — but our sex life needs a boost. We have fallen into a pattern in which he tries to capitalize on a moment when we are finally alone, and I, after a long session of tending to a child, shut him down, viewing sex as just one more thing I have to do for someone.

Given the ways sex can be sabotaged, it's amazing that new parents have any relations at all. Along with timing issues, they must cope with stress, near-hallucinatory fatigue, postpartum depression, body insecurity, and hormones, which can wreak havoc for both sexes: a University of Notre Dame study found that during the first year of fatherhood, testosterone levels drop by roughly a third — and never resume pre-baby levels.

Breastfeeding can also send libidos south, says Hilda Hutcherson, assistant professor of obstetrics and gynecology at Columbia University — and not just because you're afraid to have your husband venture anywhere near your explosion-prone G-cups. Breastfeeding triggers the release of prolactin, a hormone involved in milk production, which can make orgasm more difficult. It also causes a drop in estrogen levels, which can produce the dreaded vaginal dryness (estrogen is what keeps the vaginal lining moist and flexible).

Then there are the psychological roadblocks, such as making the transition from mom to vixen. "I have four children, and I know exactly what women are talking about when they say they don't want to," says Hutcherson, who possesses formidable credentials but a best-girlfriend demeanor. "I remember it being so difficult to switch on and off like that, when a kid has just finished sucking me dry, and my husband's lying there with an erection, waiting his turn! It's like 'Enough already, can I have some private time with *my own body?*'" And with a needy baby, she says, there is only a small window of available time. "We'd be having sex, and I'm listening for that whimper."

Yet another reason for parents' sexual paucity, says couples therapist Esther Perel, is common, but not often discussed. Mothers get tremendous physical pleasure from their children — caressing their skin, kissing their silken cheeks, staring into their eyes for hours. This enraptured union, she says, bears a striking resemblance to the physical connection between lovers.

"Let's be clear," Perel tells me, "I am not talking about sexual pleasure. I mean this is a sensual pleasure, and that sensuousness is intrinsic to female sexuality." Female eroticism, she says, is diffuse, not localized in the genitals but distributed throughout the body, mind, and senses. For some new mothers, she goes on, their sensuality is redirected to the baby — and, for the time being, "When they tell me, 'At the end of the day, I have nothing left to give,' I also hear them saying, 'At the end of the day, there is nothing more I need.'"

A sexual drought that begins with a baby's arrival is at least understandable; what is worrying is when it continues for months, or years. "I honestly can't remember the last time we did it," says my friend Kelly with a shrug. "He says he doesn't miss it, and I really don't, either. The kids just take too much out of us." (According to research from the Gottman Institute, a preschool child makes an average of *three demands a minute* on a parent.)

While it can be tough to summon up the energy, Hutcherson says it's critical to observe the Nike slogan and *just do it.* She lists the reasons why: sex releases endorphins, the feel-good hormones with a similar structure to morphine, as well as oxytocin, the "cuddle hormone" that promotes feelings of devotion and trust. "And once you get into it, you might find pleasure," she says. "I say *might* — it takes time. But in order to keep that relationship with your partner strong, you need to have physical intimacy. And you just feel better about each other after you have sex! You know?"

I tell Hutcherson that my husband and I will marvel afterward and say, *Wow, we should do this more often,* as if we're old college friends meeting for coffee. She laughs. "I find I don't get as angry the next day about the mess in the kitchen my husband was going to help me clean up and didn't," she says. "Little things just don't bother me as much, and the same for him. He's not as testy."

But Tom and I, enmeshed in our fast-moving lives, will sometimes let weeks go by without a second thought. When I say this to Perel, however, she says she doesn't buy the "busy" excuse. She often tells clients that it's not children who extinguish the flame of desire — it's the adults who fail to keep the spark alive.

But I find the typical advice doled out by magazines to be cringingly embarrassing, not to mention unrealistic. I don't want to "send him a racy text that's not safe for work!" If I did, Tom would quickly write back *Hi, hon, your account was hacked* or *Are you having a stroke? Should I call somebody?* I don't have extra funds to buy a naughty nurse outfit for role-play, nor could I credibly stay in character. And I am not going to "step into the shower with him for a sexy treat!" A small, cramped New York bathroom shower is the wrong kind of "steamy."

So I canvass experts and friends for more realistic strategies. Then I do something more difficult: I make myself bring up the subject with Tom. As awkward as it can be to talk about your paucity of action, a Georgia State University study of sexually inactive married couples found that people who argued about sex were at least more likely to be *having* it. Austrian researchers made a similar discovery: women who were given the "love hormone" oxytocin saw the same uptick in their sex lives as those who were given a placebo. Why? Because the women were also keeping diaries and discussing their sex lives more honestly with their partners — and this seemed to give relations a boost.

"Have you noticed that we don't have sex very often?" I ask Tom one night after Sylvie is asleep.

He is reading a book. "I have," he says.

"Would you like to have sex more often?" I ask.

His eyes do not leave the page. "I would," he says.

I sense that he feels the subject has been covered — but I press on, asking him if he'd like to try, just for kicks, the challenge issued in *Sexperiment: 7 Days to Lasting Intimacy with Your Spouse,* by the Reverend Ed Young and his wife, Lisa, of the evangelical Fellowship Church in Grapevine, Texas. Young, father of four, has joked that "kids" is an acronym for *keeping intimacy at a distance successfully.* Citing Corinthians 7:5 ("Do not deprive each other of sexual relations"), he encourages "congregational coupling" among his flock for seven continuous days. The goal is to get closer to each other, and to the Lord (as Young sensibly writes, "God is a great God who creates great things, like sex"). Well, why not? I propose to Tom that I would like to try out various approaches on him every night for a week. Perhaps unsurprisingly, he is game.

It feels un-sexy to arrange our encounters in advance, but many friends of mine are fans of putting it on the calendar. My friend Sally, mother of one, books a rendezvous with her husband every Tuesday, an otherwise uneventful day. "The longer the week goes on, the more likely the last days of the week are to get bogged down with stuff that didn't yet get done," she says. "At least this way I don't have to think about trying to find time for it on the weekend. And if we have sex on the weekend — bonus!"

As it happens, having sex once a week is the ideal for maximum wellbeing, according to a study of over 30,000 adults. If respondents had more than that, their happiness actually leveled off. (That finding, by the way, held true for both men and women, and was consistent no matter how long they had been together.)

But even once a week seems a little daunting, so we ease into the idea by increasing our daily amount of nonsexual touching. As Sonja

Lyubomirsky writes in *The Myths of Happiness,* "The importance of touch is undeniable, yet it is remarkably undervalued." She writes that the science of touch suggests that small daily acts such as a pat on the back or a friendly squeeze can "save a so-so marriage. When our spouse touches us, we experience a mild high, we feel less frazzled, and we experience a diminution of discomfort and distress." Similarly, neuroscientist James Coan found that married women with distressed brain activity were immediately calmed when their husbands simply reached for their hands. A stranger's hand, he found, did not have the same effect.

Along with touch, we make an effort to maintain more eye contact, another proven way to strengthen our bond. It's not something most of us think about, but a prolonged gaze is believed to release a chemical called phenethylamine, responsible for feelings of attraction. Susan O'Grady, a psychologist in Walnut Creek, California, says that many couples will go for days without looking directly into each other's eyes — she and her psychologist husband included. "When I was raising our twins and working many hours a week, I neglected to notice that my husband had shaved his mustache," she says. "He tells me it took me three days. That was a learning experience. And we work in the same office!"

On to the Sexperiment.

•••••••••••••••••••••••••••

Night one: Perel asserts that desire needs distance in order to thrive. In her research, she often hears that people are most drawn to their partners when they are away — and then reunite. "This is rooted also in absence and in longing," she says, "which is a major component of desire."

On the five days prior to our Sexperiment, Tom is away on yet another carefree assignment, this time at a robotics lab in California. I ask him to make no calls or FaceTime during his absence—he just texts our daughter a hello and that is it. While he is away, I play music that reminds me of our early days together and look at my favorite picture of him. With the all-important distance, I am able to simulate a kind of mild crush, which lasts until his return. Aaand…action!

Night two: "You can't force desire, but you can create an atmosphere where desire might unfurl," says Perel. "You can tempt, compliment, romance, and seduce. I suggest that people consciously create an erotic space, a space to *be,* not to *do,* to enjoy each other, to cultivate pleasure—a space not where sex must happen, but certainly can happen." As Tom is generally the one feeling deprived, that evening, he transforms into the Australian bowerbird, who attempts to lure females to his bachelor pad by creating a lavish courtship site, decorating it with colorful shells, berries, and leaves. When a female arrives to inspect his design prowess, the bird does a touchingly elaborate leaping and posturing dance in hopes of sealing the deal.

Tom dims the lights, brandishes a bottle of scented oil, and offers to give me a massage—not the usual stilted, two-minute Husband Shoulder Scrunch, but a twenty-minute professional rub. If something happens in our consciously created erotic space, great. If it doesn't, he says, he is willing to walk away. He does not have to walk away.

Night three: Many moms I know get tense when sex is attempted late, which cuts into their already-dwindling sleep time. "It feels like right after we turn out the lights, within a minute his member is sticking in my lower back like I'm being held up at gunpoint," says my friend Avery. "And I'm immediately doing time calculations, like, 'Okay, it's 11, we'll finish up by 11:45. I won't fall asleep for a while afterward, so I'm looking at midnight earliest. I have to be up at 6. So, no.'"

In our new spirit of openness, I tell Tom that I sometimes have similar thoughts — so he builds in an extra thirty minutes by putting our daughter to bed earlier. (Not only is she unable to tell time, but he doesn't cave and read her seven bedtimes stories, as I do.) Right before bed, he feeds her a snack that a sleep researcher once told me brings on slumber quickly: whole wheat toast (carbs raise brain levels of rest-inducing tryptophan) spread with almond butter (which contains magnesium, linked to sound sleep). *Voilà*: a free half hour. Which is plenty, according to a Penn State survey of sex researchers, who agreed that after foreplay, the optimal, most enjoyable stretch of time for intercourse is not a Tantric marathon but a mere seven to thirteen minutes.

Night four: Perel says the stereotypically male definition of sex is that foreplay is the mere introduction to the "real" thing, but often, for women, it *is* the real thing. I try a technique recommended by my friend Emma: make out for fifteen minutes, with no obligation to do anything further. Yes, it is the most obvious reverse psychology in the world, but more often than not, the slow buildup, emotional connection, rich concentration of nerve receptors in our lips, and aura of the suddenly forbidden result in some action. As is the case with us.

Night five: Perel tells me that "probably the biggest turn-on across the board" is when people see their partners holding court at a party, or doing something they're passionate about — any time that they are presenting their best selves to the world. "It's when you see your partner as radiant and confident," she said. "They're in their element; you can admire them. You look at them and they are forever somewhat mysterious, elusive, unknown. When they are in their element, they don't need you, and hence you don't have to take care of them, emotionally or psychologically." In that space cleared of needing, she says, rises the wanting of desire — in other words, in the space between you and the *other* lies the erotic élan. She likes to refer to Marcel Proust, who suggests that the real voyage of discovery lies not in traveling to new places, but in looking with new eyes.

So that night, at a loft party given by one of Tom's photographer friends, I don't go near him all night, and instead watch other women flirt with him. I see him as others do: tall, handsome, blue-eyed, fit. It is the same feeling I get when I accidentally bump into him on the street as he returns from a meeting. For just a millisecond before recognition sets in, I give him the up-and-down and think, *Hey there!* Before realizing, *Oh, it's you.*

After the party, once again: success.

"Can you not text me about this experiment anymore, or Sexperiment, or whatever it is?" my sister Dinah pleads. "It's making me really uncomfortable."

Night six: Pioneering sex researcher Marta Meana has found that being desired is exceedingly arousing for women. This manifests itself in one of women's most frequent sexual fantasies: to be ravished by an attractive man. But when they talk about being dominated, she has said that what they're trying to communicate is *I was so wanted by someone I wanted*.

Biological anthropologist Helen Fisher says that women are more aroused than men by romantic words — and that there is an evolutionary basis for this. Men, she says, derive intimacy from doing things side by side. "For millions of years, to do their daily job, men sat behind a bush together to look out over the grasslands and see where the animals were," Fisher says. "If they swiveled to talk to each other, they wouldn't be able to do their job. So you'll see two men on a Sunday watching a football game in absolute silence, both looking forward at the game. That is intimacy to men."

Women, by contrast, find intimacy in words. "For millions of years, words have been women's tools," she tells me. "Everywhere in the world, women spend much more time holding their baby, literally in front of their face, talking to it. And women, as a result, get intimacy from talking. If you and I are together, we swivel until we're face to face, do what's called the 'anchoring gaze,' and we talk. And that is intimacy to women."

I think of Fisher's remarks after we put Sylvie to bed and repair to ours. I ask Tom if we could just lie quietly together while he gives me compliments. My friend Sally often requests this of her husband: he strokes her hair, kisses her face, tells her how pretty she is, how much he loves her. "He is good at specific compliments, such as 'I love the way you read a book all scrunched in a chair surrounded by pillows,'" she says. "That's probably because I tell him, 'I want to know that you still choose me, the person.'"

Caught in our anchoring gaze, Tom is a bit rusty at first. "You're…a great mother," he says, awkwardly stroking my hair.

I sit up quickly. "You know what? That may not necessarily be the best way to, you know…"

He nods, embarrassed. "Right. Right." But when he tries again and hits upon some praise that is slightly more romantic, I soon realize that sweet words are my gateway: the method that relaxes and unlocks you, takes you away, elicits a physical response. Everyone has one, or many, even if they're long buried.

Dr. Hutcherson is right, I think as I smilingly hand Tom a cup of coffee at breakfast the next morning. *Little things don't bother me as much!*

Night seven: Renowned sex researcher Rosemary Basson discovered that women often begin sex feeling neutral, and then become aroused once the act is under way. (Men, meanwhile, are more apt to get in the mood spontaneously, hence the lower-back stick-'em-up.)

So why not obtain a little help? Some women read erotica for a few minutes and then they're ready to go. (Sales of this genre are surging thanks to the welcome discretion of electronic readers.) Friends of mine swear by porn movies, but by and large, I do not find it alluring to watch creepy dudes surrounding a glassy-eyed gal with watermelon breasts who is twisted into an uncomfortable position in some sad San Fernando Valley office with bad industrial carpeting and grimy swivel chairs.

But there are a few renegade directors who make porn that

isn't depressing, such as Barcelona-based independent erotic film director Erika Lust. Her beautifully filmed, plot-driven movies feature actors with real bodies who look like the cute tattooed baristas at your local coffee place. The settings are vacation worthy, and even the clothing they eventually remove is cute (no orange lace tank tops and Lucite stripper shoes!). Lust's production crew is almost all female; she refuses to hire any actor under twenty-three, encourages them to choose their partners, and pays them well (as she tells me, "Women care about this stuff").

My favorite feature on her website is called XConfessions, in which she solicits anonymous sex confessions and turns her favorites into explicit short films with intriguing titles such as *Meet Me in the Stockroom, Carnival Hustler, Boat Buddies with Benefits, I Fucking Love Ikea,* and, my favorite, *A Feminist Man,* based on a user's fantasy about having sex with a gender studies professor.

Ten minutes and you're good to go, she tells me, which makes her short films particularly attractive to a fried young mother. "Those films are made for everyone to relate to, even those who aren't feeling very sensual at the moment," she says. "As a mother of two, I can tell you I have my own personal experience with that. Erotic content can help you reconnect with your sexual self."

Tom peeks over my shoulder as I tune into *A Feminist Man.* "Your fantasy would probably be to have sex with a vacuum cleaner," he snickers, alluding to my next-freak tendencies. "Or a Container Store clerk, on top of a sock cubby."

But XConfessions nicely leads to a seven-day home run. In fact, we continue for ten nights — and might have gone longer, but Tom has to leave for another "business" trip (a travel piece in the Virgin Islands). I report the news of our ten-day streak to

Hutcherson, who says she isn't surprised. "It's common knowledge among sex therapists that the more sex you have, the more you want."

After Tom leaves for the Caribbean, I meet my usual crew of mom friends at the playground. As our kids play some sort of dystopian version of tag involving zombies, we discuss the news of the day, both local (Brooklyn opened its first Japanese-style cat café, in which you pay a fee, drink coffee, and pet cats for an hour) and national. Bruce Springsteen's show at Madison Square Garden was mentioned next, along with the observation that he still looks fantastic (consensus: He May Be in His Sixties, but I'd Hit That).

"Speaking of sex," I say, looking furtively around for the kids, "guess what?" My friends all lean in, faces alight. "I've just had sex for ten nights in a row. That hasn't happened since the Clinton administration."

Their eager expressions harden into disappointment as they regard me silently.

Finally one mom clears her throat. "Why?" she asks. The others nod and murmur, *That's just what I was thinking.*

I tell them about my experiment and they look at me skeptically. "I will say that your skin looks amazing," concedes one. I have noticed the same thing. As it happens, research presented at the British Psychological Society's annual meeting found that subjects in midlife who had sex at least three times a week looked between four and seven years younger than those who had less. Lead author David Weeks listed myriad reasons why: sex releases human growth hormone, which helps skin stay elastic, as well as endorphins and other feel-good chemicals that bolster the immune system, calm inflammation, boost circulation, cancel stress, and enhance sleep.

One mom looks wryly at my triumphant and temporarily unlined face. "I haven't made out with David since the twins were born," she muses. "Oh, what the hell, I'll try it." I wouldn't say that I started a trend, but she does tell me later that they made a breakthrough. "Friday *and* Saturday night," she announces, arching an eyebrow.

⟡⟡⟡⟡⟡⟡⟡⟡⟡⟡⟡⟡⟡⟡⟡⟡⟡⟡⟡⟡⟡⟡⟡⟡⟡⟡

While we never do repeat our seven-day bonanza (and three-day extension), it does serve to revitalize our sex life. Soon we revert to the proven "sweet spot" of once a week — sometimes it's spontaneous, sometimes planned, but we're always mindful that it's a critical part of maintaining our connection.

From coupling, Tom and I move on to couple time, which in our relationship is woefully lacking. While we have managed to carve out some restorative solo time using our new strategies, we haven't been out as a twosome in months. I remember a conversation with Terry Real in which he asked us what we did to "cherish each other as a couple." We couldn't come up with much and began to gabble various excuses: fatigue, heavy workloads, the eye-wateringly expensive rates of New York City babysitters (one survey tracked an average hourly rate of $17.50, and that doesn't include the cab fare home that you must often pay).

When I told him that we mostly brought our daughter everywhere, his thundering response rang in my ears. "You need to do something, because the both of you are spent! Listen, the problem with being child-centric is that the couple becomes threadbare and starts looking like you two, which does Sylvie no good! You say that you're busy, but what you really get is *lazy!*" He shook his head. "There are 168 hours in a week. How many of those do you give directly to your relationship? Get a babysitter! It's a good investment!"

The term *date night* causes many parents to smirk, but a University of Virginia study found that it is, indeed, important. People who built couple time into their schedules at least once a week were over three times more likely to report being "very happy" in their marriages, compared to those who had less quality time together. Wives who had couple time less than once a week, meanwhile, were nearly four times more likely to report above-average levels of "divorce proneness."

Perel gets incensed when she hears from parents who forsake their relationship for the kids. "They spend their entire weekends on the sidelines of these ridiculous games, cheering their children on when they finally manage to touch a ball," she says. "This sentimentalization of children has reached a complete apex of folly. There is a total depletion of the importance of the adult relationship." She tells parents to plan one curfew-free late night every six to eight weeks, in which they "lose control, let themselves go into excess, get high, drink, and dance, which connects them with the sense of freedom and possibility. And they do not spend the time talking about the children." We vow to book a babysitter once a month.

But there are ways to do date nights on the cheap as well. Perel advises creating a "family of choice" — friends and neighbors who can trade off watching each other's children. We start a standing playdate with another family in which we swap hosting for a few hours every other Sunday — so at least we have some adult time together once a month.

Many churches and synagogues run parents' night out programs for their members; various children's play spaces, YMCAs, and national kid-gym chains offer safe, supervised drop-off evening care for kids, often for less money than your average sitter. You get some couple time, and your kids enjoy a night racing around with their friends.

Terry Real was right: we have gotten lazy. Tom and I soon train ourselves to think creatively if we encounter even a small pocket of kid-free time. When we have a free hour and a half after we drop Sylvie at a birthday party, we impulsively go to a tarot card reader in our Brooklyn neighborhood whose crystal-bedecked storefront we have often passed and wondered about. This, to me, is a can't-miss: If she is off the mark, you have a laugh. If she hits on something that resonates, as our seer does when she tells Tom that he "likes cilantro and dislikes crowds," you can feel excitingly spooked. While we wait out another birthday party the following week, we jump on a water taxi that ferries people between Brooklyn and Manhattan, and savor the feeling of bouncing along on the sparkling water.

There are hundreds of ways to get creative and to relish your adult time together. We spend an hour in a bookstore, or go for a brief walk, which a mountain of studies shows can immediately lift your mood and reduce stress. Even a thirty-minute stroll can make a huge difference; benefits increase further if you are surrounded by nature, a practice that the Japanese call *shinrin-yoku,* or "forest bathing." Or we grab some bagels and coffee and sit in the park with the newspaper.

"My husband and I like to do kid stuff without the kids," says my friend Jill. "Zip-lining, go-karts, Pac-Man at the arcade. Sometimes my stomach hurts from laughing." (One study found that activities that trigger nostalgia can increase feelings of connectedness to your partner.)

My friend John and his wife occasionally tell their bosses that they will be an hour late for work because of a doctor's appointment — then steal away for a breakfast date after dropping off the kids at school. Breakfast is quicker and less expensive than dinner, and they still maintain their connection with each other.

Another father I know from my daughter's soccer class takes this idea even further: he sets aside a few of his vacation days a year, and so does his wife. Then, while their children are in school, they have a daytime date. "You can fit a lot into six hours," he says. "A movie, an art gallery, lunch. One spring, we spent the day at a sketchy carnival and ran around riding the rides and eating bloomin' onions. Which made us both sort of sick, but we still laugh about that day."

A cash-strapped friend of mine leaves her kids with her mom once every few months, and she and her husband do what they term Drunken Errands. "We live in a really walkable part of Minneapolis, so we huff down a few drinks and then do what needs to be done," she says. "We end up giggling and bumping into each other at Target, and sober up by the time we return home. Mostly." If you're home, set up the kids with dinner and a video and then have a romantic dinner *à deux* in another room.

Some neuroscientists contend that the best way for couples to bond is to try something new together. Brain scans have shown that when we are confronted by something novel, certain brain areas are activated in anticipation of some sort of reward, including the midbrain, which is flooded with the feel-good neurotransmitter dopamine. (Once the stimulus becomes familiar and the brain learns that no reward is coming, it calms down.)

Your novel activity doesn't need to be paragliding, either — anything different will do. While Sylvie is at school, I book a session at an appealingly kooky Korean spa in Manhattan that boasts rooftop hydrotherapy pools, a swim-up bar, and a sleeping room for power naps.

Tom and I revel in a long morning of hydro-massage followed by bouts of giddy disorientation as we try a stint in an Ice Igloo; something called a Chromotherapy Sauna, which flashes mood-enhancing lights; and the Infrared Zone, which emits "microscopic infrared wavelengths that are directly absorbed into the body."

"I may never forget this day," Tom whispers as a pair of sturdy Korean ladies industriously scrub off entire layers of our skin with mitts.

"That's the plan," I whisper back.

Kids: Your New Budget Deficit

The glow of one warm thought is to me worth
more than money.

—THOMAS JEFFERSON

What a bunch of crap.

—MY FATHER, J. C. DUNN

When I was pregnant, Tom and I indulged in many dreamy conversations as we took long walks (or, in my case, long, sweaty waddles) through our Brooklyn neighborhood. We speculated endlessly: Would our baby have blue eyes like Tom, or brown eyes like me? Would she be outgoing? Shy? Athletic? Bookish?

Rarely was anything practical discussed, such as how we would manage to pay for college. It was much more sweetly romantic to talk about the decor of the baby's room, or what sort of teddy bear she might like.

My father, Mr. Preparedness, was horrified. He sent me an email (subject line: *URGENT*) stating that according to the College Board, a nonprofit that tracks the price of higher education, the average cost of yearly tuition and room and board at a private four-year college for 2009 (the year Sylvie was born) was $34,000 (2016's figures have climbed to an ulcer-inducing $43,920).

Like any self-respecting retiree dad, my father phoned me five minutes after sending his email to inquire if I had received the email, before providing a helpful breakdown of the particulars of said email.

"Did you get the statistics I sent? Have you set up a college fund yet?"

"No, Dad," I said. "Jeez, she isn't even born yet."

"Uh-huh," he said grimly. "Start now, or when she's out of high school, her room and board will be a cardboard box under the bridge."

"What bridge, Dad?" I asked, just to wind him up. "The Brooklyn Bridge? Or are you thinking of one in New Jersey?"

"Go ahead and laugh," he boomed. "You won't be laughing when you have to pay your kid's tuition with your retirement fund." He went on to paint a bleak picture of Tom and me spending our golden years sleeping in our car as we travel to various parking lots for the night. Eventually, I gave in and promised him we would set up a 529 fund for the fetus. We put a hundred dollars in it, and that was the extent of any sort of practical preparation. Everything else, we reasoned, would be worked out as we went along.

Soon after the baby was born, we began to fight about money.

Most of us have money worries, and the enormous responsibility to provide for a family only tightens the vise. It seems that men in particular feel this strain: an analysis by the Institute for Public Policy Research, a UK think tank, found that when men become fathers, they earn up to 19 percent more, most likely because they put pressure on themselves to work harder — especially if their spouse is taking time off. Babies also have a habit of inopportunely arriving right in the middle of a person's prime moneymaking years. The optimists among us believe that one's salary rises as you climb the ladder; the salary profile database PayScale.com shows otherwise: men's salaries peak at the age of forty-eight, while women's top out at thirty-nine.

Tom and I had saved carefully so that I could take off two years when our baby was born, but soon after her birth, Tom was rattled by our avalanche of new expenses (our credit card debt was inching toward $15,000, the current national average). He quickly set up a command center at his computer and methodically fired off article pitches to dozens of magazine editors.

There's no way around the fact that the costs of raising a child are staggering: to bring up a baby born in 2013 to the age of eighteen, a middle-income couple will shell out $245,000, according to figures from the US Department of Agriculture. That's almost a quarter of a million dollars, not including college: factor in the statistics my father sent for a four-year private college and the total outlay is a heart-stopping $420,000. The cost of disposable diapers alone averages $864 yearly, according to the parenting website BabyCenter.

And so our money issues began to swirl in a dank cauldron of paranoia. If a package arrived for one of us, it was condemned by the other as a wasteful extravagance. One fight erupted when I received a new pair of shoes. Tom asked why on earth I needed them when I had "perfectly good ones" in the closet. "Because I'm meeting an editor from *InStyle* next week," I said loftily. "Note the magazine's title."

It was his turn to be excoriated when a larger package arrived for him: inside was a bike. I pointed out that he already had three perfectly good ones. "But this one is for gravel races," he said. "I need longer chainstays for stability and disc brakes for more braking power. It also has bigger tire clearance and a slacker head tube." As he threw more jargon at me, he watched my expression go from suspicious to confused: victory!

But it wasn't just our purchases — we fought continually about how much to spend on Sylvie's toys and activities. I maintained that fewer toys force children to use their imaginations, while Tom bought our daughter a cornucopia of sports gear, toys, and games that we couldn't afford. I liked playdates in the park, which happen to be free; he loved to enroll her in endless unusual classes and camps (a surf camp at Rockaway Beach, a robot-building class). We were at loggerheads.

Arguing about money is "by far" the top predictor of divorce, says Sonya Britt, chair of the personal financial planning department at Kansas State University. She found in her research that couples that fought about money early in their relationships — regardless of debt or income level — were more likely to split. "That is key," she tells me, "because it's saying that people have to have this good base communication, and if they don't, the problems are going to come out eventually. And if you're adding kids in the mix, the problem is just going to get bigger."

Even when people stay together, found one study, marital brawls about money were found to be "more pervasive, problematic, and recurrent" than other issues, and couples used harsher language than they did in other kinds of arguments. That is undeniably the case for us.

Making matters more fraught for Tom and me is that we are freelancers whose incomes vary wildly from year to year. Tom and I never know exactly what we will earn singly or jointly in any given year; we basically find out at tax time. We aren't alone: in a survey from the financial service group Fidelity, a full 43 percent of the respondents could not say how much their partner earned; 10 percent of that group's guesses were off by $25,000 and up.

Why the disparity? One reason is that the economy is moving from salaried to project-based jobs, so more people have incomes like ours that fluctuate from year to year. So-called contingent workers — self-employed people, part-timers, and freelancers like us — now make up an estimated 40 percent of the nation's workforce.

As our daughter grew, our finances became more complicated, and our clashes around them more intense. Then a friend who was struggling with her husband's gambling problem mentioned that she was undergoing financial therapy. A small but expanding field, financial therapy combines fiscal advice with psychological counseling. It delves into your relationship with, and emotions behind, money — still a cultural taboo many are reluctant to discuss. Money does not seem like a very touchy-feely subject, but financial therapists say that fights around it have less to do with money itself than with other emotional hot-button issues, such as the values we want to pass on to our children. What they do is try to resolve the underlying issue that causes a person to become, for example, a "serial borrower" or "financial enabler."

Unlike financial advisors, financial therapists work to make clients uncover their root fears and core beliefs about money that commence in our early years. They ask clients: Was money a source of status when you were growing up? Fear? Security? Shame? Most money conversations between partners don't probe into the past — why would they, when there is a more immediate worry of making the rent or dealing with a lost job? But financial therapists maintain that in order to dial down the stress of talking about our cash flow (or lack thereof), it's helpful to understand the "money scripts," or stories we tell ourselves about money.

Britt and an associate uncovered four basic money scripts that negatively impact a person's financial health: money avoidance (people who don't want to deal with it, or even think about it), money worship (those who believe their troubles would be over if they just had more dollars), money status (those for whom self-worth equals net worth), and money vigilance (those who are nervous about funds to the point of self-deprivation).

Even a brief money conversation makes both Tom and me fibrillate with anxiety — Britt's research found that when people watched just four minutes of financial news on television, their stress levels skyrocketed. Not only that, but with our stealth purchases, it was clear that we were growing ever more secretive with each other — something divorce lawyers call "financial infidelity."

I don't have the heart to pull Tom into yet another therapy session, yet I am intrigued by the idea. And so I find myself at the home of financial therapist Amanda Clayman — who, as it happens, lives right down the street from me in Brooklyn, and tells me she would be happy to share some insights. Smiling and warm, with a chic blond pixie cut, she ushers me into the sun-dappled courtyard of her apartment. We chat away as she pads around barefoot, watering her flowers.

The need to hang on to our money is almost primal, says Clayman as she brushes some white flower petals off a chair so I can sit down. "People think that money is a rational, concrete topic, when really it's a highly emotional subject that's hardwired into our sense of survival," she says. "So if we feel like somebody is threatening our money, we literally feel like it becomes a fight to the death." (Indeed, research shows that even a quick chat about funds can trigger the neurochemical "fight or flight" reaction.)

I tell her that Tom and I have never had a single conversation about our emotions around money. She shrugs and says that most people don't. But the way that your partner thinks about and uses money, she goes on, reflects something personal and internal about them — tease that out, and it puts you in a much more collaborative framework, diffuses the tension, and places you back on the same team.

She has clients create a system with a few intersecting components. One is that *each partner is equal* in the financial relationship. "Establish that no one has more control or decision-making power than the other," she says, "even if they make more money." This rule is especially necessary to curb resentment among stay-at-home mothers who often have to ask their partners for funds, creating an unwelcome power imbalance. I know one stay-at-home mom who has to present weekly receipts to her husband for his approval — a power-tripping, relationship-eroding move.

I tell Clayman that Tom and I make roughly the same income, so we divide our bills in half and share a joint credit card account for family expenditures — but we also have one separate credit card each, the source of our increasingly covert spending.

She recommends that after a couple has worked out a family budget, and the monthly bills are paid, each spouse gets a certain amount of discretionary spending — say, a few hundred dollars a month — which is deposited into their individual checking accounts, so that one person is not petitioning the other for cash. Nor will anyone have to justify a purchase. "Because sometimes we're not going to agree on what's a worthwhile purchase," she points out. "I'm sure if I talked to my husband about how often I get my hair cut and colored, he'd be surprised, because he's a fifteen-dollar-haircut guy."

Next, your financial management has to be *inclusive*. "Grown-ups should not be exempt from money matters," says Clayman shortly. "Both have to participate." She sees many couples in which one person handles the money, while the other claims to be "terrible with numbers." This places a burden squarely on one mate, when both should find a way to participate and be partners in a common cause, playing to whatever strengths they have. "It's also good for your kids to see a flexible back-and-forth," she says, "where both parents treat each other as competent and equally responsible."

Women, especially, shouldn't be left out of the equation: you don't want your kids to internalize that Mommy isn't good with math or perpetuate the idea that money should be handled by men: research has shown that parents talk to girls less often about money than they do boys.

Finally, financial matters between couples must be *transparent*. That means that even if there are negotiated areas of autonomy such as the discretionary spending, each person has access to all information if he or she wants to take a look.

Clayman says that transparency is healthy for kids as well — not to know your salary, necessarily, but to see a predictable choreography to your finances: mail gets opened daily, bills are paid weekly, accounts are reviewed monthly. "Children need to see that money exists within a framework of time, and that inattention to time brings a swift consequence of disorder," she says. "It shouldn't be, 'Crap! Didn't I just pay that?'"

Financial transparency between couples should also include your credit ratings. Finance guru Suze Orman advises new couples to share their FICO credit scores as early as possible. (As she cheerily proclaims, "FICO first, then sex.") Credit card companies such as Citi and American Express now provide FICO scores on their statements; each of the three credit reporting bureaus will also issue one free credit report a year.

The next day, fortified by Clayman's advice, I gather our financial information after Sylvie has gone to school. Tom and I make ourselves an omelet at our usual lunchtime of 11:30 (when you work at home, the rationale is usually "Why wait?"). Then we sit down at the kitchen table and have a heart-to-heart about money. Tom looks gloomy at the prospect of still more mutual unburdening, but I feel a rush of affection for him as he gamely tackles the questions a financial therapist would pose: What are your fears about money? What did your parents teach you about it? How do you define financial security? What is your money nightmare?

He divulges that when he was growing up, money was a source of fear and panic. After his parents divorced, he lived with his mom, who struggled to pay the bills. To this day, when he sees a bill, he quickly stashes it out of sight as if he can't bear to look at it — where it is frequently lost in the mulch of his paper piles. In other words, he's a classic money avoider.

My view of money is completely incompatible with Tom's (not necessarily a bad thing — if you have two savers, for example, you may never go on vacation). I am not as fearful about money — and one reason, I realize, is that my father made a ritual out of paying the bills. Once a month, he took out his basket of bills and set them on the coffee table, along with a roll of stamps and a pile of envelopes handily pre-stamped with our return address. Then, while a football game played in the background, he sedately took care of the bills and looked over his accounts. My childhood view of bill paying is that it was visible, consistent, and calm (we kids never saw my dad get worked up, unless the Giants were losing).

But money to me meant more than security. Growing up, I envied the rich kids in our town for the ease and self-assurance that I assumed their sizable bank accounts provided. Connecting the dots as I talk through it with Tom, it becomes clear to me that wealth has always signified self-confidence. In the fashion world that I dip in and out of, when you purchase the "right" bag or shoes, they do indeed give you more poise — they allow you, at least superficially, to "pass."

For all the fashion world's exuberance, most editors wear a uniform — lots of black, small jewelry, discreet accessories without logos. As a former Jersey girl whose father managed a J. C. Penney store, I can never quite quell the feeling that I am an outsider in this rarefied world. A gleaming new pair of shoes quiets that hectoring voice of insecurity. It seems fairly clear that my money script is "money status."

Yet I also feel guilty about ordering those shoes, and in fact rarely buy anything for myself — something Kansas State's Britt says is common behavior among mothers. "There's research that when women have extra money, they spend it on their kids and not on themselves," says the mom of two, who admits she does this herself. "And when men have extra money, they tend to spend it on fun things, like alcohol. Or music."

And our culture applauds self-sacrificing mothers who put their children first. In a study of low-income single moms in the Philadelphia area, sociologists found that mothers risked harsh criticism from other moms if they had nicer clothing than their children. As one mother in the study commented, "I can't see my son walking around with Payless sneakers on with me walking around with Nikes or Reeboks or something." (Oh, do I understand that mind-set: the limit of my self-sacrifice extends to eating only the broken bits in a box of crackers, so the rest of the family can have the whole ones.)

So Tom and I work out a system to divert our leftover mad money to separate accounts without any meddling from the other. Beyond that, we pledge to have no more financial infidelity for purchases over $150.

We move on to the subject of Sylvie. Beyond establishing a 529 fund, we have never had basic money conversations about her, either. Did we want her to help pay for her education, for instance? Was it important to us for her to have a summer job when she was old enough? (Yes, and yes.) And — a perpetual squabble — how much should we spend on her activities?

Financial therapists say that arguments like these aren't really about whether your daughter should get an allowance, or whether your son should have the pricey sneakers he claims all his friends have. The real battle here is about values: one parent may yearn for their kid to have an idyllic childhood without scrimping and the other thinks that money should be spent on basics like clothes and school supplies. Clayman says that with disagreements like this, try to zero in on what's important to you and how money factors into it, and make a practice to notice what you're doing out of emotion. If I'm afraid Sylvie is going to be spoiled, she says, dig down further and ask myself what traits I would like to see in our daughter.

Tom says that he wants her to have access to the kinds of classes his family couldn't afford when he was a kid. Why, he reasons, wouldn't you want the best for your child? And enrolling her in activities opens up the opportunity to find something she loves to do.

I counter that well-meaning parents have bought into the idea that it's our job to winnow out any hidden "passions" or talents with a barrage of lessons — how else will you discover if your child is a future Mozart? I feel that it is just as important for her to have plenty of unstructured downtime to futz around in her room or wander through a park, picking up rocks. The fact that my parents didn't have the money for various lessons, either, turned out to be advantageous for me, because I spent many hours in my bedroom, immersed in what childhood experts term "self-directed free play": dreaming, singing, staring into space, doodling, and writing. That was how I discovered that I wanted to be a writer.

I tell Tom I also have a horror of entitled children — another value revealed — and don't want Sylvie to be spoiled. When Clayman asks what sorts of traits I would like to see in our daughter, what comes to mind is kindness, empathy, generosity, and, to coin a phrase, exuberant nerdiness.

The more Tom and I talk, the calmer we feel, eventually

gaining enough courage to print out our credit scores and share them with each other (wondering about them, it turns out, caused a lot more stress than actually viewing the numbers on a page). We craft a budget around Sylvie's activities ("It has to be a compromise — you don't get to be the boss of your spouse," Clayman warns). And once a month, we start going over our accounts together. I loathe hashing out fiscal matters, but as with our other issues, transparency and communication are, for us, the only way forward. Therapists specializing in money disorders — an actual field, and one that's growing — say it's crucial to explicitly, and sympathetically, discuss money issues to alleviate ongoing financial tensions. You may not be able to make your debt go away, but you can at least come to a better understanding of where your mate stands. Research shows that communicating about your cash flow on a regular basis, rather than having a doom-laden conversation before tax time or when debt piles up, is one of the keys to a contented relationship. A study from TD Bank found that couples that talk about money at least once a week were most likely to describe their relationship as "extremely happy."

The next time I visit my folks in New Jersey, I sit in their sunny kitchen with my mom and tell her about financial therapy. I expect her to laugh, but she says it makes sense. "Because your father always did the bills when you kids were small, I didn't get involved," she says, placing two mugs of peppermint tea in front of us. "Then Jay's father died, and his mother had never written a check in her life. She was totally overwhelmed."

She squirts some honey into her tea from a bear-shaped container. "Well, that was an eye-opener. At the same time, I started working. So I finally began looking at our finances, and now I do the budget. I like that it's absolutely black-and-white. To me, the fear around money lies in the unknown."

I go in search of my father and find him in the driveway, washing my car. He does this every time I visit. "There's major pollen on your windshield," he says. "Impacts visibility." He squats down and inspects the front tires, his lips tightly pressed together. "Air's low," he informs me dourly, giving me a piercing look that says, *If you want that low tire pressure to compromise braking, cornering, and stability, be my guest. Just know that when those tires overheat and cause tread separation, it's your funeral. Your actual funeral, because you will have a nasty accident, guaranteed. But hey, do what you want.*

When I tell him about financial therapy, he snorts. "So you talk about money issues?" He wipes my car's windshield and squints at it. "Just save 10 percent of your earnings, and don't spend what you don't have. Boom. No more issues."

"Dad, it's not that simple anymore."

He disappears into the garage to fetch a clean rag, grumbling as he goes. "In my day," I hear him mutter, "we didn't have issues."

Hot Mess: Less Clutter, Fewer Fights

I am visiting my sister Heather on a rain-soaked summer Saturday. We sprawl on her couch, eating freshly baked Dunn Family Cheese Puffs (slice canned crescent rolls into one-inch squares, wrap each square around a cube of Laughing Cow cheese, sprinkle with sesame seeds if you're feeling extravagant, bake at 375° for 12 minutes).

Heather gazes bleakly around her living room at the various heaps of stuff deposited by her husband, Rob, and their two sons. "My kids' hockey equipment does not spark joy," she says, shoveling in another cheese puff. Because her teaching job typically stretches to ten hours before her second shift of shuttling the kids to practices and playdates, she is usually too overwhelmed to even think about getting organized.

I tell her I understand. One of the many traits I share with both of my sisters is that no matter what our life circumstances may be, we all bicker with our husbands about clutter and mess (to sum up: the men are fine with it, the women...not so much). Early in our respective marriages, this was a minor issue we laughed about at family gatherings (*Why does Patrick need 100 baseball caps? How many baseball cap requirements does a person have? Are there casual versus dressy baseball caps, or do most go from day to evening?).* But when children began to arrive, the quarrels in all three camps grew more heated.

Rob swerves by the coffee table to grab a cheese puff, and the sight of him leaning over a wobbly tower of unread library books and backpack detritus reminds Heather of a recent tiff. Before he manages to pop it in his mouth, she starts in.

HEATHER: Okay, I love my husband, but I have asked him every week for the past year to clean out the garage. Every week!

ROB (CHEERFULLY): And it sucks! You know why? It's never that bad to me. My definition of "bad" is when you can't walk through the garage to reach the door.

HEATHER: If he can still wind his way through the piles to take the trash out, he's good.

ME: At least he takes the trash out.

ROB: Thank you.

HEATHER: He says, "I'll clean the garage later." And "later" becomes "never."

ROB: Come on, it's a pretty big job.

HEATHER: But if you just did it once, then after that, it would turn into a small job.

ROB: But I'm so fried after working that on my day off, I just want to read. I like to relax. Otherwise, it's not really a day off, is it?

HEATHER (WEARILY CHEWING A CHEESE PUFF WITH HER EYES CLOSED): Women never have a day off.

As Rob wanders away, Heather says, "You know what I need? One of those professional organizers who sweep in and organize your life."

The preponderance of clutter is undeniably a First World problem, but the anxiety it provokes is real. A *Huffington Post* survey found that clutter was a major source of stress for Americans — ranking as high as unanticipated expenses and not having enough time for loved ones. When the retailer Ikea surveyed couples in the UK, it found that on average, fights about mess and clutter occurred twice weekly (the research effort did not probe too deeply into the question of how much clutter actually came from Ikea).

Further pushing people into the red zone is the onslaught of flotsam that comes with kids — the sports equipment, the piles of grimy shoes, the homework. And let's not forget the cavalcade of Beanie Babies: sociology professor Juliet Schor found that American children receive an average of seventy new toys a year.

Many families are drowning in stuff, so much so that the Self Storage Association estimates that nearly one in ten families stashes their excess in a storage unit. The UCLA Center on Everyday Lives of Families study cited earlier found homes that were piled to the rafters with possessions: three-quarters of the garages they studied were so crammed with junk, the homeowners couldn't store cars (at least Rob can still squeeze his Honda into the remaining crevasse).

And all that clutter, the UCLA team discovered, was particularly stressful to mothers. When moms described their spaces to the researchers during a home visit (using semi-apologetic phrases like "very chaotic"), their levels of the stress hormone cortisol, measured in saliva samples, spiked. Meanwhile, when the fathers conducted a similar house tour, the mess didn't bother them — for most, the excess stuff (or, in researchers' parlance, "artifacts") was a source of pleasure, and even pride.

"Clutter is a nagging reminder of things that are left undone, and contributes to a sense of overload," says Darby Saxbe, one of the researchers on the UCLA project (who nonetheless genially admits that she's a "total slob"). "Another reason why we potentially got this result from women and not the men in our sample is something called the social evaluative threat," or fear of being judged, mentioned earlier as a persistent anxiety among women.

Compounding the chaos is this: according to the US Census Bureau, nearly 10 percent of all employees work from home at least one day a week. In our case, Tom and I both work at home full time, so sitting down to dinner often requires clearing the table-that-is-also-a-communal-desk of a variety of laptops and files. "We now live in this kind of hybrid space, where the clutter from your workspace can enter into your domestic space," Saxbe tells me. "It's not like the old days where you'd work at the office for eight hours, and home was a sanctuary."

As I take the train back to my Brooklyn apartment after my visit with Heather, I keep picturing her unhappy, exhausted face. Then it hits me: *I write for women's magazines, for God's sake — decluttering is an "evergreen" story that readers never tire of. I know plenty of professional organizers.* I promptly place a call to a green tea–powered human typhoon named Barbara Reich.

Reich, author of *Secrets of an Organized Mom,* streamlines the capacious multiple abodes of New York's one percenters, tidying purse closets in Manhattan (yes, a closet just for purses) and arranging pool maintenance in the Hamptons. Reich began her career as a management consultant (she has an MBA from NYU). When she downscaled to part-time work after having twins, she found herself getting antsy on playdates and straightening up other families' toys. A new career was born: now she's one of the country's best-known professional organizers.

A month after my call, Reich, so intent on bringing order to my sister's house that she picks up a speeding ticket along the way, strides purposefully into the hallway with her now-teenage neat-nik son, Matthew ("He's my intern"). She stands, hands on hips, a chic fairy godmother in immaculate white pants, gold-edged T-shirt, and gold Prada espadrilles. "Right," she announces, glancing around briskly. Then she and her son march back to the car and swiftly unload it: containers, label maker, contractor bags. "Do you want me to take off my shoes?" she asks Heather. "Because I keep socks in my bag." Of course she does.

My parents, never one to miss a show, arrive at Heather's early in the morning, virtually tailgating in the driveway — all that is missing is the popcorn and the foldable stadium chairs. My mother, getting into the spirit of maximum productivity, volunteers to take notes, while my father says he will join the men in whisking the kids away to the community pool.

"I often joke that in my next life, I'd like to come back as my husband...married to me," says Reich. "I was just reminding him to get passports for a trip, and on the third time I asked, he said he didn't like my, quote unquote, tone of voice. I said, 'I asked you nicely the first two times.'" She threw up her hands. "Then *I* did it! Because women do five things at once, whereas men can do one and a half things at a time! And if your husband has an important deadline and all hell breaks loose, he'll say, 'Sorry, deadline.' But if a woman has an important deadline, she's still up at 2 a.m. checking her kids' homework. Am I right?" All the females raise hallelujah hands.

She begins, as she customarily does, by asking Heather to show her the "hot spot" in the house — the area that drives her the most insane. Deal with that first, Reich says, and your anxiety levels will drop; with this domestic triage out of the way, you'll be motivated to continue.

Heather, trailed by me and my mother, leads Reich to her chaotic coat closet in the front hallway. Reich adheres to a simple four-step system: purge, design (create infrastructure), organize (have a home for everything), and maintain. "Once you've done the purge and have infrastructure like bins or files in place, it literally takes three minutes to keep up," Reich said. "Routines work."

She charges into the purge, sorting Heather's things into three piles: keep, toss, donate. The criteria are simple: *Is it useful or beautiful? Would it help someone more than me? Does it make me happy? Am I saving this for some imaginary life I'll live in the future, or the life I'm living right now?*

While she flings old shoes into a contractor bag, she reels off rapid-fire tips to train the family to lighten Mom's load. Consider hanging a second rod from the higher rod in the front closet, so your kids can hang up their own jackets, or install a row of hooks on the back of the closet door. "In school they hang their coats on hooks," she says, "but then there's no hook at home. So they throw it on the floor."

My mother and I nod and murmur *That's right* and *So true.* Reich points to the front door. Instruct your children, she continues, to do just two things when they get home: First, when they take off their coats, stuff their hat in their sleeves and gloves in their pockets, then hang the coat on the hook you are going to install. Second, take all shoes but foul weather boots to their bedroom, so the entryway isn't piled with stuff. ("Hang a sign if you have to.") Leave the boys' backpacks by the front door every day, she goes on, so everyone knows exactly where they are. "And remind them to put their homework into their backpack right when it's done, so this behavior becomes ingrained."

My mother unearths a large box out of the depths of the closet. "It's filled with electronic doodads," she says, rummaging through it. "Are these chargers?"

Reich gives it a quick perusal. "Okay, I find this in every home," she says. "Everyone has a dusty box or a bag filled with electric cords and chargers. No one knows what they're for, but everybody is *very afraid* to throw them away." (Especially men, she says, who like to hold on to the previous technology of any consumer category.) Heather cringes, but doesn't protest, as Reich tosses it. "In the highly unlikely event that you need another cord, go to an electronics store," she says.

My mother nods. "My husband has a box of that stuff with VHS cords in it," she says. "I'm putting it on the curb tomorrow. To hell with it."

Pulling out a random hockey stick, Reich tells Heather to keep sporting equipment in the bags the boys carry to the activities, and to store out-of-season gear under the beds. "And this is very important," she says. "Print out four copies of the kids' annual doctor's report so you have medical forms for sports and camp ready to go."

Heather nods. "I've made three trips to the doctor this year already to pick up copies."

Taking a three-second break, Reich zooms into the kitchen to grab a green tea, flushing out my father and Tom. "We *are* the clutter," says my father as they herd the kids out the door. On to Heather's bedroom. The contractor bags multiply as Reich banishes the pernicious offenders she sees in almost every family home: freebies such as mugs and T-shirts ("Almost none are useful or attractive"), catalogs ("Bad for the environment, they litter the house, and encourage unnecessary spending"), and old sheets and towels ("You only need two towels per person, and two sets of sheets per bed — one to keep and one to wash"). Heather holds up a square of green cloth. "I don't know what this is," she says.

"Then it has to go," snaps Reich, rocketing it into a contractor bag.

There is something remarkably freeing about viewing objects through her merciless eye. Heather holds up a flowered duvet cover. "I'll allow that," says Reich. "It's cute." We all grow giddy and slightly unhinged, having clearly reached the ketosis stage of decluttering. If only they made a house-size contractor bag, we could just stuff the entire dwelling in there!

My mother slides open one of Heather's now-half-empty dresser drawers and gloats. "Oooh, this is nice," she says.

"Right?" says Reich. "You want to open up a drawer and feel happy."

When Reich runs downstairs for more containers, Heather whispers in my ear, "I don't want her looking in my underwear drawer, okay? Will you say something?"

But Reich has already burst into the boys' rooms, where the

phrase "underwear drawer" is a foreign concept. She points to the soccer uniforms spilling from drawers, looking like the room had been ransacked by the local narcotics unit. "Uniforms should be kept in a single location, whether it's a bin or designated drawer," Reich rules, "so no frantic hunt for soccer socks."

She dumps out the drawers of Heather's elder son, swiftly folds his T-shirts into thirds, sleeves tucked in, and arranges them vertically instead of horizontally. This not only creates more space, she says, but each T-shirt will be visible and thus get used more often. "No chance," Heather says to me under her breath. Later, however, she calls me to recant, saying that the new system has provided her son with a whole new wardrobe of previously unworn clothes (research shows we wear only 20 percent of what's in our closet).

In the younger boy's room, Reich inspects an easel. "Does he use this?" Heather says no, and Reich wrestles it into another bag. "Easels take up space, and kids are just as happy drawing on a table," she says. "If large, unwieldy items aren't being used, get rid of them." As she inspects a shelf of trophies and medals, she furrows her brow. "Were any of these given to every member of the team?" Heather nods. Barbara calls to her son, who is busily arranging shoes in Heather's closet. "Matthew, what do I say when everyone gets a trophy?"

"Out they go," comes the muffled reply.

As she ruthlessly banishes a half dozen "participation" trophies, Reich tells us that parents should do toy purges twice a year — once before birthdays, and once before December holidays, when they have leverage. Parents, she says, are often the ones hanging on to old toys, unwilling to accept that their child has outgrown them. I tell Reich that I am sentimentally holding on to Sylvie's old games and coloring books and she shakes her head. "I tell clients, 'You can have a home, or a toy museum.'" And toss junky birthday party favors within twenty-four hours ("By that time, they're sick of them, anyway"). Then she unloads a stack of clear plastic containers ("Always clear, so you save time by seeing what's inside") and swiftly sorts toy cars, her hands a blur.

• •

How many toys is too many? My friend Lindsay, mother of three boys, can pinpoint the precise moment when she knew she had to cut down. "My sons' pet frog Sammy had jumped out of his cage, and no one could find him," she says. "Well, I came across him months later, buried at the bottom of the kids' toy box. Thank God the boys were at school at the time, because Sammy looked like a leather wallet."

Decluttering expert Peter Walsh advises parents to set limits by storing toys in a set number of bins — say, four. When the bins are full, children can add a toy, but they must donate another. This trains them to be generous, Walsh has said, and to understand that unlike Veruca Salt in *Charlie and the Chocolate Factory*, they can't own everything. Toy swaps also keep the clutter down: sometimes we'll arrange for Sylvie and a friend to bring five toys on a playdate and then trade them for the week. She gets a fresh supply of toys, and I don't spend a dime.

Children are just like adults when it comes to too many possessions, writes *Simplicity Parenting* author Kim John Payne. An avalanche of toys, he contends, can make a child feel anxious and

231

distracted. Even the senior director of the Play Lab at the toy company Fisher-Price once admitted that too many toys can feel "overwhelming to some children."

In his book, Payne advises cutting back on toys that are too complicated (elaborate, joyless "educational" toys), too fixed (ones that require zero imaginative input, such as a huge furnished plastic castle with a cast of thousands), or too commercial. The more a child can use their imagination with a toy — initiating the action, rather than having it prescribed for them — the better. A Barbie lifeguard can work only as a Barbie lifeguard, but a big cardboard box can be a bus, a house, a spaceship. Boredom, asserts Payne, is a gift; out of it comes engagement and creativity.

I've seen this many times. Once, when I refused to entertain my daughter on a snowy afternoon, she drifted into her bedroom. She emerged a while later and announced that she had turned into our superintendent, Doug. She had constructed Doug's tool kit out of an old shoebox, and a ring of "keys" out of paper clips (although she stopped short of chastising our neighbors for neglecting to separate the recyclables from the trash). She spent the afternoon industriously doing "odd jobs."

In a now-famous German experiment, two public health workers persuaded a Munich nursery school to pack away their toys for three months. For the first few days, the children, faced with nothing to play with but tables, chairs, and a few blankets, wandered around listlessly. But then they began to come to life: they constructed forts with the blankets and tables, and played games like "family," "vampires," and "bogeyman." They pretended to be in a circus. At the end of the three months, the researchers found that the children played more cooperatively with each other and showed more concentration and focus than a group who had not undergone the experiment.

Back at my sister's, Reich moves on to the desk of Heather's younger son. She holds up an outline of a dinosaur he had colored in. Children's artwork, she says, making eye contact with all of us for emphasis, should be kept only if it shows creativity and personality—that means no worksheets and no homework, unless it's an especially inventive essay. To save even more space, she goes on, scan or do a digital photo of artwork and put it on the computer. Reich preserves her children's most special creations and mementos in 12-by-15-inch document boxes, color coded for each child.

The contractor bags for donation multiply as we all crowd into the bathroom, chattering excitedly. Reich excavates some lightbulbs from the bathroom cabinet. "I saw lightbulbs in the front closet, too: you should always store like with like. Knowing where things have a home saves tons of time." Then she quaffs more green tea and lays down a game-changer: store stain remover where the kids take off their clothing, like the bathroom, and teach them at a young age to spritz their stained garments. We gasp. Of course! "When they're little, they think it's fun," she says. "It's all about routines, so they don't even think of it as something they're doing to help, it's just something they do. Like if we're all watching a TV show together, I stick the laundry bag in front of them and everybody folds. They don't know any different."

Her routines extend to homework, which is done at a set place and a set time every day (in her case, at the kitchen table, after her twins have rested and had a snack). "And I keep homework supplies nearby so they don't get up," she says. "Once they get up, you've lost them." She calls to Matthew, who is unloading another teetering pile of clear plastic bins in the hallway. "Right, Matthew?" A distant assent. "Routine is one of the best ways I know to curb arguments — it's only when things are unclear that there's anything to fight about." (This rule also applies to spouses, she adds.)

A short while later, Reich flits down to the kitchen, entourage in tow. She scans the cereal boxes stored on a high shelf and tells Heather if she wants the kids to get their own snacks, she must put them on a low shelf — the more autonomous they are, the less scrambling you will have to do. She pulls out a small magnetized notepad and slaps it on the fridge. "And tell your kids that if they use up something and don't put it on this grocery list, they're not allowed to come complaining to Mom. Make everyone responsible."

She spots Heather's large family calendar posted on the wall and approves: a monthly family calendar, either paper or digital, is crucial. Every family member should be accountable for their appointments to avoid surprises and "oops" moments; make yearly doctor's appointments around every family member's birthday, so you'll always remember. "And I'm very much in favor of a family meeting on Sunday nights for scheduling," she says, and then winces. "Although I tried to implement this and my husband laughed at me in front of the kids, undermining me. So I guess I would say to start that when the kids are young."

We take a quick pizza break, with Reich holding forth as we eat. "What you want is fewer things circulating in your brain, and for as many things to run on autopilot as possible, such as meal planning," she says, taking a delicate bite of pizza. I am suddenly aware that I am wolfing my own, and attempt to slow down. I'm always the parent at kids' parties happily eating oil-filmed lukewarm slices while the other mothers look on in pity.

Reich is still firing off tips. Because she also consults with clients about management, she throws in a few about decluttering your schedule. Make your days less tumultuous by simply saying no. "It's entirely valid for moms to ask themselves if they *want* to attend a particular event, if their family will actually enjoy it, and if their presence will be missed," she says. "There's no reason to go to three birthday parties in one day! Carve out time for the things you really love!"

We don't comment and she senses, correctly, that we need a tutorial. "Okay, here is how to say no," she says. "First rule: think before you automatically answer. Two: say no, *not why*." My mother scribbles this down and underlines it twice. "This is how you do it: 'Thanks so much for the invitation. We're so sorry we can't attend; it sounds like a great time.' If you're asked to volunteer, say 'I'm sorry, but I can't.' That's all. No reason is necessary!"

I try it out. "I can't, but I wish you well, because it's such a worthwhile cause."

She claps her hands. "Exactly. Don't make excuses, and don't lie. If you tell your friend you can't go to a party because your kid has swim lessons, she may be upset that you think swim lessons are more important."

(I suddenly recall what Brené Brown tells me is her "boundary mantra": choose discomfort over resentment. As she says, "Ask yourself, 'Am I saying yes because it's more comfortable to say yes now, but I'll be more resentful at the end?'")

Reich thinks for a moment. "Also, if you have multiple children, it's easier to have them all in the same sport, because it's all in one place, and also you can hand down equipment." One of Heather's friends — mother of five boys under twelve, including the set of triplets mentioned earlier — has all five sons play hockey for that very reason. "Now that they're older," she tells me, "I can just drop all of them at the rink and not have to come back to get them until four."

Reich glances at the clock: our magical day is drawing to a close. Heather is beaming. "I feel lighter," she exults, giving me a fierce hug. No surprise there — clutter pulls you down psychologically and slows you physically. Heather now has fewer things to deal with, and is able to find and organize what remains more quickly. Is there a sweeter gift for a frazzled mother than order, peace, and priceless extra time not spent hunting down a missing shin guard?

Reich, without the slightest trace of fatigue, is heading purposefully for the door. "I just want you to know that the goal here is not to be perfect, or to be crazy like I am," she tells Heather as she slips on her gold shoes. "It's to be able to make it easier to get out the door in the morning in time for school. And if that isn't a quality-of-life improvement, I don't know what is."

It's certainly better for your marriage: according to one study, eliminating clutter can reduce housework (and the ensuing chore clashes) by up to 40 percent. My friend Jason institutes a Family Declutter jamboree every other month or so. Once each family member has filled a large trash bag for tossing or donation, they go to their favorite ice cream place for sundaes. "When your house is decently orderly and you know where everything is," he says, "it prevents so many of those fights that start with 'Where the hell did you put the wipes?' and escalate from there." And once the clutter is under control, order is easier to maintain: a Dutch study found that people tend to litter considerably more in messy environments than in clean ones.

After Reich leaves, the men file warily into the house. "Jay," my mother announces gaily to my dad, "we're stopping at the Container Store on the way home!"

"Oh, good," he says, wearily fetching his keys.

⋅⋅⋅⋅⋅⋅⋅⋅⋅⋅⋅⋅⋅⋅⋅⋅⋅⋅⋅⋅⋅⋅⋅⋅⋅⋅

When I return to our apartment, I embark on a deep purge of the one area of our home that I haven't obsessively straightened: our front closet. Tom watches with alarm, afraid that I may toss one of the many empty boxes he has hoarded in case he needs to "send something back." When my mother sends a photo via group text of her newly pared-down basement, I ask Heather if Rob has caught the fever and cleaned out the garage. It was the one part of their house that Reich didn't tackle — that would be a multi-day project, and her services, while effective, are not cheap.

Another weekend over, and the garage is worse than ever, Heather texts back, with the forlorn tone of a diarist on a doomed arctic expedition. Then I remember my conversation with Dr. Gary Chapman. In his book *The Five Love Languages,* he writes that a woman had come to him, distressed, because her husband wouldn't paint the bedroom after she had been asking him for nine months straight. Chapman told her not to mention the bedroom again. ("He already knows.") Then he suggested that every time her husband did something good — haul out the trash, pick something up at the market — she was to give him a verbal compliment.

The woman wondered how, exactly, that would get the bedroom painted. Chapman said, "You asked for my advice. You have it. It's free."

237

After three weeks of receiving lavish compliments, the man painted the bedroom.

I tell Chapman that I find this advice frankly irritating. "Why should I have to praise my husband, like he's a golden retriever, for things he should be doing in the first place?"

He laughs and says he understands. He explains that he isn't suggesting that women should pump up the male ego — rather, that the need to feel appreciated is universal. Who among us does not love praise and kindness? "This isn't manipulation," he tells me. "Look, none of us, by nature, wants to be controlled with demands. He's already heard fifteen times that you want something done. Now that he's feeling loved, that task comes back to his mind and he wants to respond. I can't tell you how often I've seen this work."

But you can't score-keep, he warns: you must offer compliments in the spirit of giving.

I tell Heather about Chapman's technique and she is aghast. "You've got to be kidding me," she says. "Why don't *I* get any praise?"

"Just do it," I say, summoning my still-potent authority as eldest sister.

And so for weeks, Heather carefully tamps down her disgust and forces herself to pile compliments upon Rob whenever he does anything even marginally helpful. Like my husband, Rob is not a naturally suspicious person, so he has no idea that he is part of a test and cheerily accepts this pleasing new turn of events (whereas if the situation were reversed, Heather would have immediately checked his wallet for receipts from Volcanic Eruptions Gentleman's Club, which exists in, where else, New Jersey).

Then, early one Saturday morning, Heather calls me. "He's doing it," she whispers excitedly. "He's shoveling out the garage." It takes all weekend, but he clears away the entire mess.

I then conduct my own trial on Tom, in an attempt to get him to excavate his closet after months of hounding. Like Rob, he is oblivious to my sudden avalanche of approval, aside from one observation that I "seem to be in a good mood." I deeply dislike being put in the position of having to motivate him, although I will admit it is funny to see his chest puff like a quail when I proclaim him a "genius" after he performs a minor repair on a kitchen cabinet.

And it works: one morning, Tom announces that his closet needs a "rethink," and begins industriously hauling out the contractor bags.

When I tell some mothers on the playground about the praising experiment, my enthusiasm is met with silence. "I can't do it," one of them finally says.

I know. I know. And this little happy ending mirrors so many pieces I have written for women's magazines, in which I must try something out — a new diet, a sleep regimen — and unerringly deliver a positive outcome. ("You know the drill," an over-it editor once told me when she had me do a piece on practicing gratitude. "Be a little cynical at first but then, at the end, realize how fortunate you are, and all that shit.")

But it is the absolute truth that because Tom felt valued, he blossomed in almost comical fashion — even throwing a few compliments my way.

If only the effort to stop my eyes from rolling wasn't so tiring. As Heather tells me, "Dr. Chapman was right. It worked. I'm never doing it again, but it worked."

Know That Eventually It's Going to Be Just the Two of You Again — Well, Unless Another Recession Hits

> *When you first get married, you have a*
> *relationship that's so important to you, and*
> *you're working on it together. But then you*
> *have a kid. And you look at your kid and you*
> *go, "Holy shit, this is my child. She has my*
> *DNA. She has my name. I would die for her."*
> *And you look at your spouse and go, "Who the*
> *fuck are you? You're a stranger."*
>
> —COMEDIAN LOUIS C.K.

At long last, it seems as if deeply entrenched gender roles are changing. Millennial men — those age eighteen to early thirties — have said in studies that they fully plan on being hands-on dads who split childcare and housework equally with their mates. Millennial women seem to support this idea: 88 percent of them told the Pew Research Center that a good husband is someone who will "put his family before anything else." Notably, being a breadwinner was not seen as vital — only a third of mil-

240

lennial women said that a good husband "provides a good income."

All this was said, however, before the respondents actually had babies. Once those people became parents, their soaring ideals landed with a loud *whomp*. When the new fathers confronted the reality of work policies that were not exactly family friendly, the same studies found them quickly backsliding into more hidebound gender roles.

Still, the culture has begun to shift. Sociologist Michael Kimmel says that younger men are now realizing that policies that achieve a work-family balance — flexible work time, on-site childcare, and maternity and paternity leave — aren't women's issues, but parents' issues.

"Actually," Kimmel says, "it's not about parental leave — it's about family leave. For those in the sandwich generation, it will be about leaving work early on Friday afternoon to coach your daughter's soccer game *and* take your eighty-six-year-old mom to the doctor. This is a demographic thing — we're marrying later, we're having children later, and our parents are living a lot longer." While women have traditionally borne the brunt of caring for both the elderly and children, "increasingly, men are going to be called on to do this sort of stuff, so we need these reforms," says Kimmel. "While I don't think we're going to become Norway anytime soon, I do think that men as well as women are going to be insisting on it."

Some firms have already listened to their younger workers. Tech companies, unsurprisingly, lead the pack with progressive work-life policies. Facebook offers full-time employees four months of paid parental leave, Twitter grants twenty weeks, and Netflix provides fully paid leave for up to one year.

But for the majority of parents, paid parental leave is not even remotely within reach. The Family Medical Leave Act allows employees to take twelve weeks of parental leave, but it's available only to workers in medium and large companies — and it's unpaid. "It should be a national embarrassment that there are only four countries that offer no paid parental leave to anyone," says Kimmel. "And they are Lesotho, Swaziland, Papua New Guinea — and the United States."

Most men are forced to cobble together their own paternal leave using vacation time and personal days — that is, if they take it at all. The Boston College Center for Work and Family surveyed nearly one thousand fathers in large companies and found that about three-quarters of them took off a week or less when their baby was born; 16 percent took no time off whatsoever.

Survey after survey shows that men want to spend more time with their kids. But even among those who can take parental leave, many hesitate to do so for fear of damaging their careers, and because of lingering social stigma. However, as more high-profile men take parental leave and show that it's a priority, the more socially acceptable it will likely become. Facebook CEO (and millennial role model) Mark Zuckerberg took off two months to care for his newborn daughter, posting photos of himself changing her diapers for his 56 million Facebook followers.

Kimmel says that Zuckerberg's actions made a huge impact. "In corporations, impulses come from the top, so it really does matter when you have your CEO saying, 'This is important to me, and I want my employees to be able to do what I've done, because it's awesome.'" When companies provide benefits such as paternal leave, he adds, it's a win-win. "There is in fact greater productivity, higher job satisfaction, lower labor turnover. So it's actually cost effective."

Along with industry titans, professional sports figures hold similar sway. Golfer Hunter Mahan left the PGA tournament he was leading to rush to a Dallas hospital when his pregnant wife went into labor a month early. Mahan, making a very public choice, forfeited his chance to win a million dollars to attend the birth of his daughter. Chicago White Sox baseball player Adam LaRoche walked away from a contract that would have paid him $13 million because his manager told him that he could no longer bring his son to daily pregame practice. LaRoche, who promptly retired, issued a statement saying, "Of one thing I am certain — we will regret *not* spending time with our kids, not the other way around." LaRoche was applauded by his fellow pro athletes, one of whom used the Twitter hashtag #FamilyFirst.

Men are gradually being portrayed differently in ads, too, as the stereotype of the clueless or remote dad looks increasingly dated. A print ad for wealth management firm UBS shows a handsome entrepreneur lost in thought in his skyscraper office. *Am I a good father?* reads the copy. *Do I spend too much time at work? Can I have it all?* In my dad's day, the man in the ad would be brooding about the time he's missing on the golf course. (Although it should be noted that while UBS grants women a generous six months of fully paid maternity leave, men receive just two weeks.) A spot for Kohler generators that ran on ESPNU during a college football game featured a family dancing in the living room to some music before the power goes out. Dad, significantly, is vacuuming.

As *Mad Men*'s Don Draper used to say, "If you don't like what's being said, change the conversation." That was the case in 2015, when a group of fathers campaigned to change the unfairly monikered Amazon Mom program, which offered parenting products such as wipes, to Amazon Family. Nine months after the protests started, the company quietly altered the name.

Laundry detergent companies are now studying the emergent and increasingly important male consumer. Not long ago, Procter & Gamble, for the first time ever, stopped referring to the average Tide consumer as "she" in its internal discussions. Whirlpool, meanwhile, has added a cycle in its washers to keep colors from blending, because they've found that men are doing more laundry these days — but aren't keen on sorting it.

Most encouraging is an ad for Ariel India, a Procter & Gamble laundry detergent brand. When it ran in 2016, Facebook COO and *Lean In* author Sheryl Sandberg called it one of the most powerful videos she had ever seen. It begins as an older man who is visiting his grown daughter apprehensively watches her return from work and simultaneously make dinner, shove clothes into the washer, and tend to her husband. We hear his voice-over:

My little baby girl, you're all grown up now. You used to play house, and now you manage your own house. And your office. I am so proud. And I am so sorry. Sorry that you have to do this all alone. Sorry that I never stopped you while you were playing house. I never told you that it's not your job alone, but your husband's too. *(The camera cuts to her husband, who is relaxing in front of the television.)* But how could I say it when I never helped your mom, either? And what you saw, you learned.... But it's not too late. I will make a conscious effort to help your mom with the household chores. I may not become king of the kitchen, but at least I can help out with the laundry. *(A shot of him unpacking his suitcase and taking the clothes to the washer while his wife watches, astonished.)* All these years I've been wrong. It's time to set things right.

At this point when I view the ad, I can barely see the tagline *(Why is laundry only a mother's job?)* because the tears are dribbling down my face.

These examples may warm the heart, but we still have a long way to go.

In an annual letter released by Melinda and Bill Gates, which outlines their philanthropic priorities for a teenage audience, Melinda Gates dedicates her section to the heavy load of unpaid work on the world's women.

She writes that globally, women spend an average of 4.5 hours a day on unpaid work — cooking, cleaning, and caring for children and the elderly. Men spend less than half that amount. "It's not just about fairness," she writes. "Assigning most unpaid work to women harms everyone: men, women, boys, and girls. The reason? Economists call it opportunity cost: the other things women could be doing if they didn't spend so much time on mundane tasks."

To narrow the unpaid labor gap, she goes on, "the world is making progress by doing three things economists call Recognize, Reduce, and Redistribute: Recognize that unpaid work is still work. Reduce the amount of time and energy it takes. And Redistribute it more evenly between women and men."

On a more micro level, she issues a call to change what we think of as normal — "not thinking it's funny or weird when a man puts on an apron, picks up his kids from school, or leaves a cute note in his son's lunchbox." Gates told the *New York Times* that she did some Redistributing in her own home. When she was unhappy about making the lengthy commute to her daughter Jennifer's pre-school, her husband, then the chief executive of Microsoft, said he would drive Jennifer two days a week. "Moms started going home and saying to their husbands, 'If Bill Gates can drive his daughter, you better darn well drive our daughter or son,'" she said. (Or, more likely, *You better get your ass in the car.*) If you're going to get behavior to change, she goes on, you have to model it publicly.

Or as feminist author Caitlin Moran tells me, "A culture is the stories that we tell ourselves about who we can be — our possible futures. And when you still don't see that anywhere in the culture — in TV shows, in films — then how would we even know how to do that? It's still up to an individual woman to go, 'I've just invented this idea of us being equal in a relationship!' and then sell it to her partner, when she's surrounded by a culture that does not support that decision, doesn't show her how to do it, and doesn't present it as the right thing to do. So that's where culture is incredibly important."

If women were running Hollywood, she adds, "and they were able to present their lives and their realities, and their dreams for what they think the future should be, we'd be able to sort this shit out pretty fucking quickly. If there was a film or TV show where there was an incredibly sexy actor that everybody fancied who was seen to be a fantastic parent — that would change things pretty quickly, too."

That is one reason why I pushed to have Tom chaperone Sylvie's class trip — and then, to volunteer for another one. Every time he does something in which he's the only guy amidst a sea of moms, he proves to himself that he can do it, proves it to his daughter and the other kids, and also to the other moms, who might then go home and nudge their husbands to show up next time. In this way, he moves the needle forward just a little.

Until we have halfway decent policies that support parents and families, social change must begin in our homes and spread outward. As the saying goes, change doesn't come *from* Washington, it comes *to* Washington.

A little over a year later, of course we still fight — but with sustained effort and self-control, we do it like grown-ups. Well, almost: I find I can't quit my beloved sarcasm, which, in my view, adds a dash of creative spice to our interactions. (I must say I enjoy thinking of various toffs throughout history that I can call Tom if he's acting entitled.) But, for the most part, we have gotten so used to resolving disputes in a relatively calm way that if we raise our voices, it sounds jarring and strange, like an unexpected disturbance in a library.

Tom, once a reluctant but resigned participant in this endeavor, now sees the wisdom of planning, negotiation, and transparency. "It's better just to be up front about things and deal with them ahead of time," he tells me one day before our mundane-but-necessary Saturday meeting, which we *zhush* up with some chocolate-studded bread from Balthazar Bakery, which I highly recommend. "There's a preventive medicine aspect to a lot of this — it's a lot easier to take a five-minute flu shot than lie in bed for a week," he goes on, cutting himself a hefty slice. "Having things be unspoken is corrosive. There's a long-term toll if you're fighting over these little things; it bleeds into other things until you might begin to think you're dissatisfied with the relationship, when it's really these more surface issues."

But in order to restore peace and harmony, we both had to be willing to get real, go to the hard places, and keep at it. (Despite research that it takes an average of sixty-six days for a habit to form, it took more like fourteen months for us to right the imbalance in our household.) A happy, functional family doesn't happen by accident, but by concerted effort from the different members of the family to do the sometimes-difficult work of getting along with each other. Marriage is an institution with a lot of day-to-day business—and institutions function better when they're running well.

I am still the reluctant house manager, and likely always will be. I still must continually insist, quietly but firmly, that Tom do his share around the house. But the mental bandwidth I use to do this is nothing compared to the energy I used to devote to drudge work. Negotiation is an endless, tiring, often clinical but necessary process—one that we will clearly be doing into our dotage—but it's much better than constantly feeling oppressed and angry. Our new harmony has been worth every stilted family meeting and therapist-scripted exchange. I now know the following:

He can't read your mind. He's not even close to reading your mind.

I can't believe how many hours I squandered fuming, in the hopes that Tom would intuitively leap in and help me out. With hindsight, I see that my expectations probably increased because I spend so much time around moms who offer constant and unthinking support: when Sylvie recently ran toward me on the playground, crying with a bloody knee, one friend handed me a wad of tissues, another a bandage, a third a lollipop for Sylvie, all without a break in our conversation.

Tom, meanwhile, rarely seems to notice that I need a hand — so my resentment would inevitably build until I exploded. My first helpful step on the path to real change was to stop playing the victim. In the wonderfully concise words of Terry Real, "If you don't like something, change it, leave it, or embrace it. If you neither change nor leave it, own it."

Stop complaining and ask clearly for what you want.

Yelling didn't work. Muttering under my breath didn't work. Neither did my trademark dramatic speeches. Yet somehow it rarely occurred to me to simply tell Tom what I wanted, rather than complain to him and anyone else who would listen. As Real says, "I'm always amazed that in this age of personal empowerment, people still subscribe to the truly nutty idea that an effective strategy for getting what you want from your partner is to complain about it *after* the fact. This boxes him in and leaves him nowhere to go." Tom's behavior changed only when I learned to tell him, calmly and specifically, what I would like to have happen.

With a Herculean effort, I now strive to keep my requests to one sentence — or even just silently involve him in what I am doing. If I'm emptying the dishwasher, I hand him some bowls. (What is he going to do — throw them on the floor?) If I'm folding laundry, I push a pile his way. If I'm making dinner, I hand him a knife and some vegetables. This tactic works a lot better than brooding, or raging that "I'm doing everything around here," an observation that swirls around with nowhere to land.

You don't always have to eat the broken crackers.

One of the most difficult things I had to do was develop a little entitlement of my own, and get fully behind the idea that I need help around the house, as well as rest and leisure time. It was tough to shake the attendant guilt, and the sense that somehow I should be able to handle everything. It helped a lot to repeat the mantra supplied by therapist Ann Dunnewold: *When I take time for myself, I come back and I'm more the mother I want to be.* By taking care of myself, I become a better caretaker.

If a fight is brewing, start with "I" statements.

I love the Gottmans' method of using a "softened startup" during conflict — simply beginning a statement with "I" instead of "you" ("I feel like you're not listening" rather than "You're not listening"). Not only is this disarming, but taking a pause to focus on how I am feeling, rather than immediately resorting to criticism, lowers my blood pressure and makes me feel more in control.

So does drawing a few deep breaths as I diagnose the "soft emotions" behind my anger. Usually, I feel betrayed — what happened to the evolved guy I married? It was as if parenthood revealed his inner man in the gray flannel suit. And my pride is often hurt, too: Does Tom believe in his heart of hearts that those in possession of a uterus are more suited to menial work? With even more digging, I have to admit that sometimes I am simply jealous that he feels no guilt whatsoever about taking time to relax.

Kids can see you fight if you do it fairly.

Conflict, I repeat, is not bad for children. What is bad is persistent, low-level tension that erupts into full-fledged battles in a manner that baffles them, and that never get resolved. Fighting fairly is not only good for a child to see, it's a useful skill for the whole family to have when a kid reaches the ornery teen years. One of the most compelling cases for having your child see you hash things out without rancor was revealed by psychologists at the University of West Virginia. They asked 157 thirteen-year-olds to describe the biggest disagreements they had with their parents, and video-taped their answers. Then the tape was played back to each teen with a parent in the room.

As the two watched the teenager describe the dispute — typically, an issue involving chores, grades, friends, sibling spats, or money — the psychologists observed the parent's reaction. Some parents rolled their eyes. Some laughed. But others jumped in and through the dispute with their teen in a healthy way — no yelling, each side listening to the other. As it turns out, those teen-agers who were able to confidently disagree with their parents dealt with their friends in the same manner. In a follow-up study when the kids were fifteen and sixteen, those same kids were 40 percent more likely to stand up to peer pressure when offered alcohol or drugs. The kids who shied away from conflict with their folks, meanwhile, were more susceptible to peer pressure.

All teenagers quarrel with their parents — but again, it's the *way* in which you argue that makes a critical difference. When kids learn to calmly but persuasively stand up for themselves, the study author says, they build a lifelong skill that will help them deal with obstreperous coworkers, friends, and partners.

Push through his pushback.

When I announced to Tom that the party was over, he was sensibly reluctant to give up his single-guy-within-a-family lifestyle. Why would he want to forgo long, carefree bike rides and three homemade meals a day? In effect, I was asking him to hand over his leisure hours to me.

So what motivated him to change? For starters, he was fully aware that he had been getting away with doing very little — he told me so later, and admitted that he constantly felt guilty about it. He knew that I had reached my limit, and that I was burned out and frustrated.

When he started helping me out, he did it strictly to keep the peace. But the more he did his share, the happier I was — a tangible benefit for him. The idea that you can create an "upward spiral" of happiness was, in our case, true. When Tom pitched in, I was relieved and grateful. Our sex life improved. We were more polite to each other. I stopped falling asleep at 9 p.m. from sheer exhaustion, and stayed up with him to watch his depressing Romanian films. I baked his favorite ginger cookies, unasked. And our naturally upbeat child was even cheerier when we didn't fight, so our family life had a newfound ease and effervescence.

As University of Oregon sociologist Scott Coltrane has observed in his research, while men often report some difficulty assuming more responsibility around the house, "initial frustration is typically short lived."

Treating your spouse with consideration does not mean you are "caving."

As FBI crisis negotiator Gary Noesner points out, all human beings want to be treated with respect. Terry Real instructed us to make a commitment that nothing we say to each other should drop below the level of simple respect. It seemed impossible at the time, but I'm here to say that it can be done. If you're about to blurt out something disrespectful, says Real, "then, with all due respect, shut up."

Say "Thank you," and say it often.

For us, thanking each other was what *The Power of Habit* author Charles Duhigg calls a "keystone habit" — an influential habit that creates "chain reactions that help other good habits take hold." A prime example of a keystone habit is exercise, which prompts people to eat better; so is having regular family dinners, which seems to correlate with children who have better homework skills, higher grades, and greater emotional control.

Voicing your gratitude takes almost no effort, and to my mind, it's nearly impossible to thank someone too often. I told Tom repeatedly for months until it lodged in his head that women don't like to feel invisible. A simple "thank you" renders you visible and takes away the feeling that you're a stagehand, silently engineering the props while the others have all the fun.

Divest yourself of the "story you are making up."

Rising Strong author Brené Brown calls it her "number one life hack" for relationships that go the distance, and it was one of the most helpful things I learned. Brown, as I wrote earlier, says that we often construct an elaborate motivation for someone that may have nothing to do with reality (if a coworker doesn't return your smile, then obviously you offended her somehow and she can't stand you).

Whenever I find myself writing a custom thought bubble above Tom's head (which usually has a gloating or evil tone), I follow Brown's recommendation and share it with Tom. This deflates tension and helps both of us understand the other's perspective. Tom doesn't seem quite as evil when he informs me that what he was really thinking about was electronic cord management strategies, not how he can trick me out of having to help with the chores.

It's been illuminating to learn from the observational psychology research and insights from experts such as biological anthropologist Helen Fisher the role that optics can play in relationships: how sometimes men can take what is closest at hand for granted not because they are hopeless jerks, but because they just don't see it. On the flip side, when women focus too closely on matters at home, it can make them fail to see more pressing ones on the horizon.

Use your power.

If Tom was under a tight magazine deadline in the summertime, I would occasionally take our daughter to my parents' house for a few days to give him space to work. Our absence created a recognizable pattern: For the first two nights, Tom celebrated his liberation with takeout food, a violent-film festival, and international computer chess tournaments that stretched into the wee hours. But by the third day, a low-grade funk had darkened his mood and he would mournfully inquire when we were coming home.

My friend Marea, a stay-at-home mom, describes a similar scene when she and her daughter take their annual summer trip to visit Marea's father in Pennsylvania. Her husband doesn't accompany them because summer is a busy time at his advertising office. "My dad cooks us dinner every night," Marea tells me. "He cooks well, and it is such a gift to have a lovely, delicious, healthy meal placed in front of you — I always think, 'Wow, this is what Sean must feel like every day of his life.' Meanwhile, Sean is back in Brooklyn falling apart. He aimlessly comes home from work to an empty apartment. He calls me too much. During one of those calls last summer, he told me what he had for dinner: a hot dog bun with cold shredded cheese on it. I'm like, 'You couldn't even heat it up?' Well, I didn't feel sorry for him. I just said, 'Grandpop made apple pie. I have to go.'"

Women, as it turns out, have more leverage than they think: two-thirds of all divorces among Americans over forty years of age are initiated by *women,* not men. "As our recent research shows, marriage and parenthood are no longer negotiated on men's terms alone," sociologist Scott Coltrane wrote in the *Atlantic.* "One of the biggest shifts in recent years is that many women will simply not put up with partners who don't contribute at home."

And your husband may be more emotionally dependent on you than you realize. Sociology professor Terri Orbuch recommends an exercise to help women understand their importance in a marriage. She has each spouse draw five concentric circles, like a target. She instructs them to write their names in the bull's-eye, then has each partner list the five people they feel closest to, with the inner circle signifying the most intimate and the other circles representing decreasing closeness.

The responses of men and women are radically different. Women tend to cram all five people in that bull's-eye, and often ask Orbuch if they can list seven or eight. Husbands, meanwhile, put their wives right next to them in the inner circle. The rest, including children and other close relatives, are usually relegated to outer circles.

When Tom and I try it, he places me and our daughter in the inner circle. I put in five intimates and wish I could ask Orbuch if I could list seven or eight. "For women," Orbuch writes, "the knowledge that you are the main provider of reassurance and intimacy for your husband gives you incredible power. Most women have no idea they have this much ability to influence their husband's long-term happiness and short-term behavior."

Know that no matter what you and your spouse tell yourselves, your child is affected by your arguing. Period.

If you think otherwise, as I did, ask your child, and see if you can live with her answer.

Symbolic gestures: minimal effort, maximum effectiveness!

Tom now makes dinner once a week. Even though I cook dinner the other six nights, I still appreciate it. I don't care that it is not equal — I feel supported, and that perception is important. Scott

Coltrane has noted that when men share "routine repetitive chores of cooking, cleaning, and washing," women feel they are being treated fairly, they're less likely to become depressed, and the couple has less marital conflict.

I am amazed (and sometimes a little dismayed) at how much mileage some of Tom's largely symbolic gestures have resonated with me. He doesn't need to toil with me side by side: if he takes our child to the park for forty-five minutes so that I can putter happily around the house, I'm good for the day.

Some of his largely symbolic actions resonate with our daughter, too. Aside from chaperoning those class trips, Tom, for the first time ever, attended a parent-teacher conference and a birthday party solo, and took Sylvie to the doctor when she had pinkeye. All of those gestures — and I'm aware they were mostly gestures — took a total of a few hours, but she was thrilled, it deepened their relationship, and the goodwill he received from me lasted for weeks.

Finding the tasks your mate can't tolerate if they're neglected, and then foisting them on him, is an exciting game of strategy.

Couples therapist Joshua Coleman's advice is ingenious: once I trained myself to notice, I discovered many tasks that Tom couldn't tolerate if they were left undone. He has to have coffee first thing in the morning, for instance, in order for the consonants to reappear in his speech. Why, then, was I the one making the coffee? He is a stickler for being prompt — one quality that I loved about him when we were first dating, after a series of boyfriends who would keep me waiting, sometimes for hours — so it drove him nuts that I could never seem to get our daughter to soccer on time. Aha: *you* take her!

Does your husband twitch if grocery supplies run low or your dog needs a bath? Here you go — all yours, hon!

Couples counseling is not always, in the words of my father, "a buncha crap."

Especially, I would add here, if you can find a therapist who yells at your husband, "Stop with your entitled attitude, get off your ass, and help her out!" Heaven! And couples counselors needn't cost what Terry Real charges — many therapists, particularly those at university psychiatric centers, have sliding-scale fees. Some facilities offer counselors in training for a reduced cost; others will do Skype sessions if parents are crunched for time.

It may well be that Tom's motivation to change had nothing to do with me, and is entirely based on a deep fear of returning to Terry Real. I'm fine with that.

Children learn what they live.

As child psychologists like to repeat, kids often register what you *do* more than what you *say*. I can't count the number of soaring speeches I gave to our daughter about how girls — and women — can do anything. Girls rule! Then why was she given to observations like "Moms do the boring stuff, and dads do the fun stuff"? Because day after day, it was her mom who was doing the boring stuff. That is what she saw, so that was what she knew. Again: you can't be what you can't see.

Prevent future arguments by tackling the big questions about parenthood in advance (not just the fun ones such as "Should the crib mobile have ducks or bunnies?").

Many people with a baby on the way spend weeks or even months online, researching the best crib, the safest car seat — but spend little if any time thinking about the titanic impact the baby will have on their marriage. Couples therapists John and Julie Gottman run a national program called Bringing Baby Home, in which expectant parents spend a total of twelve hours learning how to resolve fights, divvy up chores, and navigate touchy topics like leisure time and sex.

Many psychologists and hospitals now offer similar classes. Of course, there are plenty of issues that can't be worked out in advance, no matter how much preparation you do. But never is there a better time to do a life hack than pregnancy, when time itself seems to move very slowly, and your life is dictated by forces that are still slightly in your control. Tom and I could have avoided so many post-baby battles if we had taken the time beforehand to simply address some of the issues the Gottmans explore in their workshops.

A sampling: *Should we have mealtimes together? Who will take care of the kid when she is sick? How should we include our relatives in our baby's life? How much television should we allow? How do you feel about the child sleeping in the same bed as us? Will religion play a part in her life? Write down three to five things that you liked about how you were parented that you plan to include in your parenting, and three to five things you did not like that you plan to avoid.*

Many of the questions the Gottmans provide are useful even for parents of older children, because they drill down quickly to your values, many of which you may never have identified in any meaningful way (certainly, we haven't). The Gottmans say that parents can quickly and easily build intimacy just by asking open-ended questions like these: *In what ways has our child changed our relationship? How do you think we could have more fun in our life? How have your goals in life changed since we had a child? What things are missing in your life? Who is your role model as a parent? What are your biggest worries about our future?*

Most parents tend to ask closed-ended questions that can be answered with a brief mumble: *Where is the Go-Gurt for her lunch? Well, why didn't you buy it when you were just at the store? You do know that if you just made a grocery list, you wouldn't have to run back there later? Are you even listening to me? Okay, what did I just say, then? Wrong!*

If you are able to swing paternity leave, your marriage, and your baby, may benefit hugely.

Research shows that having an involved father early on is essential to forging a more equal division between partners as the child grows. The benefits actually begin if Dad is present in the delivery room, as is the case for 91 percent of US men: research has shown that it reduces hostility later on between mothers and fathers.

A study of four countries — England, Denmark, Australia, and the United States — revealed that dads who had taken even short amounts of paternity leave were more likely to bathe, dress, feed, and play with their offspring long after their time off had ended. Nearly half of the leave-taking American dads were more apt to read books with their toddlers than men who hadn't taken time off.

Sociologist Scott Coltrane, who has studied the role of men in childcare and housework for decades, has found in his research that men who take time off for family reasons are more likely to take a hit in their long-term earnings. But the benefits of paternity leave, he argues, can outweigh the loss of long-term income: wives are happier (and, in one study, had lower rates of postpartum depression), children thrive from having two dedicated caregivers, and men develop better nurturing skills.

When fathers experience skin-to-skin cuddling with their newborns, the babies go to sleep faster, cry less, and are calmer than babies who did not have the same contact with Dad, research has found. And Swedish researchers discovered that men who take paternity leave *live longer* than others — with those who took the longest leaves reaping the greatest rewards. They speculated that the fathers' deepened involvement curbed some of the "damaging behaviors traditionally linked to men," such as alcohol abuse, risk taking, and violence. Talk about long-term benefits.

Date nights: a corny necessity.

Some of my more capable friends manage weekly date nights, but the most Tom and I can do is once a month — and it is still one of the most important ways of reinforcing our bond. How liberating it is to talk without having a kid interrupt you forty times! How freeing not to have to assemble your face into an attentive expression as your child drones on about the intricacies of Minecraft! Instead, you can bring up inappropriate subjects, flirt, reminisce,

261

and speculate on which members of the restaurant waitstaff are sleeping with each other!

On a daily basis, it is transformative to take just ten or fifteen minutes a day to talk about anything — anything — except scheduling, our child, or the fact that we're running low on paper towels.

Be mindful of the ways you are shutting your husband out, or making him feel incompetent.

Maternal gatekeeping comes in many sneaky forms. When I was texting with a group of moms recently about an incident at school, Tom asked me what was going on. "Oh, you wouldn't be interested," I said, and then stopped myself: Why was I excluding him?

I now make a concerted effort to stop this automatic, offhand dismissal, especially after my daughter, not yet the recipient of a birds-and-bees talk, made this observation: "You and I are related because you grew me in your stomach. But Daddy's just some guy that lives with us."

When I am engaged in a kid-related activity, I have noticed that I often reflexively leave out the men, assuming they will be bored. One day, Tom and I took my parents to lunch at their favorite Chinese place in New Jersey, which is festively housed in a giant red and gold pagoda. En route, Sylvie, my mother, and I were playing a word game we devised in which you name a brand — say, Legos — and the next person must name a brand starting with the final letter of that word — say, Superga. It's an excellent game for young kids in particular: toddlers who can't name a single country can unsettlingly rattle off a hundred brand names.

Then I noticed something: when Sylvie got stuck on a brand beginning with the letter *M,* I saw my father mouthing "Michelin tires." When my mother was stumped by a *T*, Tom quietly uttered, "Thermos." They wanted to play!

Now I actively try to include men in the kid stuff.

What does it cost you?

This unerringly useful advice, given by professional organizer Julie Morgenstern, has prevented many a scene. If your mate wants a nap or a run or a night out with friends, what is it *really* costing you? Is it increasing your workload or robbing your child of precious quality time — or is it just annoying, because you would never presume to take a nap?

One Saturday morning, Tom was sleeping in (per our new arrangement). Sylvie and I spent the morning coloring and creating a tea party for her stuffed animals, a chance for her to surreptitiously eat cookies ("Look, they ate five Fig Newtons! They sure were hungry!").

At around 11 a.m., I went into our bedroom for a sweater and saw Tom quickly stash his phone under his pillow and shut his eyes. Normally my impulse would be to announce, "Okay, quit hiding — time to get up." But I was having a lovely morning with my daughter. His lingering in bed wasn't costing me a thing — I was just irritated on principle. So I pretended not to notice his ruse, and shut the door.

Don't pee on the gift.

Terry Real's maxim is correct: if I tell Tom I'm okay with him playing a long Saturday soccer game, I cannot pull the silent treatment when he returns. (And as Che Guevara once put it, "Silence is argument carried out by other means.")

Don't suffer (for) the little children.

It's perfectly valid to ask if a kid event will be fun for you, and to reconsider if it isn't (remember the research about how children are upset when their parents are tired and stressed?). As professional organizer Barbara Reich points out, you don't have to go to three kids' birthday parties in one day. (Although I would happily attend if all three featured magicians; if they're hostile, or drunk, all the better.)

My weekends were transformed when I simply took a little time to build in some fun for myself instead of handing over those days wholesale to my child. Why can't parents have a bit of levity, too? For instance, I devised a plan before Easter for the grown-ups in my family to have an Easter egg hunt of their own. We stashed the kids in my parents' den with a film that they had all been clamoring to see, and set them up with treats.

Once the kids were sufficiently narcotized by the movie, I staged an egg hunt for the adults, along with various backyard games. Winners were directed to an upstairs Prize Room where they could choose among bottles of Scotch and wine, gift cards from various big-box stores, fancy chocolates, and firming moisturizers. The years dropped away as my mother forcefully bodychecked my sister Dinah in order to snatch the golden egg. ("I wanted to win that Scotch," she said, serenely brushing herself off.)

At Thanksgiving, I once again stashed away the kids with a movie, then furnished every adult with a coin and a pile of scratch-off lottery cards, with enticing names such as Instant Frenzy and Triple Tripler. Not a word was said as everyone set upon those cards with greedy concentration. My father won fifty dollars and announced that he was going to buy a 100-count box of contractor bags at Costco — his idea of a madcap splurge.

Let him do things his way.

If every father-daughter outing involves a giant milkshake, so what? If he dresses her in plaids and stripes, who cares?

So many aspects of childcare that I have assigned a gendered valence to, such as feeding kids or putting them to sleep, are just as easily and competently performed by the other gender. Children don't care one way or the other who is handing them Goldfish crackers.

The FBI's methods of paraphrasing and emotion labeling are remarkably effective.

As the FBI's Gary Noesner (and just about every psychologist) tells me, all people want to be understood. Everyone wants to feel validated. Part of the reason I would get so furious at Tom is that I felt he wasn't listening to me, so we were condemned to repeat a lifelong loop of demand/withdrawal. He still sounds wooden when he attempts to restate how I'm feeling in his own words (paraphrasing) or names my feelings instead of ignoring them (emotion labeling). But I always appreciate it, and it usually succeeds in calming me down—sometimes because his guesses are so off that I have to laugh ("You're feeling dejected. No? I meant, you're feeling uneasy. Right? No?").

Small things often.

This edict from the Gottmans has raised our game considerably. Small, specific, everyday gestures of affection that require almost no energy—giving a quick shoulder squeeze, buying the special salsa your spouse likes, sending a funny text—can make for big changes over time. What you do every day, the Gottmans claim, matters more than the things you do once in a while. Usually in the afternoon, I make Tom tea and bring him a cookie on a plate. When I was growing up, one of our nuttier family customs was that a paper napkin folded on the diagonal was "fancy," while one fashioned into a rectangular shape was "everyday." So I put a "fancy" napkin next to the plate, for an added dash of glamour.

Just a few kind words here and there are extraordinarily effective. Try this test on your mate: meet his gaze, raise an eyebrow, and tell him, "You know, you're looking really good to me lately." Then watch the comical procession of expressions that will cross his face: surprise, followed by narrow-eyed suspicion that you are making fun of him, cautious pleasure once he grasps that you are serious, and, finally, the most poignant sort of hopefulness.

Forge an alliance for the teen years.

As one of my friends with older kids put it, "Get your relationship together while your kids are young, because trust me, you and your husband are really going to need each other for emotional support when your kids are teenagers. Like Jason and I are constantly muttering to each other, 'What the hell was *that* about?' You sort of have this new esprit de corps."

Another friend tells me about an argument she had with her teenage son over his curfew. "It was in his room, or should I say, I stood outside his room," she tells me. "I don't like to go in there because there's dirty plates everywhere and piles of sneakers, and the whole place just smells like the reptile house at the zoo." Soon they were yelling—not helped because he refused to turn his music down—and she stomped downstairs in disgust.

Her husband was in the kitchen, stirring tomato sauce on the stove, shirtsleeves crisply rolled up, NPR playing quietly in the background. He silently handed her a glass of the pinot grigio he had poured when he heard her thump wrathfully down the stairs. Entering the orderly, adult atmosphere her husband had created in the kitchen was like leaving a chaotic Third World airport and boarding a quiet flight in first class.

Your child can, and should, help you out.

It is a little disconcerting to see how many tasks a child can take off your plate. Little kids really do want to help (and per Brown psychiatry professor Richard Rende's advice, you'll get better results by calling a kid a "helper" rather than asking them to help, because, touchingly, they want to be viewed as a good person). Why was I continually picking up after my child, when she could do it herself? As I bent to scoop up her toys, I used to rationalize insanely, *Well, at least all this bending is good for my abs. It's sort of like doing crunches.* Giving her just a few daily chores has freed up fifteen precious minutes of my time.

Again, it is imperative to lock in this behavior well before the commencement of preteen attitude.

Look for the good.

Therapist Guy Winch's exercise of having me notice and write down all Tom's kindnesses was an eye-opener. I had gotten so used to staying in the comfort zone of being resentful that the many good things he was doing, for both me and our child, slipped by me. In my martyred state, I noticed only the bad, which led to what's known in cognitive science as a confirmation bias: a tendency to pay attention to information that confirms your pre-existing beliefs, while ignoring anything that might challenge those beliefs.

I am the only person who can decide how I am going to feel. So I continue to make an effort to see his acts of caring, some of which normally flit under the radar — such as monitoring and stocking a precisely arranged cabinet of seven sizes of batteries for Sylvie's various toys. When he shepherds Sylvie and me across a busy crosswalk, he makes direct and uncomfortable eye contact with the driver waiting at the light, after reading research that this reduces a pedestrian's chances of getting hit.

Tom is more than "some guy who lives with us." As comedian Chris Rock has said, "Think about everything a real daddy does: pay the bills, buy the food, make your world a better, safer place. And what does Daddy get for all his work? The big piece of chicken. That's what Daddy gets."

●●●●●●●●●●●●●●●●●●●●●●●●●●

One of the greatest gifts you can give your child is a loving relationship with your spouse — and with it, a sense of security, peace, and permanence. Investing in your marriage while your children are young, or even before they arrive, is vitally important for your kid's future: research shows that children whose parents have happy unions are much more likely to have stable relationships themselves as adults.

Tom has proven that he cared about my unhappiness, and was willing to lean in, which touches me. It's embarrassing to admit that I started this project because I was worried about the effect our fighting had on our daughter, whereas it was barely a concern that my relationship with my husband was deteriorating. Instead, Tom has become the ally I didn't know I had.

Together, Tom and I are sharing the experience of watching this goofy, exuberantly happy child navigate her way through the world. We're profoundly and permanently connected, because of—and despite—the arrival of our child. Our marriage is far from perfect, but it has improved immeasurably. Now the distress we cause our daughter occurs mostly when I give Tom a kiss after he has jumped up to unload the dishwasher.

"Gross," Sylvie says, covering her eyes.

ACKNOWLEDGMENTS

I am enormously grateful for the incisive intelligence, dedication, and profound kindness of my editor and friend, Vanessa Mobley.

My deepest gratitude to the sterling and supportive all-stars at Little, Brown: Reagan Arthur, Katharine Myers, Nicole Dewey, Lauren Passell, Jayne Yaffe Kemp, Karen Wise, Sarah Haugen, and Carina Guiterman. Thanks also to the universally beloved Laura Tisdel, an early supporter of the book, as well as the generous and thoughtful Jocasta Hamilton at Penguin Random House UK.

Heartfelt appreciation goes to my agent, the brilliant, hilarious, almost absurdly charismatic Alexandra Machinist at ICM.

I offer my sincere thanks to the mothers and fathers who shared their stories and advice for this book. It is endlessly moving to see how my fellow parents support one another in doing "mankind's hardest job."

I am so lucky to have such a wonderful family: my parents, Jay and Judy Dunn, my sister Dinah and her husband, Patrick, and my sister Heather and her husband, Rob.

And, most importantly, I am forever grateful to my husband, Tom. I can't think about what you mean to me without reaching for a box of tissues.

ABOUT THE AUTHOR

New York Times bestselling author Jancee Dunn grew up in Chatham, New Jersey. She is the author of five books, including a memoir, a children's book, and *Cyndi Lauper: A Memoir.* Her essay collection, *Why Is My Mother Getting a Tattoo?* was a finalist for the Thurber Prize for American Humor. She is a frequent contributor to the *New York Times, Vogue, Parents,* and *O, The Oprah Magazine.* She lives in Brooklyn with her husband and daughter.